CW01262159

Guilty Victim

GUILTY VICTIM
Austria from the Holocaust to Haider

HELLA PICK

I.B.Tauris *Publishers*
LONDON • NEW YORK

Published in 2000 by I.B.Tauris & Co Ltd
Victoria House, Bloomsbury Square, London WC1B 4DZ
175 Fifth Avenue, New York NY 10010
Website: http://www.ibtauris.com

In the United States and Canada distributed by St. Martin's Press
175 Fifth Avenue, New York NY 10010

Copyright © Hella Pick, 2000

The right of Hella Pick to be identified as author of this work has been asserted by her in accordance with the Copyright, Designs and Patents Act 1998

All rights reserved. Except for brief quotations in a review, this book, or any part thereof, may not be reproduced, stored in or introduced into a retrieval system, or transmitted, in any form or by any means, electronic, mechanical, photocopying, recording or otherwise, without the prior written permission of the publisher.

ISBN 1 86064 618 2

A full CIP record for this book is available from the British Library
A full CIP record for this book is available from the Library of Congress

Library of Congress catalog card: available

Typeset in Goudy by Dexter Haven, London
Printed and bound in Great Britain

CONTENTS

	Acknowledgements	ix
	Introduction	xiii
I	The 1980 Silver Jubilee: Austria Finally Emerges from the World War	1
II	Occupied Austria: Cold War Hostage	16
III	Austria Under Occupation: Liberated but not Free	33
IV	The Occupation Ends – Neutrality Begins	49
V	Bruno Kreisky – Not Yet Chancellor	64
VI	Beyond the Corridors of Power: Cultural Icons as Opinion-formers	84
VII	Chancellor Kreisky – A Post-imperial Emperor	101
VIII	Kreisky's Middle East Ventures	118
IX	The Golden Age of Economic Prosperity	136
X	Austria in the Dock – The Waldheim Saga	149
XI	From the Mozartkugel to Klimt and Schiele	170
XII	Exit Waldheim, Enter Haider: Have the Lessons of the Past Been Absorbed?	181
XIII	The Restitution Go-slow	203
XIV	Small but Far from Insignificant: A Personal Assessment of Austria	222
	Bibliography	236
	Index	241

ILLUSTRATIONS

Plates 1–9, 11, 14, 15–19 and 23 © Votavafoto Wien
Plates 10, 12 and 13 courtesy of Bildarchiv, ÖNB Wien
Plates 20–22, 24, 26, 28 and 29 courtesy of Matthias Cremer
Plate 25 courtesy of Georg Lembergh
Plate 27 Diether Endlicher

For the friends who helped me back to my Austrian roots

ACKNOWLEDGEMENTS

How has the outside world treated Austria since 1945? What is the country's image in the international community?

In search of answers I have obviously taken close account of Austria's post-war history. But in so doing I have given a personal perspective on the country rather than a chronicle of Austria since the end of World War II.

When I embarked on this book, two years ago, I rashly assumed that it would be a relatively easy task to meet the publisher's deadline. But it did not take long to realise that I had underestimated the research required to describe or explain the circumstances that shaped Austria's position in the world since 1945.

It could never have been tackled without extraordinarily generous help from three outstanding experts on Austria's post-war history: Professor Gerald Stourzh, Dr Oliver Rathkolb and Dr Hugo Portisch. I owe them a huge debt, though I must emphasise that they cannot be held responsible for the views expressed in this book.

Professor Stourzh, Austria's pre-eminent constitutional historian, found time for extensive conversations, even while he was preoccupied with the final stages of his *magnum opus*, the revised history of the Austrian State treaty, *Um Einheit und Freiheit*. He explained much that I had previously ignored, pointed me to new material he had found in Soviet archives and, hopefully, improved my understanding of the Treaty negotiations.

Dr Rathkolb, research director of the Kreisky Archiv, and specialist in Austrian contemporary history, whose capacity for work never ceases to astonish me, once again gave me access to invaluable material, just as he had when I was writing Simon Wiesenthal's biography. But he did far more: he took time out to discuss many aspects of the issues I have tackled; he gave me a shoal of relevant books and articles; he also read the manuscript with great care, pointing to errors and filling in gaps.

Dr Portisch is an Austrian friend of long standing. His well-known TV documentaries and his books on the First and Second Austrian Republics could not have been made without the most detailed knowledge of the period and unrivalled access to the key actors of the post-war era. He has taken a close interest in this project, steered me into a better grasp of the issues, and made some of his research material available to me.

One of the dividends of writing this book has been to renew old acquaintances and make some new ones. I consider myself very fortunate that Austria's former Primate, the distinguished Cardinal Franz König received me on a number of occasions. He allowed me to raise sensitive questions and to share in some of his reminiscences. It is a privilege to be treated as a friend.

A few of the early architects of the post-1945 Second Austrian Republic are still, happily, around. Among those who agreed to talk with me were the ex-President Dr Rudolf Kirchschläger, former head of the Trade Union Federation Anton Benya, former cabinet minister Franz Olah, and Dr Martha Kyrle, daughter of Austria's second post-war President, Adolf Schärf.

Among those who worked with Dr Bruno Kreisky, I am particularly grateful to Frau Margit Schmidt, Dr Peter Jankowitsch, Dr Willibald Pahr, Dr Heinz Fischer and Dr Thomas Nowotny. I first met Dr Hannes Androsch when he was Chancellor Kreisky's Finance Minister and we have always kept in touch. He has given me valuable insights for this book and I want to thank him.

Friedrich Peter, the former leader of the Freedom Party, gave me new material on his relations with Bruno Kreisky and the Social Democrats. Ex-President Waldheim answered questions about his tenure as Foreign Minister under Chancellor Klaus. Dr Georg Hennig, whom I had also known since Waldheim's time as UN Secretary-General, also briefed me generously. But President Klestil, who had been Austrian Ambassador in Washington during the Waldheim crisis could not be persuaded to give his impressions of US attitudes towards Austria at that difficult time.

In addressing the post-Kreisky period, it was a great help to secure first-hand impressions, among others, from ex-Chancellor Klima, ex-Chancellor Vranitzky, Dr Manfred Scheich, Austria's former Ambassador to the European Union and his successor in Brussels, Dr Gregor Woschnagg. Dr Eva Nowotny, then still close at hand in London as Austria's Ambassador, has been very supportive, helping me not only with her first-hand experience of working with Dr Vranitzky but also with her wide-ranging knowledge of the ups and downs of Austria's standing in the world since 1945. Britain's Ambassador to Austria, Sir Anthony Figgis and Lady Figgis offered consistent encouragement, and were exceptionally generous with their hospitality.

Outside the political and diplomatic framework, my thanks for filling important gaps in my knowledge go especially to the head of the Austrian resistance organisation, Dr Wolfgang Neugebauer, to the Vienna Philharmonic's Secretary-General, Dr Clemens Hellsberg, Vienna State Opera Director Ioan Holender, Austrian PEN writers' club President Dr Wolfgang

Fischer and his wife, Jutta Fischer, and the Austrian actor and author Miguel Herz-Kestranek.

Outside Austria, this book gave me the opportunity to debrief David Cornwell (John Le Carré) on his time in Austria as a junior intelligence officer. Former German Chancellor Helmut Schmidt and former British Chancellor of the Exchequer Denis Healey gave me their perspectives on the Kreisky era. It was enlightening to have Lord Roll's views as a banker who has maintained close links with his native Austria. Contact with Dr Robert Knight of Loughborough University led towards a much better understanding of the tortured history of restitution to Austria's victims of Nazi persecution.

The list of those to whom I owe a debt of gratitude is much longer, and includes friends in Vienna who turned my 'working visits' into pleasurable occasions and helped me to rediscover my roots. Friends in London cheered me on as I complained of the mountains of work involved in finishing this book on time. But without mentioning all their names, I want to single out Rosl Merdinger in Vienna, whose research work for me was invaluable – this book could not have materialised without her – and also Eric Silver in Jerusalem, who once again dug up information I would not otherwise have found; in London, Evi Wohlgemuth, who read each chapter as it emerged, and whose queries and comments were as invaluable on this occasion as they had been with my Wiesenthal biography.

As a long-time admirer of the wide-ranging list of books published by I.B.Tauris, I was particularly pleased when the publisher, Iradj Bagherzade, decided to include this book in his Spring list for the year 2000. The book has been updated to take account of the political fallout from the 1999 election, when the controversial Jörg Haider scored an important electoral advance.

Last but not least, my thanks go to my ever-patient and helpful agent in London, Mike Shaw of Curtis Brown.

INTRODUCTION

'How can you bear to go to Austria? Why do you want to write about Austria?' Inevitably these questions were put with still greater vehemence after Jörg Haider's Freedom Party was invited to join with the Austrian People's Party in forming a new government at the beginning of the new millennium

I have been challenged so often to explain my motives for involving myself with my native Austria – and by no means only by Austrian emigrés, but also by a great many people, most, but not all, of them Jewish, who have no direct connection with Austria, or experience of the Holocaust. Many seem to feel more strongly about Austria than they do about Germany. They say they are uneasy, uncomfortable in Austria; they suspect Austrian *Gemütlichkeit*, and they often question whether Austrians will ever be able to admit to themselves fully the extent to which they willingly collaborated with Nazi Germany and became party to the Holocaust. They wonder how Austrians can stake a claim to have been Hitler's victims, when the evidence is plain that so many of them were perpetrators and counted among Hitler's willing executioners, and when around one third of Austria's voters now support Haider and his misnamed Freedom Party.

I have plenty of reservations about Austria, and about a mind-set that facilitates Haider's rise towards power. But I have always rejected the wholesale condemnation of the country and its people. Unlike many other Austrians who were forced to leave the country after the Anschluss, I have never had any reservations about going there on visits – both on assignments for my newspaper, the *Guardian*, or on holiday. In 1995, after I began to work on Simon Wiesenthal's biography, I spent a great deal of time in Vienna, interviewing him and researching the book. As my circle of friends grew, and I could see, close-up, the debates swirling around Austria's cultural and political life, I became more and more intrigued with the facile, often distorted, image that Austria appeared to have abroad.

So, when it was suggested that I should write a book about foreign attitudes to Austria since 1945, I readily seized the opportunity. I knew there would have to be a sub-text: a search for an answer to the question whether Austria is victim or perpetrator, or both.

Even though I was already familiar with Austria's domestic politics and political leadership, it added a new dimension to look at the country through the prism of the international community, both observing the country and building its relations with Austria through more than 50 years of post-war history. I learned a great deal to extend and deepen my understanding of the Austrian scene. Not least, I have realised that Austria's critics are either ignorant or deliberately ignore the responsibility which the four wartime allies must share for allowing Austria to see itself as Hitler's victim. It was they who incorporated the idea that Austria had been Hitler's 'first victim' in their 1943 Moscow Declaration; and it was they again who allowed this to be written into the 1955 State Treaty. No wonder Austrians made use of this gift.

In this book my aim has been to explain the interaction between external influences on Austria and the country's search to establish a new, foolproof, internationally credible identity for itself after the Nazi era.

The period since 1945 divides itself roughly into three periods. First, there were the ten years after the war, when Austria under four-power occupation was a kind of incubus for the Cold War. Austria was used by the Great Powers for their own different ends; its own identity, even its future as an independent state, was of secondary importance.

Second, after the State Treaty in 1955, and especially during the 13 years while Bruno Kreisky was Chancellor, between 1970 and 1983, Austria became a successful democracy, possessing a flourishing economy and a much admired welfare system. As a neutral country it was cutting its own path between the Cold War combatants.

Third, there has been the period since Kurt Waldheim's election as head of state in 1986, during which official Austria was finally driven to acknowledge responsibility for the country's involvement with Nazi crimes, and had to abandon the historical lie that Austria had been Hitler's first victim. Austria's Chancellor decreed, even while Waldheim was still in office, that it was time to blow away the myths, to face reality and try to make amends; to deal with restitution issues more expeditiously; to make peace with Austrian emigrés; to improve the teaching of history in Austria's schools. Austrians of all ages had to learn that they must understand the Holocaust and its depravities, and not just shrug it off either as something too remote to affect them or of which they had most likely been victims, if involved at all.

Now, with Haider so prominent on the political scene, the question arises whether Austria is on the verge of a perilous step backward into the political twilight, where the extreme right will impose new definitions of political correctness, and put at risk Austria's considerable achievements. Certainly Austria's partners in the European Union, together with the US, have demonstrated with their reactions to the Freedom Party's entry into government that they fear the worst. Perhaps a new revisionist phase has begun in Austria's post-war evolution, with dangerous consequences for its international standing and economic growth. Will Austria turn in on itself, and once again try to reject a balanced view of its recent history?

Though this book is written in chronological order, I have not attempted to write a definitive history of post-war Austria. It is intended primarily as an account of the role this small, strategically situated country in Central Europe has played in the geopolitics of the post-war world and, as a result, how it has positioned itself in the international order.

I have quoted extensively from contemporary newspaper accounts because they contain graphic illustrations of Austria's changing image in the world. I have also drawn on my own experience as a journalist who often went on assignments to Austria. But I have also had access to unpublished sources, and have benefited from interviews with a considerable number of key players involved with Austrian affairs, both within the country and from abroad. It has been a salutary lesson to discover the extent to which a number of individual Austrians have battled to bring home to their fellow citizens the importance of conscience and of ending their self-deception about the Nazi era.

At the end of my quest, I remain as convinced as I was before that there is no straightforward answer to the questions about Austria's character and moral standing. The country is both victim and perpetrator. But there is no equivalence between the two: Austria has been far less victim than perpetrator.

Austria has made great strides in coming to terms with its history and establishing itself as a valued member of the European Union. But, as Haider's political advance has shown, the country still has a long way to go to establish its credentials.

I

The 1980 Silver Jubilee

Austria Finally Emerges from the World War

For the second time in his long political career, Harold Macmillan stepped out from the Great Marble Hall and looked across from Schloss Belvedere to the roofs and spires of Vienna and beyond to the vineyards and green hills that skirt the city. It was 15 May 1980, and Macmillan, the grand old man of British politics, was eighty-six years old.

As Britain's Foreign Minister, he had stood on this balcony a quarter of a century before in 1955, moments after Austria's State Treaty had been signed and sealed by the US, the Soviet Union, France and the UK. Ten years of four-power occupation had been about to end; Austria would again be master of its own fate, circumscribed only by a commitment to remain a neutral country. That day in 1955, as the euphoric cheers from the phalanx of people gathered in the gardens below wafted through to the Marmorsaal, Macmillan had urged the other Foreign Ministers – John Foster Dulles, Jean-François Poncet and Vyacheslav Molotov, together with Austria's Leopold Figl – to show themselves on the balcony. 'Oddly enough, they were reluctant,' MacMillan recalled. 'I suppose they had never before experienced such acclaim and may have worried that it might turn into an addiction. However I had already had the doors opened, and they had no alternative but to go out.'[1]

Thus it was that a last gesture of occupation power saw to it on that momentous day in 1955 that Leopold Figl emerged from the diplomatic conclave inside and appeared in public, joyously waving the bulky treaty and proclaiming, 'Austria is free!' As a snapshot of a more peaceful world ahead, the scene is etched into the annals of the Cold War.

Now, in 1980, 25 years later, the decade of post-war occupation had faded into history. Austrians had fashioned for themselves a solid post-imperial sense of national identity. The belief that Austria was part of the German nation, and desire for union with Germany, so widespread in the inter-war period, had faded to insignificance. The impoverishment and insecurities that had dogged Austria since 1918 were a distant memory. Austria had blossomed to prosperity, and independence was taken for granted. Committed to neutrality since the achievement of the State Treaty, Austrians were proud of their country's success in navigating around the Cold War protagonists, and of its growing international standing.

In the mellow climate of May 1980, nothing was allowed to disturb Austrian complacency, not least because the outside world was still prepared to conspire with Austrians in maintaining the fiction that their country, far from embracing the Nazi annexation in 1938, had been Hitler's first victim. There was as yet no external pressure on Austrians to take a candid look at their recent history and to confront the unpalatable truths about their attitudes and actions during the Nazi era.

Since the end of the Second World War, and to some extent already in the war's closing stages, Austria has always attracted more attention and, in the wake of the Waldheim affair and Haider's rise, more controversy than its small size appeared to warrant. To study its changing image abroad and how other countries have handled their relations with Austria is to take the pulse of the post-war era; it is to observe both the strategic factors that have shaped the new Europe and also to realise how deaf the Western alliance, and not only the Soviet Union, was to moral argument in determining their policies.

— * —

In 1980, a time of renewed bitterness in the Cold War over the Soviet invasion of Afghanistan, Austria's image as a neutral country eager to facilitate East-West dialogue could hardly have been bettered. Clearly there was much to celebrate at this Silver Jubilee of the State Treaty. Yet, the crowds in the Belvedere Gardens were much thinner than in 1955; perhaps no more that 600 people, and among them tourists who had little idea what was going on. 'Must be some secret conference,' observed an American among them as the soberly dressed politicians displayed themselves once again on the Belvedere balcony. For Macmillan, however, the ceremonial of the State Treaty anniversary had a magic quality – it was a reminder of an exceptional achievement that had bucked the trend and survived in a troubled Europe caught up in East-West confrontation. Austria's freedom, and with it the withdrawal of its occupation forces, had revealed itself like an aberration from the Cold War, one of the rare post-war decisions in which the Soviet Union and the Western Allies had been able to overcome their differences. 'When I look back over the last 25 years,' Macmillan reflected, 'it seems to me that the Austrian state treaty has turned out to be the only genuine foreign policy success of this whole period'.

For Austria, 1980 deserves to count as the high point of the country's achievements during the closing half of the twentieth century. The country had won widespread admiration as a small unified nation which had at last come to terms with post-imperial shrinkage and had pulled itself up successfully from the rubble of the Second World War to establish itself as a responsible member of the international community. In 1980, Chancellor Bruno Kreisky was valued as an influential figure in world councils. Kurt Waldheim was still known only as an anodyne UN Secretary-General, with no hint of the storm to come. Austrians were proud that one of their own occupied such a key position in the world organisation. The war crimes charges against Waldheim still lay in the future. The outside world was more interested in Austria's post-war achievements than in its Nazi record, its antisemitism or its reluctance to face up to its past; and the four wartime Allies still had no qualms about endorsing Austria's status as Nazi Germany's first victim.

Certainly this commemoration of the State Treaty was considered important enough to attract to Vienna an uncommon kaleidoscope of guests from the international community of politics and the arts. Austria's national sovereignty, and its identity, were now so securely anchored that there was not the slightest sense of apprehension when soldiers from the four former occupying powers were once more seen strutting in formation on the streets of Vienna. The soldiers had been brought back for ceremonial purposes, and their presence was welcomed as a picturesque exercise in nostalgia as they paraded through the city.

Among the older people, some remembered and hummed the post-war jingle 'Four Men in a Jeep', and thousands came to applaud a joint military tattoo in which the Soviets played the 'Soldatenfreundschafts-Marsch' – 'The March of Soldierly Friendship' – and where the British, in the full dress uniform of the Queens Dragoon Guards, strode to the drumbeat of 'Marching On'. The Americans, alone among the Allied forces to include women instrumentalists in the band, played first 'The Star-spangled Banner' and then went to distinctly non-military entertainment with some Gershwin tunes. The French plunged straight away into the popular chanson, 'Auprès de ma blonde'. Finally all the bands together, with Austrians in the lead, ceremoniously ended the tattoo with the evergreen Radetzky march. 'Peaceful – but loud,' I wrote in my notebook as I watched the end of the spectacle.

Only a handful of the Austrian leaders who had been involved with the State Treaty negotiations were still around in 1980. Kreisky was one of them. This time it fell to him to play a leading role in the festivities. Twenty-five years before, as a junior member of the team which had negotiated the Treaty, he had only been allocated a back seat. Still only an Under Secretary in the Austrian Foreign Office in 1955, Kreisky's political career had most certainly undergone a spectacular transformation. In 1980 he had much to celebrate. President Jonas had died in 1974, and in his place Rudolf Kirchschläger had been elected head of state. Julius Raab, the country's Chancellor in 1955, was gone. More than old age had eroded Austria's post-war political profile. In the period between 1955 and 1980 the country's political profile had been radically transformed.

No longer dominated by the conservative People's Party, the Social Democratic Party was now firmly in power with an overall majority. Kreisky, though beginning to suffer ill-health, had already been Chancellor for a decade, and towered over the country's political and economic life. He remained dedicated to his self-imposed task of carving out for Austria a significant international role far in excess of that which its small size might justify. In 1979, Kreisky had triumphed with his third successive election victory, on this occasion securing the highest number of parliamentary seats yet won by the Social Democrats.

The Silver Jubilee of the State Treaty came less than a month after Kreisky's tenth anniversary at the helm of Austria's government. He was combative and often controversial. But his popularity was undisputed, and he dominated the political scene as no other Austrian has done since 1945. At the end of his first decade, the Chancellor had already achieved enough to persuade most of Austria that the country was living through a period that merited its description as 'the Kreisky era'.

Abroad, Kreisky was seen in less grandiloquent terms; but even among those who were sharply critical of aspects of his foreign policy – most notably of his initiatives in the Middle East – there was a widespread view that Kreisky had shown great inventiveness in constructing an activist form of neutrality and had projected Austria as a constructive influence on the world stage. Those interested enough to follow his domestic policies, chief among them fellow socialist leaders abroad, were also impressed by Kreisky's single-minded pursuit of full employment in tandem with economic progress and the creation of a model welfare state.

Austrians, being romantics and fond of nostalgia, enjoy the ceremonial of their anniversaries. Kreisky shrewdly calculated that the Silver Jubilee of the State Treaty offered a unique opportunity to illuminate – and magnify – the country's progress, and to project Vienna as an ideal European hub for diplomacy, serving as a neutral meeting ground where

East and West, North and South would feel at ease even during the most intractable negotiations.

— * —

Preparations for the anniversary were begun months ahead. Kreisky wanted to create a truly international event with plenty of ceremonial formality, but above all where an elite group of notable figures from home and abroad would accept invitations to take stock of Austria's achievements since 1955. He sought out three principal groups: foreign leaders, the foreign media, and Austrian emigrés. All would be steered firmly to focus and review the post-State Treaty era since 1955.

Plainly Kreisky had no wish to trigger a more fundamental debate about Austria during the Nazi period, or about the desultory approach to denazification and to restitution for the victims of Nazi persecution. Nor did Kreisky want to draw attention to his own and the Social Democrats' readiness to work with former Nazis and his controversial flirtation with the far-right Freedom Party. Kreisky's reluctance to stir up the unpalatable found a ready echo at home, and was matched by indifference abroad. They all took cover behind the contention that between the Anschluss in 1938 and the war's end in 1945, Austria had ceased to exist as a legal entity and could not be held responsible for the actions of Hitler's 'Ostmark'. Only individual Austrians could be judged for their actions. The notion that a society can only flourish through awareness of its true history was left dormant. Instead there seemed to be a general consensus that sleeping dogs be let lie. So it was that in all the acres of speeches, articles and commentaries delivered around the State Treaty's silver jubilee, Austria's handling of Nazi-related issues remained a virtual taboo.

Almost single-handedly, Simon Wiesenthal, beavering away in his Documentation Centre in Vienna and seeking to bring Nazi mass murderers to justice, harangued Austria for its failure to face up to unpalatable facts, and accused Kreisky of opening the corridors of power to war criminals. But few took note or thanked him for his efforts to stir up Austria's conscience. In 1980 Austrian public opinion – led by Kreisky – treated Wiesenthal as a hate object. Where matters of Austrian involvement with the Nazi ideology and Nazi crimes were concerned, his strictures fell on deaf ears. Austrians themselves did not want to be hectored or reminded of unpleasantness; and the world outside was in no mood for searching questions and moral judgement on Austria. There was an almost complete absence of pressure from any influential quarter on Austrians to emerge from their comfortable cocoon of victimhood, face up to their history during the Nazi era in its true light and assume responsibility for their share in the Holocaust.

As Austria drew up the 1980 guest list, it was a *sine qua non* that Harold MacMillan and Antoine Pinay, the two surviving signatories of the 1955 treaty, must be persuaded to come, joining the current Foreign Ministers of the four signatory states. Ministers from Austria's neighbours and from member states of the Non-aligned Movement would also be invited. Eleanor Dulles, sister of the late John Foster Dulles, was asked to Vienna both because her brother had been a key figure in negotiating the State Treaty, but also in her own right as US Financial Affairs Attaché in Vienna during the first two post-war years. As US Secretary of State, John Foster Dulles had become convinced that in Austria he had succeeded in rolling back the iron curtain. Eleanor Dulles, like her brother, thought in certitudes and had no hesitation about claiming that she had been instrumental in securing a lifeline for Austria by persuading the US authorities to extend massive economic aid to the occupied country: 'Without seeking praise for myself, I can honestly assert that I saved the Austrian economy'.

Though Kreisky could not have foreseen it when the preparations for the State Treaty anniversary were initiated, external events played into his hands. The May 1980 event turned out to be fortuitous for high-level East-West contacts. There was a new US Secretary of State, Ed Muskie, who welcomed the opportunity to make himself better known to his colleagues. There were pressing matters crying out for high-level discussion. East-West relations were again in crisis over the December 1979 Soviet invasion of Afghanistan. The Americans had a further concern: desperate for ways to free their hostages in Iran, they had nevertheless already rejected Kreisky's proposal to use the PLO leader, Yasser Arafat, as intermediary. Now the US hoped that the meetings at the margins of the anniversary might produce other ideas for ending the deadlock with Iran over the hostages.

With key ministers in Vienna, a whirl of meetings was organised. But no progress was achieved towards a solution of either the Afghanistan or Iran crises. Even getting to know Muskie was of limited value as, only a few months later, Jimmy Carter was the loser in presidential elections. Under President Reagan, a new, more hawkish, less human rights oriented cast of US officials was about to occupy centre-stage.

But even if the high-level encounters in Vienna failed to narrow East-West differences, with respect to Austria's own national interests, Kreisky was eminently successful in highlighting Vienna's qualifications as an international meeting ground. Media coverage was massive, and generally very friendly. Much was made of Austrian prosperity and how the country, living in the dangerous terrain between the Eastern and Western camps had nevertheless carved out for itself a positive image as a European capital for the United Nations and a useful, highly respected venue for international diplomacy.

Already in the weeks preceding the Treaty anniversary, several major newspapers had carried extensive, admiring surveys of Austria under the rule of 'Emperor Bruno'. Though some journalists warned of potential storm clouds ahead – an economy about to slow down, controversy over nuclear power, question-marks over the durability of the social consensus between employers, unions and the government – surveys in the *International Herald Tribune*, *Financial Times*, *Guardian* and other papers were overwhelmingly positive. It was as if critical faculties had been suspended: 'The shops, commercial centres, restaurants and theatres are booming. Heavy buying is evident everywhere. In factories, order books look encouraging. There is very little unemployment among the youth, slums are virtually non-existent. Indeed this small, prosperous country still fares better than the nine Common Market countries put together,' wrote Axel Krause in the *International Herald Tribune*.[2] He reflected that 'Austria's Chancellor, Bruno Kreisky, towers over his country like no other Western leader.'

'Austria – the showcase of the politics of consensus turned in a spectacular, strong growth, low inflation performance in 1979, but the rising price of energy and loss of external reserves are setting Austria problems for the 1980s. The prevailing view in Vienna is that these challenges will not produce confrontation, but a closing of ranks.'[3] That is how the *Financial Times* headlined a survey on Austria at the beginning of 1980. The headline writer in the *Guardian* described Austria as 'Europe's trendbender'. A series of articles I had written about Austria to highlight the 1980 jubilee were prefaced thus: 'In a 1979 public opinion poll, 76 per cent of Austrians agreed that Austria today can serve as a model for the rest of the world. The nation has good ground for optimism – stable government, neatly poised foreign relations, low unemployment and inflation, rising incomes and GNP.' My articles, the newspaper said, would be 'an account of the triumphs of consensus politics'.[4]

A more cynical note was introduced by Sue Masterman, a long-time resident of Vienna, in a mood piece entitled 'Long faces in Harry Lime country'.[5] 'Spring in Vienna,' she wrote, 'the crocuses bloom. Thirty demonstrators sit on the grass in the Burggarten Park because it is forbidden to sit on the grass. The police unused to such overt civil disobedience in a city where one can still, more or less walk in the streets alone at night in safety, say they have been provoked to the extreme. Next time they might lose their tempers... A forlorn group of Russian Jewish emigrants leave the train which brought them to freedom and are shepherded by commandos bristling with with arms and ammunition through the Südbahnhof station hall to the waiting buses which will spirit them away to temporary quarters before they pass on to Israel or America. Their first glimpse of the civilised West is the station hall, the meeting place for Vienna's Yugoslav and Turkish foreign workers and city vagrants.

'Vienna has a population of around one and half millions, and is affectionately known as the Wasserkopf, the hydrocephalus. In this one word, the Viennese, who are their own best critics, have summed up the essence of the problem. Vienna is too big a capital for the rump of empire left to it after two world wars. It was built for the Austro-Hungarian empire's dimensions, and is populated by people whose roots have been rudely amputated by the Iron Curtain. Vienna is always a crucible. This is where, in a Meidling doss-house, the young Adolf Hitler spent his formative years, while a few miles away the man who was later better known as Joseph Stalin eked out his existence as a gentleman's gentleman.'

There was much, much more of the same in other foreign newspapers, and even if the Soviet and other Warsaw Pact media couched their reviews of Austria in their standard turgid communist jargon, their conclusions too were positive.

With the superpowers and so many other countries certain to be represented at the Treaty anniversary, Kreisky naturally anticipated that the event would trigger a fresh avalanche of coverage from the foreign media. Even so, the Austrian authorities took out an insurance policy by organising a symposium of journalists, all of them foreign policy experts. I was among them. We were asked to assess 'Twenty-five years of the State Treaty'.

The workload was light. We were treated as VIPs, housed in Vienna's best hotels, and flattered with invitations to all the ceremonial events. Kreisky and his senior colleagues, though busy with their ministerial guests, were even more accessible to the foreign press than normally. Not surprisingly, such media massage worked to Austria's advantage: we all wrote extensively about Austria as a success story and about Kreisky as an international statesman with constructive views about the conduct of East-West relations and the search for peace in the Middle East that rightly deserve to be given a hearing. The *Guardian* was envious: 'Austria is 25 years old, and except for the professionally malevolent, everyone wishes the Austrians well. They do no one any harm. They entertain superbly, and they prosper. They have the highest economic growth rate of any industrialised country in Europe, the rate of inflation is 6.1 per cent, and unemployment stands at 2.1 per cent – another figure which puts most of the rest of Europe to shame... Austria has been steadfastly neutral and at peace and has managed without any of the conditions imposed on the Finns by the Russians. Much of the credit for this belongs to Chancellor Kreisky and his socialist government.'[6]

Those were days when the European Left still had great faith in public ownership and the planned economy, and believed that Keynesianism held the key to fairly-shared prosperity. The *Guardian* felt that Austria was a vibrant example of such verities. 'The Austrians prosper because by agreement they submit themselves to an incomes policy; because the government uses the riches of the considerable public sector to regulate the economy sensibly, because Mr Kreisky's ministers are intelligent and skilful men, and because the people trust them. The Austrians have proved that democracy and socialism can complement each other.' Furthermore, 'in the international field the Austrians have shown that neutrality need not mean idleness'. Kreisky 'and Kurt Waldheim' – an unsuspecting editor wrote – 'have done more than most men to assuage the world's conflicts and will do so again. Many happy returns.'

Even if the presence of foreign leaders and the effort to attract the attention of the foreign media were Austria's top priorities, Kreisky also seized on the anniversary to persuade Austrian emigrés to visit their former home. This had a twin purpose. Kreisky wanted to convince them that the Austria of 1980 had changed its colours, and must no longer be confused with the country that had embraced Hitler with open arms in 1938 and welcomed its annexation to the greater Germany, forced many of them to emigrate and shared responsibility for the Holocaust. Within the domestic political context, Kreisky had insisted on drawing a line under the past; now he shrewdly hoped that Austrian emigrés could be persuaded to adopt the same attitude and associate themselves more closely with their country of origin.

Kreisky's other aim was to persuade some of the best brains among the Austrians driven out by the Nazis, and now settled abroad, to work more closely with Austria's depleted intellectual capital, and to fill some of the gaps in the country's cultural life. To that end, a list of achievers among Austrians abroad, a large majority of them Jews who had fled Nazi persecution, was drawn up. It was an extraordinary roll-call of talent lost to Austria. It included such well-known names as the child psychologist Bruno Bettelheim, the pianist Alfred Brendel, the management expert Peter Drucker, the journalist Henry Grunwald (later to become US Ambassador to Austria), the economist Friedrich Hayek, the film director Billy Wilder, the banker Eric Roll, the philosopher Karl Popper, the writer Hilde Spiel, the art dealers Wolfgang and Jutta Fischer, and the publisher George Weidenfeld.

Put aside, or better still ignore altogether, that many of these people were forced to tear up their roots and hounded out of the Ostmark in 1938 and 1939, that many members of their families had been killed in concentration camps, that their worldly possessions had been seized. Now, in 1980, the official watchword was to honour the Austrian emigrés as representatives of the 'tenth' province (under its federal constitution Austria is divided into nine länder), irrespective of whether they were Jews or not, or had fled from persecution or left because of their political beliefs. There was a positive bias to the headline theme they were asked to discuss: 'Transformation into a nation – from the state that nobody wanted to the island of the blessed'. These ex-Austrians certainly had the background and the varied expertise to assess Austria's social evolution, its economy, its scientific progress and its culture. The organisers had selected their guests wisely. They were not disappointed by the conclusions reached during the debate.

Fritz Molden, a leading publisher in Austria charged with organising this aspect of the State Treaty anniversary, set out[7] a threefold agenda for the visiting Austrians. They were sure to bring fresh minds to bear on 'how the world regards Austria and its achievements' and the reverse side of the coin, on 'how the world could gain a better understanding of Austria,'[8] he wrote in a confidential memorandum for the Chancellor. In addition, all this would also serve, Molden hoped, to deepen the contact with Austrians abroad, and lead them to a better appreciation of their former home. The Molden offensive made little headway with the numerous emigrés who long ago decided that Austria's Nazis had placed the country beyond redemption. Quite a number of invitations were turned down – and not only because of prior engagements.

However, of those emigrés who did accept Austrian government invitations, most had a sufficiently open mind about post-war Austria to welcome the opportunity for a far-reaching exchange with leading Austrians. Whether they made the most of it is questionable. Much of the debate behind closed doors centred on a demand for the right to an absentee vote for Austrian nationals living abroad. Some also questioned why the Austrian government devoted such massive funds to the loss-making public sector. There was a heated discussion about the extent to which Jewish emigration had led to a lasting impoverishment of the Austrian cultural scene.

But there was no demand for Austrians to acknowledge responsibility for their actions under the Nazis; nor any organised pressure for a more generous approach to restitution issues. It was as if the expatriates had made a secret compact not to ruffle their hosts' feathers during the State Treaty anniversary. Instead, the group conveyed the impression of believing that it was possible to remain true to their adopted countries and yet play a more active role in their country of origin. That at any rate is how Lord Weidenfeld, at the end of the meetings, chose to sum it up on behalf of the expatriates. President Kirchschläger and a collective of Austria's great and good were in the audience to hear him spread his message of good-will.

Rightly, Weidenfeld pointed out that those who had accepted this invitation to Vienna had implicitly come to terms with the past. But he went further, arguing that the Kreisky government deserved to be praised for its aid to the victims of the Holocaust, and he cited some carefully selected examples.

While avoiding sensitive issues such as denazification or restitution, Weidenfeld singled out Austria as virtually the only European country which had allowed the transit of tens of thousands of Soviet Jews, and given them temporary refuge on their way to Israel and elsewhere. He hinted at the dismay felt by many Jews over Kreisky's recent decision to recognise the Palestine Liberation Organisation, but said that the conference participants had been unanimous in acknowledging that Austria, acting in the spirit of President Sadat's initiatives, had helped to bring Arabs and Israelis to the conference table at Camp David.

Weidenfeld drew a sharp distinction between the inter-war generation of Austrians which had lost its bearings and welcomed union with Germany, and post-war Austria's strong belief in its own national identity. 'Those among us who witnessed the tragedy of the Anschluss, also know of Austria's fight for understanding, and for its own political and cultural identity... When I was a youth, Austrians – on the left as well as on the right – were ambivalent about their identity. A majority believed in the all-German concept, and readily sung the Renner national hymn: "German-Austria, this wonderful country, we love you"... The first seeds of a new reality developed under pressure of external force and occupation and the extinction of Austria, under the suffering of the country's patriots in the concentration camps and Hitler's prisons. Today the country's youth are convinced Austrians... Today the whole world values Austrian culture and civilisation.'

Weidenfeld had high praise for the new Austria: 'Successive Austrian governments, while staying true to the country's traditions and its history, have developed a role and an image for Austria that goes far beyond the size or significance of such a small country. Austria's neutrality is neither colourless nor fearful; instead it is creative and bold... All men of goodwill will agree that Austria's motives are of the best... A country that became a display case for racism and genocide has now adopted a prominent place in the provision of help to the victims of those terrible times.'

In his summing-up, Weidenfeld was still more fulsome. Expatriates had drawn up a resolution of thanks to the Austrian authorities: 'Irrespective of our reasons for leaving this country, we who live outside its borders are thankful that we can acknowledge today's Austria as our country of origin... We take pleasure in today's Austria, and hope that our links will be maintained into the distant future.'

In the journalists' forum, in which I was a participant, we also seemed to draw an invisible veil over Austria's links with Nazi Germany, or the inadequacy of denazification in Austria. Unlike myself, few among the journalists had been refugees. But even if the others were not schooled to raise sensitive issues about Austria's past, with the wisdom of hindsight I find it difficult to explain my own silence in 1980, my own pleasure, undiluted by reservations, at being able to share in Austria's celebrations.

Having left Austria in a children's transport in 1939, and grown up in Britain, I had made my first return visit in 1949, and had been back many times. There had been holidays in the Tirol and the Salzkammergut; but more recently, and with growing frequency, I had been in Vienna on assignments for the *Guardian*: Austria belonged to my 'parish'. I had none of the hesitations about visiting Austria that so many other refugees experienced. But I had nevertheless always been uneasy in Vienna: I felt the outsider looking in on a foreign country; there was no sense of belonging, no instinctive sense of belonging to my Austrian *Heimat*. It was to be several years after 1980 before the relationship became closer and warmer; but also before I came to reflect more deeply on Austria's Nazi record.

— * —

Needless to say the praise lavished on Austria in 1980 and the non-judgmental attitude of the *Auslandsösterreicher* was music to the ears of the Austrian leadership. If the survivors of Nazi prosecution could adopt such attitudes, why burden the Austrian people with unpleasant inquests into past behaviour and with a closer look at the legacy that the new Austria had inherited? Austria's elite, the ministerial guests, and the media – even Israel's – evidently preferred to focus on the record of the recent past: on 25 years of Austrian achievement in the arts, in their cooking, in their laid-back way of life.

General Mark Clark, who had commanded the US forces in Austria during the first two years after the war, wrote from his retirement that the twenty-fifth anniversary brought back sentimental memories of happy days in Austria. 'My fondest memories of Austria are those of the wonderful people and the beautiful countryside. To have lived in the cities of Mozart and Beethoven was exhilarating, and to have walked in the footsteps of the Habsburgs was humbling. The people of Austria were magnificent. Doctors Renner, Figl and Gruber, along with countless other patriots selflessly shouldered the burden of the unbelievably difficult and dangerous (in the light of Soviet kidnappings) task of restoring self-rule to the country which had led Europe and the West for so long. The statesmanship of Dr Renner and his colleagues, who time and again overcame enormous obstacles, was inspirational.'

Patently, Clark had acquired a one-dimensional view of Austrian politics. Everything was judged in terms of halting the spread of communism. 'The complete repudiation of the Austrian Communist Party in the November 1945 elections and the subsequent ingenious handling of the thorny "German assets" question by Dr Figl's government confirmed my conviction that the Austrian people understood the Soviet threat.

'Austria thus became the first post-war failure of communism, and although my role in achieving this was a modest one, as a student of history, I take great satisfaction in thinking that Austria, which was for so long a bulwark of the West and of Christianity, has again assumed its historical mission as a sovereign independent state.'

General Clark had not been well enough to come to Vienna in person in 1980, and we shall never know whether he would have been as effusive about Bruno Kreisky as he had been about Renner and Figl. But groups of young people from the former occupying countries who were invited on a two-week study tour of Austria, which included a meeting with Kreisky, were impressed. 'We have learned that the Austrian Republic is more than the land of the Lippizaner horses and of the Viennese *valse*. It has used tradition to create a modern, progressive state, whose world role we have only now come to appreciate,'[9] wrote the American professor in charge of the US student visitors.

Many more testimonials to Austrian virtues and the country's contribution to world peace, prompted by the State Treaty anniversary, have been filed away in archives, kept for posterity. But the most important ones were put into two volumes published soon after the 1980 celebrations. An official government publication, handsomely bound in red, contains all the key speeches made by Austrian leaders and their foreign guests, and also reproduces a wide selection of newspaper accounts from home and abroad. The second book, a special number of the Austrian journal *Europäische Rundschau* has a series of specially commissioned articles from prominent leaders and thinkers who were asked to evaluate the circumstances that led to the State Treaty and the impact the settlement with Austria had had on world affairs.

Common themes run through both volumes: implications of the state treaty for East-West relations, the evolution of Austria's 'active neutrality', and the factors that brought about the 1955 treaty. Much is made of the contention that the State Treaty was a unique event in post-war Europe – only the Soviets insisted that it was the beginning of a process of detente and peaceful co-existence. Everyone else maintained that the Austrian peace accord (which perversely could not be labelled a 'peace treaty' because Austria, having been designated as Hitler's victim, had not been considered at war against the Alliance) was a one-off product, a collector's item.

In 1980, just as in 1955, the Germans were alone in questioning whether the Western allies had been right to sign the accord with Austria in the absence of Soviet assurances that a peace treaty with the Federal Republic would swiftly follow. In 1955, Chancellor Adenauer had scarcely hidden his bitterness. Of course he understood that Austria's small size, its geography and its post-war history added up to a combination of factors that could not be applied to Germany. But this did not prevent the German leadership from insisting that the Allies should have held out for progress on a settlement with Germany.

A quarter of a century later, Germans acknowledged that they had pursued a chimera, that Austria could not, and should not, have been held hostage to a German treaty. But though reason told them that the Austrian treaty was no precedent for a German settlement, the Germans were not deterred from revisiting their misgivings of 25 years before and reminding the world of the dangers of leaving the German question unresolved.

Foreign commentators in 1980 also ruefully acknowledged other miscalculations. Those who had imagined in 1955 that Soviet withdrawal from Austria marked a lasting turn towards East-West detente and a loosening of the Communist grip on Eastern Europe had been proved quite wrong. They had to look no further than Hungary in 1956, Czechoslovakia in 1968, Afghanistan in 1979. At the other extreme, those who, in 1955, had doubted that the Soviet Union would tolerate an independent Austria for any length of time had also misjudged the situation: the new Austria had proved itself a durable product which had won the Kremlin's seal of approval and was now beyond the Soviet Union's destructive arm. 'The great achievement of Austrian policy during the last 25 years is reflected in the fact that East and West alike regard Austria as an important factor for stability in Central Europe, and that its active neutrality is interpreted as a useful instrument of international relations,' the *Frankfurter Allgemeine* noted.

There was further consensus that Austria had established for itself a singular brand of neutrality, unlike that practised by Europe's other neutral states. Kreisky had known how to use Austria's neutral status constructively. Western contributors, wary of drawing attention to the distinctly pro-Western brand of neutrality, nevertheless took covert pleasure in emphasising the careful balancing act between Austria's commitment to democracy and affinity to Western culture and its determination to demonstrate neutrality in the conduct of foreign affairs.

Soviet Foreign Minister Andrei Gromyko and his Communist colleagues also gave Austria a squeaky clean bill of health, but preferred to dwell on Austria's eagerness, as a neutral member of the UN and of the Conference for Security and Cooperation in Europe (CSCE), to play a full role in the collective search for peace. It was no accident, Gromyko said, that Vienna had established itself as an international meeting ground or that several international organisations had their headquarters in Vienna.

In all the speeches and writings linked to the silver jubilee, the Soviet Union and its friends dispensed with critical analysis and described the State Treaty in familiar propaganda terms as a Soviet contribution to peaceful co-existence, and as an event whose time had come in 1955. Not so for the others: Western politicians, academics and journalists all pondered at length in speech and print on the history of the long-drawn-out, frequently frustrating, treaty negotiations and on the circumstances that had finally, almost unexpectedly, led to Soviet concessions and produced an accord which had miraculously given lasting satisfaction to all sides.

At one end of this welter of analytic inquest Stalin's successor Nikita Krushchev emerged as the key figure, overruling Politburo opposition to give the go-ahead for the conclusion of the Austrian accord. At the other end – or rather at one of the beginnings of the process that culminated in the State Treaty – was the 1943 Moscow Declaration signed by the Soviet Union, the US and the UK (and supported by the Free French government of General de Gaulle). Under the terms of that Declaration, the wartime allies formally accepted that Austria had been Hitler's first victim. From this flowed the commitment to restore Austria's independence. The Moscow Declaration also includes a rider that Austria could not escape responsibility for its involvement in the war on the side of Hitler's Germany; but this turned out to be a dead letter when the State Treaty came to be finalised.

The Treaty came a decade after the war's end, and only after endless delay and frustration. It set the country free politically, but it put no obligation on Austria to free itself from the moral shackles of its recent history. During a brief period after the end of the war, Austria had attempted to face the unvarnished truth about its involvement with the Nazis. But encouraged by the example of Chancellor Figl, who had been a concentration camp inmate, Austria rapidly recast itself as a victim nation.

The three Western occupying powers liberally encouraged Austria to live this lie. And then in 1955 even the Soviet Union endorsed the unqualified victim version: during a dramatic last-minute intervention in the long-running Treaty negotiations, the Austrian leadership prevailed on the Soviets to remove from the draft text any wording that would have obliged Austrians to shoulder responsibility for past behaviour.

A further 45 years were to pass before Austria's leaders finally bowed to moral pressure – and to international furore over Kurt Waldheim's election as head of state – and called on Austrian society to re-examine their post-imperial history and come to terms with their true role during the Nazi era and the Holocaust.

NOTES ON CHAPTER I

1 *Die Presse*, interview, 17 May 1980.
2 *International Herald Tribune*, March 1980.
3 *Financial Times*, special report on Austria, 25 February 1980.
4 *Guardian*, special report on Austria, 10 December 1979.
5 *The Times*, letter from Vienna, 29 March 1980.
6 *Guardian*, 15 June 1980.
7 'Osterreich – 25 Jahre nach dem Staatsvertrag: Eine Bestandsaufnahme zu Beginn der 80-Jahre (unpublished memorandum), May 1980.
8 Kreisky archive.
9 Letter from Prof. Walter Lohnes, Stanford University, California, to Bruno Kreisky, 10 November 1980.

— II —

Occupied Austria

Cold War Hostage

In contrast to the joyous Vienna of May 1980, Moscow in 1943 was a drab city grieving for the millions who had died repulsing the Nazi invader, but also confident after so much suffering that victory was on its way. This was the time and place where, with little awareness of the likely consequences, commitments were made concerning Austria that would have a profound influence on the strength and character of the post-war Austrian Republic.

Three towering figures, Roosevelt, Churchill and Stalin, made up the supreme directorate still united by their common goal of defeating Nazi Germany. The grand alliance had convened a meeting of its Foreign Ministers.

The tide of war has turned against Hitler's Wehrmacht. Alongside military action to complete the defeat of Hitler and Mussolini, the time was ripe for mapping out the political architecture of Europe in the aftermath of victory. As Vyacheslav Molotov, Cordell Hull and Antony Eden gathered in the Kremlin, the search for a lasting dismantlement of German power was the most pressing feature of their discussions. The three Foreign Ministers and their officials remained in session for close on two weeks. The future of Germany took up most of their time. But on the periphery of the Moscow Declaration published on 1 November – and endorsed by General de Gaulle's Free French government-in-exile on 16 November – the document also addressed itself to Austria, the country that Hitler had renamed the 'Ostmark' after its annexation in 1938.

The three Foreign Ministers had different perceptions of Austria's role and significance in the post-war world. So did the Free French, not yet present at the top table. None of the allies foresaw that Austria, though nominally free and with a democratically elected government, would remain under four-power occupation and used as a Cold War battlefield for a whole decade after the war's end. The State Treaty negotiations directed at translating the commitment to independence into reality, drawn out over a decade, were to become a benchmark to measure and mark the overall state of East-West relations. The tortuous process towards the Treaty can only be understood in the context of the Cold War, of Soviet expansion in Eastern Europe and of seemingly unbridgeable East-West differences over settlement of the German question.

— * —

Austria is crucially placed geographically on the dividing line between East and West. During the ten years it took to finalise Austria's State Treaty, the country was profoundly affected by the way the wartime Allies used and abused their presence on Austrian soil to pursue Cold War goals. Austria's post-war leaders recognised the need for solidarity to defend Austrian interests against the machinations of the occupying powers. The experience of the 1930s with the bitter divisions Austria had experienced, would anyhow have persuaded the country to aim for consensus in its political and economic life.

But the presence of the occupying powers served to reinforce the determination to underline national unity by building a new democracy based on co-operation rather than the rough and tumble of parliamentary political strife. This approach more than served its purpose while the new republic was young. But much later, when Austrian sovereignty became securely anchored, the emphasis on consensus threatened to become an albatross that weighed heavily on Austrian democracy.

During the first decade after 1945 it was not only the long duration of the occupation, but also the Moscow Declaration itself that was to have a profound impact on Austria's post-war evolution. With a few short phrases, the 1943 Declaration commits the grand alliance to securing the re-establishment of a free and independent Austria. It describes Hitler's 1938 annexation of Austria as an 'occupation' and names Austria as Hitler's 'first victim'. However the Allies also add that Austria would have to shoulder its share of responsibility for its participation in the war alongside Hitler's Germany. 'The governments of the UK, the Soviet Union and the US are agreed that Austria is the first independent country, that became victim to Hitler's typical policy of aggression and which must be liberated from German dominion. They regard Austria's occupation by Germany on March 15, 1938 as null and void... they declare their commitment to the restoration of a free and independent Austria... Austria must however be reminded that it carries responsibility for its participation in the war on Hitler's side...'

By no stretch of the imagination could the Allies in 1943 have envisaged that their seal of approval for Austria's perception of itself as Hitler's victim would determine the image that Austrians were to cultivate both for their own peace of mind and for defining the thrust of their foreign relations for decades to come. Nor did the authors of the Moscow Declaration, least of all Molotov, realise that in 1955 the Soviet Union, as well as the more complacent Western powers, would allow the other half of the equation – the rejoinder to Austria to assume its share of responsibility for fighting on Hitler's side – to remain a dead letter.

— * —

Underlying the Moscow Declaration was the determination of all three Allies to prevent the resurgence of a strong Germany. In mapping a way forward for Austria, the wartime alliance was driven both by political considerations and by military factors to do with speeding up the end of the war. The British position reflected Winston Churchill's romantic vision of Austria. He wanted an assertion of Austrian independence not for its own sake but because he believed that this would open the way to a Danubian federation. He envisaged some kind of republican resurrection of the former Habsburg empire, one that would serve as bulwark both against Germany and, even more, against Soviet expansionism in Central Europe. At the same time, the UK, like the US, calculated that the promise of independence would energise the Austrian resistance movement enough to ease the way for the Western military advance as their forces fought their way up from the Italian front into Austria.

A British draft was used as the basis for the Moscow Declaration on Austria. The US asked for a few minor modifications, but President Roosevelt was preoccupied by the war in the Pacific and endorsed Churchill's approach without giving it much attention. At the Moscow Conference, the commitment to secure Austria's independence also happened to suit Joseph Stalin; not, however, for the same reasons as Churchill or Roosevelt. The Soviet leader, already bent on Soviet hegemony over Eastern and Central Europe, was determined to prevent a Danube federation, which he believed would be used as a means of constructing a pro-Western zone of influence designed to undermine his aims. Thus Stalin calculated that it was in the Soviet interest to have an independent but weak Austria on the borders of the future Communist bloc. And while Stalin assumed that Austria possessed a reservoir of committed communists, well placed to convert liberated Austria into a popular democracy, this was never his highest priority. The Soviet leader was always more interested in post-war Austria as a rich source of industrial products and equipment for the starved Soviet economy. Rather than turn the country red, Stalin wanted to bleed the country white.

In 1943, the Soviet Union insisted on two crucial amendments to the British draft declaration. Rather than calling on the Austrian people to remember their actions on Hitler's side, he demanded that the onus be placed on the Austrian state, and that Austria as a nation, and not just Austrians as individuals, be sternly reminded of its responsibility for Hitler's actions. Stalin won the day for his amendment. By holding the Austrian state responsible for collaboration with the Nazis, the Soviet Union believed it had secured legal claims on Austria's economic wealth.

Austrians, however, have always interpreted the clause very differently. On the grounds that the Austrian state had ceased to exist after the Anschluss, they contended that only individual Austrians could be held to account for their Nazi links. It followed that the Moscow Declaration could not be used to hold Austria to a collective responsibility for its wartime behaviour. And there was nothing in the Declaration that required individual Austrians to account for their actions. It took four decades for the Austrian leadership finally to decide that Austrian society could not hide behind such legalisms and that it must recognise its collective responsibility for what had happened while their country was a quasi-province of Nazi Germany; when it was designated as Hitler's Ostmark.

— * —

The Moscow Declaration had momentous consequences – good and bad – for Austria. On the plus side, I share the view that the 'victim' version of history spurred Austrians to develop a strong sense of national identity and to reduce to political insignificance the latent yearning for the greater German nation that had played such a destructive role during the inter-war years. The importance of this can hardly be exaggerated: one only has to recall the weakness of the first, post-1918, Austrian Republic, and the lack of conviction then, even among the elites, about Austria's separate identity.

Even so, the negative fallout from the Moscow Declaration surely outweighs the positive. Nothing could have produced as serious a distortion of recent history as the decision to classify Austria as Hitler's first victim. The Foreign Ministers thus conferred a watertight alibi on a nation that has consistently painted its small, often quarrelsome, resistance movement on a heroic scale, and has sought to draw a veil over Austrian complicity in the Holocaust.

The Moscow Declaration allowed Austria as a whole, and not just the Kurt Waldheims, to live a lie, without facing up to the truth of their headlong rush into Hitler's arms. It enabled Karl Renner, Austria's first post-war leader, to perform an about-turn, to ignore the fact that before the war he was among the keenest advocates of Austrian fusion with Germany, and to be accepted by the Allies in 1945 as a true Austrian patriot wholly committed to a free-standing democratic Austrian nation. To turn a blind eye to history is corrosive. Nothing illustrates this better than the dilatory way in which Austria pursued denazification. The Western Allies are as guilty in this respect as Austria itself: between them, after an initial effort to root out Nazis from public service, depriving them of the vote and bringing a number of war criminals to trial, denazification processes were allowed to lapse. The vote was restored to former Nazis, and permission given to them to form the nucleus of a new right-wing party – which ironically received financial help from Austria's socialist party. Austria began to search its collective conscience on these fundamental matters only when its international credibility was dramatically reduced by the election of Kurt Waldheim as head of state in 1986.

— * —

The preparatory drafts and negotiations leading up to the Moscow Declaration, made it glaringly obvious that the Allies were less concerned with the country itself, or with its people, than with geopolitical considerations involving their wider post-war interests in Europe. There is no need to labour the point: Austria occupies a strategic area in the heartland of Europe.

During the final phase of the war, Hitler looked to Austria's mountains in the Ausseerland as an alpine redoubt where he might be able to regroup his forces. During this time, the Allies were primarily interested in Austria as a staging post in the military campaign against Germany, and in pursuit of their aim of securing Hitler's unconditional surrender. A British diplomat wrote in 1944 that 'Where we want to be severe with Austria, we should regard her as part of Germany... Where we want to encourage her, emphasising her liberation rather than the need for purging and control, we should use new proclamations or orders specifically drafted for Austria.' Another British diplomat, exasperated with the feebleness of Austria's resistance movement, wrote: 'if it were not for the strategic importance of keeping Austria separate from Germany, we would let this feeble country stew'.[1]

After the war's end in 1945, Austria became even more of a strategic pawn of Great Power diplomacy than it had been during the conflict's closing stages. Once the iron curtain was in place and East-West relations had become polarised, Austria was tossed hither and thither in an increasingly deadly game between the Communist and the Western camps. The Western Allies saw their occupation zone as a forward military defence base. The Soviet Union looked to its zone as a security buffer, and a possible launchpad for expansion, while it consolidated control over the Communist bloc. Austria was a minnow in a sea of sharks.

Arguably, Austria's role in the State Treaty negotiations, except at the very end, was marginal. Even the commitment to neutrality, a key aspect of the settlement, owed more to US initiatives than to Austria itself. Austria's own proposals and submissions were of little effect while Stalin remained alive. Its influence on the outcome of the negotiations only grew after his death in 1953 and the emergence of Krushchev as the Soviet Union's new leader. Krushchev felt that a timely settlement in Austria would provide adequate evidence of Soviet commitment to peaceful co-existence. He also needed the treaty to satisfy the demand of Yugoslav leader Marshal Tito for Soviet withdrawal from Austria as his price for normalisation of relations between Moscow and Belgrade.

A 'peace' treaty with Austria was ruled out from the beginning. As an appendage of Germany after 1938, the country itself was not considered to have been in a state of war against the Soviet Union and the Western allies – and that was not only because the 1943 Moscow Declaration had labelled Austria Hitler's victim, but also because ironically the Allies had recognised the legitimacy of the Anschluss, and accepted that Austria had, temporarily, lost its sovereignty.

The State Treaty alternative to a peace treaty was broached by Austria's first post-war government within weeks of the general election in November 1945. But the key moves came from the US administration. In February 1946, a memorandum from a senior US State Department official, James Dunn, embraced the version of Austria as a liberated country and urged the early conclusion of a treaty for the restoration of Austrian independence. He backed his proposal with a perceptive analysis of the Soviet Union's aims in Central Europe. Dunn argued that the four-power occupation of Austria needed to be ended as soon as possible, if only to eradicate any Soviet pretext for retaining troops in Hungary to keep open lines of communication to their Austrian occupation zone.

The Dunn memorandum was no isolated draft. In his famous Fulton speech, Winston Churchill delivered his stark warning that an iron curtain had descended on Eastern and Central Europe and that many of Europe's greatest cities, Vienna included, now found themselves in a Central Europe 'reverting to the dark ages'. 'This is not the liberated Europe we sought to build up,'[2] Churchill asserted. US President Truman, endorsing Churchill's analysis, adopted the 'containment' policy advocated by the American diplomat George Kennan: the Soviet Union, Kennan argued, was in a mood to expand, and must be contained. Austria was one country in which Stalin's advance had to be halted.

Like Germany, the country had been divided into four occupation zones, and its capital split into four sectors under the Allied Council which administered Vienna. It did not take the West long to rule out

Churchill's ambition of promoting a Danube federation. The West was now convinced that the same ruthless determination that had guided Stalin in securing the Wehrmacht's defeat in the Soviet Union would inform the Soviet leader's quest for hegemony over Eastern and Central Europe. A Danubian federation was guaranteed to fall into Russia's grip. Since that was obviously an undesirable option, Austria would have to be helped to stand alone.

In the summer of 1946, the four powers met in Paris to conclude peace treaties with Germany's wartime allies. Austria, Hitler's 'victim', was automatically excluded from this list. Just as Dunn had warned, the Russians, in the negotiations over Hungary and Romania, used the Austrian occupation as justification to secure treaty rights to maintain a Soviet troop presence in those two countries. Soviet forces in Romania and Hungary were essential, they insisted, to keep open their communication lines to the Soviet zone of occupation in Austria.

This argument only reinforced US pressure for an early settlement with Austria. If the Russians were to be pushed back from Central Europe, the Western Allies would have to secure an Austrian treaty that required the evacuation of the occupation forces from the country. The Americans immediately went on the diplomatic offensive, tabling draft treaty proposals and pressing the other three wartime allies to enter into early negotiations. The UK and France were initially hesitant, with both countries arguing that they had higher priorities. They were more concerned by the need to achieve the smooth working of the Allied Control Commission throughout Austria, and especially of the Allied Council in Vienna. The French also held back, arguing that it would be unwise to go ahead with Treaty negotiations before there was evidence of more energetic Austrian action on denazification. French and British hesitations could have been overcome. But the Russians frustrated all US attempts to put an Austrian treaty on the agenda of the Paris Peace Conference. The meetings continued intermittently between July and mid-October 1946. Molotov advanced any number of arguments to exclude Austria: the Paris Conference, he contended, was already too busy; denazification in Austria was too dilatory; the restoration of normality in Austria was being delayed by the presence of too many displaced persons; Austria, having been classed as a victim country could not be put into the same negotiating basket as enemy states.

The true reasons behind Soviet delaying tactics were of course very different: Stalin was determined to consolidate control over Eastern and Central Europe. A settlement with Austria would thwart his designs, because it would certainly have required a rapid military withdrawal from the country. In 1946, Stalin very likely calculated that if the Soviet Union held on long enough in Austria, the country itself could still be edged into the Soviet zone of influence. Besides, he also wanted plenty of time to pillage the Austrian economy and transfer anything movable to strengthen the Soviet economy. In his paranoia, Stalin even suspected that the West was pressing for an early settlement in Austria as a way of delaying Soviet economic recovery.

Having failed to break the deadlock over an Austrian settlement in the early aftermath of the war, the Western powers also came to see advantage in delay. With the Cold War increasingly bedevilling East-West relations, the Western military presence in Austria was seen as an important strategic asset.

— * —

Throughout the decade, the ups and downs of the State Treaty negotiations can only be properly understood in the context of external events. In an era where the world's most powerful nations were obsessed with fear of nuclear war, there was no chance that Austria's plea for a settlement would be judged in isolation on the merits of its case for full independence. Instead, an Austrian treaty had to be handled within the framework of Cold War confrontation and events such as the Berlin blockade, Communist coups in Hungary and Czechoslovakia, and the war in Korea. Against this sombre background there was no way of securing consensus across the East-West divide to finalise the Austrian State Treaty and provide for four-power withdrawal from Austria.

Beginning in 1946, Western military planners were drawing up contingency scenarios in response to a possible Soviet invasion of Western Europe. They assumed that Austria would be in the Western camp, and that there would be local skirmishes instigated by the Soviets and their Austrian communist supporters. Picturesquely entitled 'Pincher' (1946–7), 'Broiler' (1947–8), 'Bushwacker' (1948–9) and Half Moon (1948–9), all four scenarios envisaged that US conventional forces would be too weak to make a stand in Europe. Instead, they provided for withdrawals from Continental Europe, leaving the US free to conduct an all-out air campaign against the Soviet Union without fear of Soviet reprisals capable of reaching US military targets. As the Soviet Union did not yet have 'the bomb', the US plans even envisaged the use of nuclear weapons. To achieve a successful withdrawal, a 'Dunkirk II' scenario was drawn up for allied forces in Austria.'

None of these ideas reached the point where they were adopted by the US administration as policy projections. All the same, the mere fact that such war games were designed – and taken seriously by the military – underlines just how little concern or understanding there was for Austria's direct interests. Given the nuclear dimension of US strategic planning, Austria would, after Allied evacuation, almost certainly have become a nuclear target. Yet the Austrian authorities were not even told about these plans.

Pincher, Broiler, Bushwacker and Half Moon all assumed that Western withdrawals would only be implemented in response to acute emergency. The planners evidently took it for granted that under all other circumstances Allied occupation forces would remain in place in Austria, ready for conventional defence against Soviet expansion. After the Communist coups in Prague and Budapest, the Austrian zones under Western occupation had become one of the most sensitive frontline areas of Western defence. In line with this realisation, another plan, 'Pilgrim Dog', was devised in 1949 by France and the US. The British were not involved. The plan provided for the use of Austrian partisans – to be known as Police Brigade B – to co-operate with Allied forces to resist a Soviet invasion of Austria, and possibly also to help with the defence of Northern Italy.

Unlike the other scenarios for Austria, Pilgrim Dog was for real – to the extent that arms piles were stocked in secret locations, men were recruited and trained for special units of the Austrian gendarmerie, and money to pay for all this channelled to Austria with the connivance of the US trade union movement and a handful of carefully picked Austrian leaders.[4] Among those taken into American confidence were two senior Austrian politicians, President Schärf and trade union leader Franz Olah.

Western concern that Austria was being drawn into the epicentre of the Cold War first became acute during the 1948–9 Berlin blockade. They feared that the Soviet Union might also attempt to blockade Vienna. Unlike Berlin, where the Allies had Tempelhof airport and rapidly constructed a second one at Tegel, Vienna's airfields were all in the Soviet zone. The Americans built small airstrips at Schönbrunn and in the Karl Marx Hof in the 19th District, and decided to construct an airfield at Kaiser-Ebersdorf. Emergency dumps of food and coal were built up in Vienna even though US military planners doubted that the West would have the resources to mount an airlift to Vienna as well as Berlin.[5] The British were even more dubious, questioning not only military feasibility but also US political strategy. The UK's military commander in Austria, Major-General Sir John Winterton, sent a forceful note to London opposing the US moves and arguing that the responsibility for supplying Vienna rested 'squarely on the shoulders of the Austrian government'.

However, Lt-General Geoffrey Keyes, the general commanding US forces in Austria, persevered with airfield construction and stockpiling. The operation was given the codename 'Operation Squirrel Cage'. It was all supposed to be done under conditions of the utmost secrecy, but inevitably the Russians became aware of these plans and kept up the suspense over their intentions by provoking minor aggravations on the access routes to Vienna. Late in 1949 they also resorted to one of their favourite ways of signalling displeasure, and used the tightly controlled

Soviet media to launch a tirade of warnings about resurgent fascism and dangerous militarism in Austria.

Fear of a Soviet blockade of Vienna continued even after the Soviet Union had ended its efforts to drive the Western allies out of Berlin. Early in 1950, Truman considered the threat serious enough to authorise a secret directive on 'US policy in Austria in the event of a blockade of Vienna'. It instructed American forces to exercise their full rights in Austria, but avoid all provocation of the Soviet authorities or the Austrian population. Whether the Soviet Union ever seriously contemplated a Berlin-type blockade of Vienna remains unclear. The Soviets certainly knew that they could have interrupted access to Vienna without provoking another Western airlift. Truman's 1950 directive contained no provisions for an airlift. Without access to adequate airfields in Vienna, it would have been impossible to sustain such operations.

But under the Marshall Aid Plan for Austria, emergency food piles continued to be replenished until 1954. Early in 1955, only 1800 tons of canned horse-meat were left, and these were then sold off as dog-food, 'An ignominious end to a once grandiose plan to sustain Vienna in the face of Soviet aggression'.[6]

After the conclusion of the NATO treaty in 1949, Western military commanders had become adamant that a significant force presence must be retained in Austria. NATO strategy had to be based on a forward defence by conventional forces backed by a massive nuclear umbrella. Austria was part of the forward defence line, all the more important since the NATO treaty included a guarantee to protect allied occupation forces in any part of Europe against Soviet military action. Some military experts even proposed that the Western zones of Austria should be incorporated into the alliance.

General Emil Béthouart, the French High Commissioner in Austria insisted that the Austrian Alps were a vital strategic link with Italy and the Mediterranean theatre, and that the Allied occupation must be maintained. 'The Austrian Alps must remain under allied control. They are vital for the defence of Western Europe, as they provide cover for Italy and the Mediterranean... The occupied zone legitimises the allied presence in Central Europe, enables us to pose a permanent threat to the [Soviet] enemy, and offers hope to the oppressed peoples [of the Communist bloc].'

The US High Commissioner in Austria, General Geoffrey Keyes, agreed that the Western forces in Austria were essential for Allied forward defence during the Cold War. The occupation had to be maintained not because of any wartime commitments but because Austria had to be used as a military base. 'We must recognise that the occupation of Austria is not only necessary because of our wartime commitments, but also because of the ideological conflict between East and West. The original justification for our occupation of Austria has become secondary. The main purpose of our presence in Austria is to combat communism and to oppose the Soviet Union's economic and political aggression against the West. This alone justifies a decision to maintain our [the West's] military presence in Austria.'[7]

Dean Acheson, the new US Secretary of State, remained unconvinced, however, by such strategic considerations, and made plain that he would have preferred to conclude the State Treaty on condition that it obliged all four occupying powers to accept an early withdrawal from Austria. The UK's Foreign Minister, Ernest Bevin, and France's Georges Bidault shared this view.

When the three Western Foreign Ministers were joined in Paris by Molotov in May 1949, they detected signs that made them believe the Soviet Union was edging towards conclusion of the treaty. Bevin became sufficiently optimistic to tell Acheson that 'it appears quite clear to me that Stalin has instructed that within reason, an effort should be made to clear up this matter'.[8] Not long afterwards, on 17 November, Truman determined 'that it should be US policy to agree at an early date to a draft Austrian treaty on the best terms available'. This was followed up by important economic concessions to Soviet demands in the treaty negotiations.

But Western optimism proved premature. The Soviet Union again became obstructive. Stalin had decided after all that Soviet interests would be damaged by conceding military withdrawal from Austria. Austria still counted as an important Soviet bargaining chip in the quest for Communist consolidation in Eastern Europe and for the demilitarisation of Germany. The country remained hostage to the Cold War. If Western political leaders were disappointed, their military planners were pleased with Stalin's wrecking tactics. They had not changed their minds about Austria as a vital component of Western defence.

The negotiations were to remain stalled for close on a further five years. The Cold War had become a freeze, and disagreement over Germany's future remained unbridgeable, leaving no room for compromise over Austria. The Soviet Union continued to use its occupation zone in Eastern Austria as a convenient buffer between East and West. However much Austria pressed for the State Treaty, its needs were pushed aside by the Great Powers. By 1952, Austrian frustration had grown to such an extent that the government even appealed to the UN General Assembly to support its cause. A resolution in support of Austria was duly passed – and fell on deaf ears in the capitals where it mattered.

Negotiations were never broken off altogether: there were proposals and counterproposals, and some issues inched forward. But the political will to bring matters to a conclusion was missing. It was tantalising. But for all the work involved in the negotiating sessions, it is hard to think of it as more than a charade, with Austria again and again caught up helplessly in the East-West contest.

— * —

After Stalin's death in March 1953, superpower interest in a settlement over Austria at last looked as if it might be genuine. Krushchev was consolidating his power, cautiously seeking to correct some of his predecessor's mistakes. In the US too, there was a new President, General Dwight Eisenhower, who had chosen John Foster Dulles as his Secretary of State.

Dulles promised to roll back communism. But the Soviet Union had caught up with the US and was now also a nuclear power. The brief uprising in East Germany during the summer of 1953 demonstrated that NATO had no intention of coming to the aid of 'the captive peoples' – as the US labelled them – in territories under Soviet control, where intervention carried the risk of triggering another world war – a nuclear one.

After Soviet forces helped to put down the East German uprising, Krushchev over-ruled Politburo critics and decided to abandon the old Stalinist goal to secure a unified but demilitarised and neutral Germany. The division of Germany seemed inevitable. The Federal German Chancellor, Konrad Adenauer, was pressing NATO to allow the Federal Republic to become a member. As a counter, the Soviet Union would put its full weight behind the German Democratic Republic and draw up the Warsaw Pact Treaty, with the right for Soviet troops to be stationed in member countries. The East-West divide was being firmed up. Two zones of influence in Europe were set in political cement. Austria was sandwiched awkwardly between them.

Krushchev began to advocate the idea of peaceful co-existence as a way of easing tensions between the two blocks. Suddenly an Austrian State treaty began to have attractions for the Soviet Union. A settlement there would be a tangible sign of detente. According to a Soviet defector, Krushchev's thinking had already evolved towards military withdrawal and the establishment of a fully independent but neutral Austria as early as the summer of 1953. 'The talk in the Soviet mission [in Vienna] when I arrived [in September 1953] was all of the neutral Austria which Krushchev was now ready to accept... The general assumption was that Krushchev had decided that the isolation of the Stalin era had to be ended and that an Austrian Treaty was the cheapest entry ticket back into civilised society. It might even bring advantages, though that would depend on how the link-up with the main problem of Germany could be made, and nobody knew yet how that would be worked out. Yugoslavia was another important factor. Marshal Tito had apparently made it clear to Krushchev that if he wanted a reconciliation with Belgrade, he had better remove the Red Army from Austria first.'[9]

Krushchev was faced by another problem: Molotov's adamant resistance to a deal over Austria that involved Soviet withdrawal from the country. The veteran Soviet diplomat, Anatoly Dobrynin, recalled the Kremlin's heated discussions about the Austrian treaty: 'Only Molotov spoke out against it. He said, "we are very comfortable there. So why should we go?" But most of the Soviet leadership thought we should make a goodwill treaty. Krushchev succeeded in outmanoeuvring Molotov.'[10]

Krushchev's arrival on the international stage had prompted Austria's leadership into renewed efforts to break the deadlock over the State Treaty. The Soviets had eased their iron grip on censorship over the media under their control in Austria and were no longer demanding reimbursement for their occupation costs. Austria had a new Chancellor, Julius Raab. He sensed that, at long last, Austria's time had arrived; that the negotiations over Austria were now centre-stage in the search for improved East-West relations. Talks about an Austrian settlement had become more than a convenient Cold War temperature gauge.

Raab decided to sound out international statesmen with good contacts in Moscow. In June 1953, India's Prime Minister, Jawaharlal Nehru stopped off in Switzerland on his way to Moscow. The Austrian Foreign Minister, Karl Gruber, was dispatched to Burgenstock, where Nehru was staying, to consult with him over the kind of approach that might persuade Moscow to move towards a settlement. Nehru provided useful pointers to Russia's problems with the State Treaty, notably their concerns over Austrian links with Germany, and Austria's future relations with the two power blocs.

This resulted one week later in an Austrian memorandum – intended for use by the Indians when they raised the issue in Moscow – which included an offer to reject all future links with military alliances in return for the restoration of full sovereignty and the withdrawal of all occupation forces.

Bruno Kreisky, as State Secretary for Foreign Affairs, was involved in drawing up the document, which turned out to be doubly significant: it was remarkably prescient in mapping out the key elements of the settlement that was reached two years later in 1955; and it also contained the first indications of Kreisky's ideas for Austria's future world role. The memorandum argued that the best guarantee that Austria could give the Russians would be a unilateral declaration to be ratified by the Austrian parliament to the effect that Austria would remain outside all military pacts, and could therefore not be used as a Western military base. By adopting a status similar to Switzerland, Austria envisaged a neutralised zone in the heart of Europe. With the strategic Alpine region outside any military alliance, Kreisky argued that the Soviet Union, and not only the Western powers, would also gain an important security guarantee.

'Austria is, in any event, determined to safeguard its independence against all sides [in the East-West conflict].'[11]

Even though this was not yet tantamount to a proposal to volunteer permanent neutrality, it was a hint in that direction. The Indians duly discussed these ideas in Moscow. But they ran into the Molotov buffer, and negotiations remained at standstill until January 1954 when the Foreign Ministers of the four wartime allies met again after a five year break. For the first time at any high-level meeting since 1945, the Austrian question figured high on the agenda.

Dulles came to Berlin armed with a crucial concession from President Eisenhower, who had said that 'he could see no objection to the neutralisation of Austria if this did not carry with it demilitarisation. If Austria could accomplish a status comparable to Switzerland, this would be quite satisfactory from a military standpoint.'[12] Plainly the President no longer shared the concerns of US military experts who wanted to retain some hold over Austria as a communications link with NATO's southern flank. Dulles was more dubious, but reasoned that a Soviet withdrawal from Austria could be interpreted as a roll-back that could set a precedent for Eastern Europe. And, while he remained implacably opposed to Germany's neutrality, he accepted that a neutral status was acceptable for a small country like Austria.

At the Berlin conference, Dulles stressed that Austrian neutrality could only be meaningful if it was voluntarily adopted, and not if it was forced on Austria as part of its obligations under the State Treaty. This interpretation had been formalised in consultation with France and the UK, and fully reflected Kreisky's thinking. But Molotov held different views. He wanted a binding treaty commitment that Austria drop all coalitions and military pacts. Taken literally, this amounted to an impossible restriction on Austrian membership of multinational institutions. 'A neutral status is an honourable status,' Dulles declared, 'if it is freely chosen by a nation. Switzerland has chosen to be neutral, and as a neutral she has achieved an honourable place in the family of nations. Under the Austrian State Treaty as heretofore drafted, Austria would be free to chose for itself to be a neutral state like Switzerland. Certainly the United States would fully respect its choice in this respect... However it is one thing for a nation to choose to be neutral. It is another thing to have it forcibly imposed on it by other nations as a perpetual servitude.'[13]

Molotov refused to be convinced. The Soviet Foreign Minister produced another bombshell – he put forward a further condition, one which guaranteed the breakdown of the negotiations over Austria. Once again, he insisted on a link between an Austrian settlement and accord on the larger German question; and he demanded that some occupation troops should be allowed to remain in Austria until a peace treaty with Germany was achieved. But of course a German peace treaty was nowhere in sight. The Western Allies rejected Molotov's proposal out of hand. While they had come to Berlin ready to satisfy Austrian demands for full sovereignty, the Soviet Union had again reverted to using Austria as a tool to pursue their wider ambitions in Europe.

— * —

By February 1955, Germany was on the verge of joining NATO; the Soviet Union intended to respond with the Warsaw Pact Treaty, which secured them the right to station Soviet forces on the territories of their Eastern European satellites and removed any need to use the occupation of Austria as a figleaf for their military presence in Hungary or Czechoslovakia. A number of Soviet experts suspected that unless a settlement was speedily reached, Austria might end up as a member of the NATO alliance. Krushchev decided that Molotov's intransigence towards Austria could not any longer be allowed to dictate the Soviet negotiating posture.

On 8 February 1955, Molotov, acting on Krushchev's instructions, was himself obliged to announce the Soviet *volte face*. Austria, he told the Supreme Soviet, could have its State Treaty with full independence even without a German peace treaty. The only vital condition for concluding the Austrian treaty was a firm guarantee against Anschluss with Germany. It took a further three months to iron what had earlier been insuperable difficulties over the Soviet Union's demands for 'German assets' in Austria. During this time agreement was also reached on the process by which Austria would voluntarily accept the status of neutrality.

With the Western allies acting in broad support of the Austrians, Raab and his colleagues were at last able to have a decisive say on the terms of the State Treaty. Initially the Austrian leadership was uncertain whether a declaration of neutrality was in their best interests. An image has grown up around Kreisky that it was his idea and that he proposed a status of 'permanent neutrality' for Austria during a negotiating session in Moscow. In fact, he disclosed many years later that he had argued against a neutrality declaration on the grounds that it might go too far in circumscribing Austria's freedom of action. He had feared that the Soviet Union, France, the UK and the US would all have different definitions of neutrality and might ignore Austria's own interpretation. It would be far wiser, he had believed at that stage, for Austria to steer clear of the neutrality concept and limit itself to a commitment to remain outside any military alliance. 'I was well aware of the different concepts of neutrality. So I asked myself why we should use a word that would be interpreted differently in Moscow, London, Paris and Washington. Our own interpretation would carry the smallest weight of all. Far better to make a commitment to permit no military bases [in our country].'[14]

— * —

On 14 May 1955, the four Foreign Ministers, Dulles, Molotov, Pinay and Macmillan assembled in Vienna. Not since the Potsdam Conference in 1945 had the four wartime Allies found themselves in complete agreement over a major issue. They were unanimous in approving the Treaty text. By the end of October, all their forces would have gone from Austrian soil. Only then would the Austrian parliament declare Austria's permanent neutrality.

The four ministers beamed politely and nodded: next morning they would sign the Austrian State Treaty. Then it was the turn of the Austrian Foreign Minister, Leopold Figl, to drop a potentially wrecking bombshell. He had one more request, that the preamble to the Treaty repeated the 1943 Moscow Declaration's formula that Austria was Hitler's first victim, but had to bear its share of responsibility for its participation in the war on Hitler's side. Austria wanted this clause removed from the State Treaty. Figl argued that it would be unfair to burden Austria with guilt about past behaviour at the very moment of its relaunch as an independent nation. Austria's internal and external development would be handicapped by such a moral slur.

With little pause for reflection, all four ministers agreed to Austria's request. The three Western allies had no qualms. But the real surprise of the day was Molotov's agreement to drop a requirement to which the Russians had clung so tenaciously – not out of moral considerations, but because from the very outset in Moscow in 1943 the Soviet Union had always seen the responsibility clause as a useful weapon to extract economic tribute from Austria.

But the timing of the Austrian intervention proved crucial. Apart from the responsibility clause, in all other aspects the Treaty text was ready for signature; and the four wartime allies were anxious to seal it and move on to test whether the East-West climate could now be improved. They were not going to allow a small paragraph to delay them. And so, without any concern for historical truth, the four powers that had fought a bitter war against Hitler's 'Greater Germany' conspired with Austria's leaders to endow this relaunch of the Second Austrian Republic with a clean bill of health.

Thirty years later, when the international community finally began to question Austria's failure to face up to its past, the four Great Power signatories might have acknowledged that they bore a large share of responsibility for creating and sustaining a misleading image of Austria. But they preferred to remain silent, and let Austria take all the blame for the long-lasting cover-up of the country's moral failures.

NOTES ON CHAPTER II

1. Internal minute written by Oliver Hardy, Head of Foreign Office Central Department, 4 July 1944.
2. Winston Churchill, at Fulton College, Missouri, February 1946.
3. Erwin Schmidl, 'The Airlift that Never Was: Allied Plans to Supply Vienna by Air, 1948–49', *Army History*, the professional bulletin of army history, Washington DC, Fall 1997/Winter 1998.
4. Franz Olah, *Die Erinnerungen*, Amalthea Verlag, 1995, pp 148–51.
5. Schmidl, 'The Airlift that Never Was', op. cit.
6. Schmidl, 'The Airlift that Never Was', op. cit., p 19.
7. Hugo Portisch and Sepp Riff, *Osterreich II: Der lange Weg zur Freiheit*, Kremayr & Scheriau, 1986, p 373.
8. Bevin to Acheson, 1 October 1949, FO 371/76451(C7962) UK Public Record Office.
9. Peter Sergeivich Deriabin, quoted by Gordon Brook-Shepherd, *The Austrians*, HarperCollins, 1997, pp 401–2.
10. Interview with Anatoly Dobrynin in Jeremy Isaac's TV documentary, *History of the Cold War*.
11. Gerald Stourzh, Um Einheit und Freiheit: Geschichte des Osterreichischen Staatsvertrag, 4. Auflage, Böhlau, 1988, pp 229–32.
12. White House memorandum of meeting with the President, 20 January 1954, reproduced in Portisch and Riff, *Osterreich II*, op. cit., p 463.
13. Statement by the Secretary of State, 13 February 1954, published in *American Foreign Policy* 1950–5, basic documents vol. 2, p 1859.
14. Interview with Bruno Kreisky in Portisch and Riff, *Osterreich II*, op. cit., pp 475–6.

III

Austria Under Occupation

Liberated but not Free

The contemporary world no longer lives in fear of nuclear conflict. The Cold War has receded to become part of the history of the twentieth century. Set in the perspective of post-war history, Austria's decade as an occupied country was a side-show – interesting but of minor importance – staged by the four wartime allies as the West fell out with the Soviet Union and battled over the division of Europe.

For me nothing could have underscored Austria's walk-on role in the Cold War drama more than my involvement in a television documentary history of that era that was made for CNN in 1998. Austria only figures briefly in one of the 24 hour-long episodes. Even then, I had a hard fight to preserve footage about the State Treaty – and that was reduced to a one-minute slot: the same State Treaty that was ten long years in the waiting and the making, while Austria had to accommodate itself to four-power occupation; the same State Treaty which launched Austria on its career as a widely respected activist neutral state and allowed the country to postpone an uncomfortable confrontation with its record during the Nazi era.

Not surprisingly, Austrian leaders surveying the parlous condition of their occupied, hungry, impoverished country at the war's end pressed for an early settlement with the Allies. The occupation was the centre of

Austria's universe. As the years passed by without agreement, the State Treaty became not so much a mirage but an obsession.

Austria is probably exceeded only by Israel in possessing a tunnel-vision about its country's affairs, and so it is that Austrian mythology attaches extravagant claims to the role of its own leaders in achieving the State Treaty through ten long years of trial and tribulation. To assert this is not to belittle the inventiveness and endurance of Austrian politicians and diplomats who explored every chink in the Great Powers' armour – and made a good stab at exploiting the differences between them. But their influence was far more limited than the myths spread in Austria about the 379 treaty negotiating sessions, spread over a decade of dangerous East-West confrontation, would suggest.

For Austrians themselves, each day counted – and not only because the country wanted its full freedom without the presence of foreign forces, but also because of the debilitating impact of the occupation powers on day-to-day life in a physically and mentally shattered nation. The Moscow Declaration had endorsed independence. But freedom and the full exercise of sovereignty was simply not attainable under an occupation regime. Interference varied with time and circumstance and the conflict between the occupying powers. Each of the four, but most notably the Russians, handled themselves differently.

— * —

During the entire decade of occupation, Austria's life at all levels revolved around the image that the US, the Soviet Union, the UK and France had each formed of Austria, and the role they envisaged for the country within the framework of their strategic aims in a deeply divided Europe. How would the occupying powers behave in post-war Austria? How far would they go in rooting out the Nazis? What importance did they attach to the country's recovery and its restoration as a sovereign nation? How would the occupation forces go about their everyday dealings with Austrians? It was only natural that such questions were articulated at every level from the grass-roots up to the political class that emerged in 1945 from concentration camps or returned from exile. 'It is a brutal fact that Austria's fate is in the hands of the victorious powers, who can if they so chose totally destroy it. Austria's political stature will be determined exclusively by the Great Powers.'[1] Such was the view expressed during one of early meetings of the provisional Austrian government which launched the Second Republic at the end of April 1945 only a handful of days after the Red Army had taken Vienna.

This conclusion, gloomy as it was for the Austrians, was perfectly justified. Austria had been allowed the trappings of independence, and possessed an all-Austrian government; but its freedom was severely circumscribed. How could it have been otherwise under military occupation, an occupation moreover where the victor countries were gearing themselves up for what became the Cold War?

— * —

Unlike Germany, in Austria the four wartime allies had, by some miracle, managed to agree that the country, though occupied, was entitled to its own government with authority over the entire country. It was a salient factor, one which made a huge difference to the post-war settlement in the two countries. In Germany, the division into occupation zones without the immediate establishment of an all-German government was the precursor of its division into the Federal Republic and the German Democratic Republic.

In Austria's case, the willingness of the occupying powers to work with a democratically elected national government sustained its unity even while it was divided into four occupation zones. Stalin agreed to Karl Renner's request to set up a provisional Austrian government within days of the war's end, even before the Western Allies also endorsed the proposal. At the time, Stalin's move was not as odd as it looks in retrospect. The Soviet leader, still intent on warding off possible Western moves to establish a Danubian federation, wanted to see in place a government that would personify Austrian independence.

But Stalin also calculated – wrongly as it turned out – that Austria's Communist Party was strong enough to secure a majority in the country's first nationwide post-war election. This helped to persuade the Soviet Union to follow up formation of the provisional government with endorsement of elections in November 1945. The Western Allies at first suspected that Renner himself was in the Soviets' pocket. It did not take them long to realise they had misjudged him. But even before they revised their views about his integrity they agreed to the provisional government and to the staging of early elections. These two decisions in 1945 were as fateful in shaping Austria's whole post-war evolution as the State Treaty was ten years later.

The unified administration meant that the Allies found it harder to run roughshod over Austrian interests, and helped Austria to resist Soviet efforts to enfeeble the country. The November 1945 election proved a disaster for the Russians – and by extension was rightly interpreted as a victory not just for Austrian democracy but also for the West – because Austria's Communist Party was so soundly beaten that any prospect of a Communist assumption of power was decisively dashed.

The powers of Renner's provisional government, and of its elected successors, were inevitably circumscribed by the fact that Austria became a Cold War theatre, and that the whole country was occupied and divided into four occupation zones, with Vienna split into four sectors under a four-power Allied Council. But at least Renner was able to put a political and an administrative machine in place, and his government's writ extended throughout Austria. Gradually, during the decade of occupation, Austria's politicians succeeded in carving out for themselves a remarkably wide space for manoeuvre and establishing a stable multi-party democracy.

— * —

Ten years of occupation were an endurance test for Austria. Yet the pessimistic predictions of at least one British observer, Charles Hiscocks, who headed the hyperactive British Council office in Vienna, proved to be very misguided. He wrote in his Annual Report for 1948 that 'the prolongation of the occupation is bound in the long run to have a demoralising effect on a people inclined by nature to live for the present and to shirk strategic responsibilities, and it makes it difficult, if not impossible for them to face the need for working out their own salvation'.[2]

Austrians did in fact work at regaining control over their lives. Yet for the duration of the occupation the country's politics, economy, institutions – including the Church, the media and trade unions – and ordinary people were all intimately affected by the way the outside powers handled themselves in Austria, judged the country's character and leaders, and exploited the occupation for purposes unconnected with the country's own best interests. Arguably only the arts were left – relatively – undisturbed to lift spirits in what was otherwise a bleak existence for Austrians and often the occupying forces alike.

There was an obvious contradiction between the claims of all four wartime allies to have liberated Austria and the ten-year delay in ending their occupation until a pause – certainly not an end – in the Cold War led to the conclusion of the State Treaty. Austrians were left in no doubt that external powers were trying to manipulate their future. But it was Austria's good fortune that the three Western powers concluded that their Cold War objectives called for the promotion of a firm sense of national identity in Austria based on democratic rights and a viable economy. There were two priorities in 1945: first to deter Austrians from seeking renewed links with Germany, and second to use Austria as a bulwark against Soviet expansionist aims in Europe.

Typically, General Mark Clark, the commander of US forces in Austria, declared in July 1945 that he did not see Austria as a militaristic nation, and promised that it would not be treated in the same class as Germany. 'Austria was drawn into the war after the Nazi invasion. Our task is to create a democratic and independent government capable of running the country on its own. It must remain separated from Germany and free of Nazi influence. Austria must be treated better than Germany.'[3]

A British expert, John Mair, who served as political officer with the British army in Austria and Germany, echoed Clark's prescription: 'The

Allies' post-war task in Austria was never primarily considered, as their task in Germany, in terms of re-education of a people, but rather in terms of the reconstitution of a state'.[4]

By no means everyone in the West was persuaded that Austria was capable of securing its own separate identity. The distinguished British historian A.J.P. Taylor defined a brutal image of Austrians when he wrote that 'the fragment of German territory called Austria has no roots in history, no support in the feeling of its people, no record even of resistance to Nazi rule... When (if ever) there is a peaceful democratic Germany, Austria will be a contented part of it. But Austria will never be an effective barrier against German nationalism.'[5]

Politicians were more diplomatic in their expressions of doubt about the strength of Austria's nationhood, but during the early post-war years there remained a widespread view abroad that Austria was an artificial construct bound to seek a return to the German embrace unless shored up by carefully administered external props.

Among the American forces who liberated Mauthausen and its nearby satellite concentration camps there were some who were so horrified by the sights they encountered that they felt unable to follow Clark's logic and follow his advice to differentiate between 'good Austrians' and 'bad Germans'. During research on my biography of Simon Wiesenthal, some of the US officers who entered Mauthausen in May 1945 revealed that nothing had prepared them either for the horrors they uncovered in these death camps or for the realisation that many of the perpetrators had been Austrian, and not only German Nazis. Colonel Richard Seibel, who led units of the US 11th Armoured Division, wrote later that he could not believe the terrible evidence of 'man's inhumanity to man' that he encountered. 'I saw the people and what had been done to them and realised the severity with which they had been mistreated. Mauthausen did exist. Man's inhumanity to man did exist. The world must not be allowed to forget the depths to which mankind can sink lest it should happen again.'[6]

Such experiences undoubtedly affected the attitude of individual soldiers towards Austria. But most of the forces that liberated the country were already at the end of their period of service abroad and were replaced by personnel who had no direct experience of the war. They had less difficulty in accepting the priorities set by the *realpolitik* of the three Western governments, even though amongst the new army arrivals were emigrés from Nazi Germany and Austria who had few illusions about Austria's Nazi record – yet willingly carried out such duties as recruiting former Nazis to become anti-Communist informers.

In London in 1945, the newly elected Attlee government felt very strongly that it should not stand in judgment over Austria, but instead concentrate on the task of building an independent Austrian state.

'Before she can achieve this independence, she must win recognition of her own and purely Austrian national identity – first among her own people, and second, among her friends abroad.' Evidently it did not occur to the British policy-makers that it would also take an end to foreign occupation for Austria to be considered as a truly independent state.[7]

However, the UK believed that it owed Austria a debt: that Neville Chamberlain's appeasement policy before the war had helped to deliver Austria into Hitler's arms. Now was the time to make amends. Ordinary British people were equally reluctant to blame Austrians for involvement in the Holocaust. 'The fact was that there were many people in Britain who found it hard to imagine a people so gay and friendly as being truly sympathetic to so rigid a creed as German Naziism... But underlying these feelings of sympathy was undoubtedly a more general sense of guilt about Britain's share in the West's abandonment of Austria in 1938, and this sense of guilt found relief in assurances by government leaders that the policy would be reversed.'[8]

Neutral Switzerland could afford a detached interpretation of the Western Allies' position. Post-war Austria had to be helped to recover both from the ravages of war and also of its experience under German 'occupation'. It had to gain the confidence of the occupation powers. In April 1945, soon after Soviet forces had taken Vienna, the *Neue Zürcher Zeitung* encapsulated Swiss thinking in an article which stressed that 'the German occupation of Austria only brought suffering, death and misery to Austria. It constitutes an unforgettable period of its history. After seven years of occupation, the character of the new Austrian republic has to be sharply differentiated from the former Republic. The key issues confronting Austria today is the elimination of the Nazis, the relationship between the old and the new generations, and the restoration of superpower confidence in Austria.'

— * —

In the heady atmosphere of victory, Soviet behaviour and attitudes towards Austrians in 1945 were ambivalent. Marshal Tolbukhin, the commander of Soviet forces in Austria, proclaimed on his arrival that the Red Army was liberating Austria from the Nazis, and promised to respect the country's social order, not to appropriate any territory, and to adhere to the principles of the 1943 Moscow Declaration to which all four wartime allies were committed. But this did not prevent the Russian occupation forces from displaying total disregard for the rights and property of ordinary Austrians: requisitioning homes for army quarters, appropriating vehicles, stealing food, raping women, placing Austrian Communists into key ministerial position in the provisional government and targeting the country for a Communist take-over. In their overall behaviour, the Russians treated ordinary Austrians as lowly beings, fit for every kind of exploitation and humiliation.

Unlike the Western occupation powers, the Russians made little attempt to win Austria's trust. If the West was cynical in its use of Austria, at least it did not seek to reduce it to an enfeebled satellite state. The Soviet Union had fewer scruples. Stalin never aimed to divide Austria, fearing that such a split would drive Austria's Western rump back into the German camp. But Stalin wanted Austria's economic assets for the Soviet Union. It also suited him politically to have an economically weakened Austria which would be open to Soviet pressures and might be conditioned to become another Soviet acolyte.

Only days after Soviet forces occupied Vienna in 1945, the Russians submitted a startling list of Soviet demands for economic tribute. Indeed for the duration of the occupation the Soviet Union never ceased to try to bleed the Austrian economy and lay its hands on anything moveable within the Soviet grasp. That the Soviet Union partially succeeded is testimony to Stalin's deviousness. Having accepted Austria's status as a victim rather than an enemy state, the four wartime allies had removed the prospect that reparations might be extracted from Austria. So the Soviet leader devised another approach to justify the seizure of Austria's resources.

In the summer of 1945, during the Potsdam conference – the last of the four-power summits – Stalin succeeded in bouncing the others into an agreement that German assets in each of the Austrian occupation zones should be assigned to the relevant occupying power. The Western Allies fell into line, even though they had little intention of seizing German-owned factories and installations in their zones. They did not see through Stalin's ruse for extracting massive reparations from Austria. While seeking to rob Austria of its wealth, the Soviets also courted Austria's new political leader. They supported Renner as champion of Austria's renewal as an independent nation, even though they were well aware of his pre-war enthusiasm for 'Grossdeutschland' and union with Germany. Austrians were themselves either oblivious to Renner's political somersaults or preferred to ignore them.

The Russians misjudged the Austrians' chameleon-like character and failed to understand that there were some gut instincts that never change. They did not realise the depth of Austrian distrust of Russia, which was rooted in their history. Nor did they foresee that this factor, now reinforced by the undisciplined behaviour of Soviet soldiery, would alienate the working classes to such an extent that communism would never find a firm foothold in post-war Austria. A US intelligence report, written in November 1945, concluded that the undisciplined behaviour of the Soviet troops was 'sufficient to provide a residue of anti-Soviet bias to their [the Austrians'] thinking for a long time to come... A tremendous amount of publicity has been given [by the Soviets] to the delivery of foodstuffs to the city, to the allocation of certain funds to the reconstruction of the Vienna Opera, to the erection of a memorial to the Red Army men who lost their lives in the liberation of Vienna etc... The main reason why all this propaganda has had very little effect on the Austrian population is obvious: looting, rape and indiscriminate requisitioning of foodstuffs create a state of mind which it is very difficult to eliminate by phrases alone.'[9]

Of course it was not all clear-cut. In the murky circumstances of the period, indelibly portrayed in the film, *The Third Man*, Austrians themselves were certainly not above appropriating other people's property; nor did every woman offer resistance to the indecent advances of Soviet, or for that matter Western, soldiery. But as with other uncomfortable facts, Austrians prefer to gloss over such unpleasantness. Soviet behaviour alone became etched into the subconscious. 'These people will never forget what the Red Army did to our women. The present feeling of the simple people that the Russians are *Untermenschen* will last as long as this generation lives.'[10]

As a young priest, Franz König – later to become Austria's much-respected Primate – had spent the war in St Pölten, and was still there during the early stages of Soviet occupation. Soviet soldiers were constantly on the search for women, and König did his share in trying to protect them from rape – even to the extent of guarding a group of nuns while they slept. 'One day a Russian officer arrived, pointed at one of the nuns and told me he wanted her. I stood up and said "that is my wife" and the Russian respected that and left!

'We were haunted by the Soviet presence. We feared that Austria would remain under Soviet domination. Throughout the occupation years we gave communism a higher priority than the question of Austria's co-responsibility with Nazi Germany. The Church did not understand early enough that it must urge people to search their consciences... We saw ourselves as victims.'[11] Later König became outspoken in exercising moral pressure on his fellow citizens to confront the truth rather than push uncomfortable matters aside.

— * —

There can be no question that between 1945 and 1955 the four occupying powers cynically exploited Austria in their Cold War strategies. As already described in the previous chapter, the Treaty negotiations became a furnishing of the Cold War. It was Austria's good luck that Western strategy often coincided with the aspirations of the Austrian leadership. Both wanted a sound democracy and a viable economy, capable of standing up to the Russians. Austria's leaders obviously wanted this for the country's own sake, to reinforce their claim that the 'victim' nation had earned its right to count as a sovereign member of the international community. The Western powers were motivated by different calculations. They wanted Austria's economic recovery as an insurance policy against the kind of domestic instability that might open the way to a Communist coup and drive the country into Stalin's clutches. A second vital objective was to bolster the Austrian identity in order to suppress any lingering aspirations for union with Germany.

At the outset, the Western powers would have preferred radical denazification of Austria's key institutions. But they soon calculated that the Cold War era was not the time to call the Austrian nation as a whole to account for its behaviour under the Nazis. The Americans lost interest in denazification, less because they were persuaded by Austrian assertions that the country could only function if a veil was drawn over the past than because of their perceived need to concentrate on the fight against communism – including the use of former Nazis as informers and as members of shadowy groups financed with clandestine American funds and formed as a defence against a possible Soviet invasion of Austria.

Arguably, even the extension to Austria of the Marshall Aid Plan, the US response to the acute shortage of food and fuel, was motivated more by Cold War considerations than by concern for the obvious suffering of wide swathes of the population. As in Germany, a hungry demoralised population had to be helped to resist Soviet efforts to make them more responsive to Communist encroachment. The answer, the Americans concluded, was generous economic assistance. President Truman's offer of aid was accepted by the Austrian government without serious protest from the Russians. However, while the Soviet occupation continued, no Marshall aid was allowed to be channelled to their zone. After the State Treaty, and with the Russians gone, the US administration behaved in a particularly generous way towards Eastern Austria, and allowed Marshall Plan credits to be used to bring the much abused economy of this part of Austria into line with the rest of the country.

Altogether, over the period of the Marshall Plan, Austria received more aid, per capita, than any of the other beneficiary countries. There were special circumstances. Berlin was under siege, kept alive only by the Allied airlift. Even if Vienna could be spared similar travails, the Americans calculated that without Marshall aid the economy might have ruinously destabilised Austria.

In 1945, Soviet hopes of Communist domination suffered a severe body blow when Austria's first post-war elections turned into a humiliation for Austria's Communist Party: they won a mere 5.41 per cent of the vote, giving them only four seats in a parliament of 165 members. But Stalin did not want to give up. Vienna remained rife with rumours of Soviet plots to seize power. Western intelligence agents were sending alarmist reports to their governments. After the Communists seized power in

Prague in February 1948, Major-General Geoffrey Keyes warned that 'Vienna is suffering from a first-class attack of jitters'. In Washington, the Pentagon's Joint Strategic Survey Committee expressed doubts that the Austrian police, equipped only with rubber truncheons, would be capable of dealing with internal subversion, and emphasised Austria's strategic importance as a cornerstone of Western defences in Europe. 'In light of the present situation in Europe and particularly the recent developments in Czechoslovakia… our position in Austria is an important part of that [demarcation] line [from Italy to the Baltic].' The Western Allies ruled out any thought of withdrawing their occupation forces. 'To undertake such a withdrawal [which conclusion of the State treaty would require] without first providing reasonable means of at least maintaining the present line of demarcation between the USSR and the Western Powers would be militarily unsound.'[12]

However, a senior US diplomat in Vienna, John Erhardt, told Washington that Austrian politicians were confident that they could prevent a Communist coup. He had been assured that they could 'prevent or suppress any attempted Communist take-over after withdrawal of occupation forces. They [the Social Democrats] base this confidence on extreme weakness and unpopularity of Communists and on non-Communist control of police and trade unions.'[13] This turned out to be an accurate judgement of the strength and steadfastness of anti-Communist sentiment in Austria. Soviet-inspired Communist-led strikes in 1949 and 1950 collapsed largely thanks to the resolve of Austria's mainstream trade union leadership and their co-operation with the Conservative-led coalition government.

The Russians put heavy pressure on Vienna's radio station, Radio Wien (RAVAG), which was under their authority, to broadcast the Communist strike committee's bulletins, to the exclusion of government information. A Soviet officer, Major Yakuv Goldenberg, appeared in the radio studio at one point and threatened the broadcaster with a 'voyage to Siberia' unless he read out a pro-Communist strikers' bulletin.[14] This attempt to intimidate failed, and in any event the US-sponsored station Rot-Weiss-Rot in Salzburg, as well as the Alpenland radio station in Klagenfurt in the British zone, broadcast accurate news about the strikes.

The Soviet Union had to come to terms with the fact that Austria was not susceptible to the Hungarian or Czechoslovak treatment, and that there was no way of engineering a pro-Communist coup in Austria.

— * —

For the duration of the occupation, each of the four powers used a mix of 'spin' and censorship to promote not just their policies in Austria but also their own achievements and political philosophies. They brought in artists, orchestras, authors, books and newspapers, and opened windows to the outside world.

The occupation zones each had radio stations and newspapers controlled by their foreign overlords. They were used as propaganda instruments. As well as the two already mentioned, the French were installed at Radio Vorarlberg. All three used their spin-doctoring sparingly, and flagged their own – propagandised – programmes so that listeners were forewarned. Even though censorship was exercised, the stations gave the Austrians a relatively free hand in programme content, and encouraged them to build up their services.

The Soviets were much more heavy-handed. Seeking to impose selective and pro-Communist content on news bulletins, they constantly interfered with RAVAG and its senior personnel. They insisted on a daily 'Russian Hour' whose contents they supplied themselves. Censorship was rigorous. The most notorious of the Soviet censors was Major Yakuv Goldenberg. Being of Polish origin and Jewish, he was an unlikely candidate for such a key function. But he was an ardent doctrinaire communist, spoke perfect German, and thrived on putting fear into the Austrians whose work he censored. 'Goldenberg spoke perfect German. His interrogations were feared. He always suggested that the Viennese were dumb; that they would never be able to resist the advance of communism. He never understood that after seven years under the Nazis, Austrians were immune to still more propaganda.'[15]

If the Western censors were less obtrusive, they also remained reluctant to relinquish control until shortly before the State Treaty was signed. The Austrian authorities at various times pleaded with the Allied command for freedom of the airwaves; but were always rebuffed. Foreign commentators often expressed surprise that the three Western powers were as determined to hold on to censorship as the Russians. With the Communists it was standard practice in their own countries. But Western democracies were, after all, supposed to believe in the freedom of information as a fundamental right. It all went to reinforce the impression that they saw Austria as a Cold War battlefield, where special circumstances applied. Oddly, in Germany the media regained full freedom much sooner than in 'liberated' Austria.

— * —

There has probably been no period since the end of the war when foreigners – from the governments of the four occupying powers to the military and intelligence services, to scientists, aid and relief organisations, writers, and casual observers – devoted as much time and thought to Austria as they did during the occupation. To put matters into perspective, at the macro-level Austria may indeed have been small fry. But at micro-level each of the four powers had a great deal at stake in shaping Austria in its own image. Governments and the military high commands were interested in Austria as part of the Cold War jigsaw; intelligence services, oblivious of the Nazi antecedents of their recruits, were outbidding each other to secure Austrian informers and to compete for German-trained Austrian weapons experts. Soldiers wrote to their families recording everyday observations of life around them; writers and film-makers identified the country's ambiguities.

My own memories of Austria during the occupation are sketchy. I was living in the UK, had become a British citizen, and was preoccupied first with my studies and later with my early excursions into earning a living. In 1949, I made my first brief return to Vienna since leaving Austria in 1939. I felt awkward and detached, a stranger without family or possessions in a place that had apparently once been my home, and where I supposedly had my roots. I bore no great resentment. I did not eye everyone with suspicion. I just did not want to involve myself. It was impossible to look at the Austrian scene dispassionately; yet the people around me seemed alien. Many years were to pass before I ceased to think of myself in Austria as a complete outsider.

In the wake of numerous studies by scholars in Austria and abroad, and with the opening of Soviet and Western archives, there has been much material to illustrate the impressions that foreign observers formed of Austria during the occupation years. I have selected the comments of three bit-part players on the Austrian scene. They sum up many of the salient points about the Second Republic during the occupation. George Clare was an Austrian-born writer who emigrated to the UK after the Anschluss and made his first return visit to Vienna in 1947. John Le Carré, the author, spent several months in the late 1940s in the British zone of occupation as a junior intelligence officer; Sir Rodric Braithwaite, a rank and file soldier with the British forces in Vienna in 1951, later became one of the UK's most distinguished diplomats.

Clare's descriptions of inter-war Austria are encapsulated in his widely-read book *Last Waltz in Vienna*. In his later book, *Berlin Days, 1946/47*, published in 1989, Clare delivered a harsh judgment on the Vienna he encountered in 1947. He recalled the circumstances of 1938 and 'the tidal wave of anti-semitism that swept over us, this Jew-baiting and Jew-beating festival with which the Austrians celebrated the Anschluss, was a violent explosion of race-hatred, the like of which even the Jews of Germany, who had already endured five years of Nazi rule, had not experienced'.[16]

At the time of his 1947 interlude in Vienna, Clare was stationed in Berlin with the intelligence section of British Information Services Control. 'Vienna had been bombed, there had been fighting in the streets. Yet compared to Berlin or Hamburg it had suffered little. The opera was burnt out; the Burgtheater too was an empty shell. But so many of Vienna's famous landmarks – churches, museums, monuments, the grand houses along the Ringstrasse and the baroque palaces of the inner city – had hardly been scratched'. Clare was invited to sit in a meeting of one of the subcommittees set up by the four-power Allied Control Council in Vienna. The atmosphere was far more cordial than in Berlin. 'Nyet' was not yet the most important word in the Russian officer's vocabulary. 'Underlying everything that was said was the Viennese belief that talking gets people together, that conciliation is better than altercation, and that a compromise badly fudged is preferable to a crystal clear rupture. It was all very *gemütlich*, but also rather provincial. Whatever happened in Vienna, I thought, was not of great consequence, but what happened in Berlin was.'[17]

Clare notes that 'denazification did not figure much in their [the committee's] deliberations. That, they explained, was because Austria, unlike Germany had its own central government. Although the Allies had the final say, they restricted themselves to a supervisory role… My impression was that in their particular field they found the whole thing a bit of a nuisance. They wanted good music, good opera, good theatre, and if an artist had blotted his political copybook – well, what did it matter in dear little Austria?'[18]

During the few days he remained in Vienna, Clare visited the old familiar places and talked to as many Viennese as possible. He arrived at an unflattering comparison between Austria's and Germany's post-war mentality: 'I found that same self-pity in Vienna so familiar to me from Germany, but with an added dimension of lamb-like Austrian innocence. Although most Germans trotted out all kinds of excuses for their involvement with the Nazi regime, they were slowly becoming uneasily aware of a kind of impersonal national responsibility for their country's past. Not so the majority of Austrians. Having mentally mislaid the Hitler years, they filled the void with Austrian patriotism – so rare in March 1938 when Fuhrer and Anschluss received his rapturous welcome. Austria was in fashion now, as symbolised by the ubiquitous peasant hats few would have worn in Vienna before the war. They sprouted on so many heads that, not long ago, had sported the brown or black caps of SA or SS. Everything German was out, even the way the Viennese now spoke that language… And in 1947 no one, at least no one I spoke to, doubted for one moment that Austria had been the first country overrun by the Germans.'

Clare tells how his Viennese contacts used selective quotations from the 1943 Moscow Declaration to justify their innocence and to ignore their responsibility. 'The Austrians, living up to their historic maxim "Bella gerant alii; tu felix Austria nube!" ["let the other nations wage war; thou, oh fortunate Austria, marry"] which encapsulates the Habsburgs' felicitous policy of extending their realm by shrewd dynastic marriage rather than by war, wooed the Americans, the British and the French with some fervour... The recent matrimonial experiment with the Germans having proved a misalliance, the country opened its arms to the semi-liberators. And not in vain. British, French and Americans responded readily to the romance of Vienna, its glamorous history, its music, its people – so polite and so seductively winsome, so apparently different from the Germans – and readily danced to and swallowed "Tales from the Vienna Woods".'[19]

Was his judgment too harsh and influenced by resentment, Clare asked himself? 'I thought not. I had not looked for sackcloth and ashes, for breast-beating. What I had looked for, and not found, was some self-doubt, some self-questioning. It did exist in Germany.'

One of Rodric Braithwaite's tasks in Vienna was to question refugees from Eastern Europe in search of visas to the West. Some of his experiences are recorded in letters he wrote home to his mother. An ardent music lover, he marvelled over the succession of concerts and opera and theatre performances he was able to attend. In a typical letter he wrote about seeing *Don Giovanni, Tännhauser, Turandot, Der Rosenkavalier, Julius Caesar*, all in the space of a couple of weeks. He notes that 'the Viennese audience has the annoying habit of laughing when somebody sings a wrong note', and thinks that *Der Rosenkavalier* 'was the only opera I have seen so far in which the production didn't come up to Covent Garden standards'. In a rare remark about his interrogator's work, he notes that most of the visa applicants he had to interview were 'Jews who had escaped from the iron curtain countries. Their histories read like something from "Scarlet Pimpernel".'

April 1951 was a warm month, and Braithwaite told his mother that the trees and flowers were coming out of hibernation in Vienna's parks. 'The Viennese seem to have nothing better to do than to sit around in the parks all day. There were even Russians wandering around – though they really aren't supposed to leave their barracks. The ones I saw were officers: I suppose they manage easier to get away with it.'

Tom, a fellow soldier, was constantly making 'gloomy remarks about people being kidnapped by Communist "friends",' Braithwaite wrote on another occasion. 'Everybody here seems to be scared of their shadows. They [British army friends] all seem convinced that we shall never get out of Vienna alive and talk about what they will do when the Russians take over... I think the Austrians suffer our presence as well as anyone. They prefer the British to anyone else, although they would prefer to be without us.

'We don't mix with the French or the Americans very much – we have no reason except in the line of duty – and we don't mix with the Russians at all. As I was told when we first got here: "The Russians are our potential enemies, and one doesn't cooperate much with one's potential enemy". Furthermore the Russian private soldier is not even allowed to fraternise with the Austrians, let alone us. The Russians have a pathological fear of cameras. Anyone carrying one is being looked on as a spy and liable to immediate arrest. An American was arrested not so long ago – he made the double mistake of carrying a camera and walking on the pavement in front of the Soviet Officers' club. The Russians rope off the pavements in front of all their buildings and post armed guards to make sure than nobody walks on them.'

Braithwaite went to the St Stephen's when the Pummerin, the cathedral's great bell, destroyed by German shellfire, was recast and reinstalled. 'Its triumphal progress from Linz was described in a blow-by-blow account by radio. The town was packed because St Stephens means a lot to the Viennese – the bell-tower being more or less the symbol of Vienna to them. The church itself was covered with flags, as were most other buildings in Vienna. It was all most pleasant and sentimental, and I can't imagine anything similar in London.' He added that he was 'getting a bit sick of political processions' and was much relieved to have seen the *Rake's Progress* twice in the previous week, and to be off to a Schumann Lieder recital by Irmgard Seefried: not a bad life.

John Le Carré is the acknowledged master of the Cold War spy thriller. In his novel *The Perfect Spy* he used his own observations of post-war Austria to describe the espionage atmospherics of occupied Vienna. His experience of Austria, as a junior officer, provided him with plenty of material. He worked mostly at British headquarters in Graz, where he helped to vet Austrian recruits for work with the British intelligence aparatus. 'I was detailed to recruit people who had connections with Eastern Europe and were prepared to go back. We were certainly not averse to former Nazis; they were not seen as a security risk. The ex-Nazis were obedient, and were "our type of chaps"!'[20] Le Carré also looked after a group of low-level spies operating in the Soviet zone of Austria. He recalls how easy it was to identify the carpet-baggers and black-marketeers among the Austrians. Many young men who had served with the Nazis showed him their SS tattoos 'without any sense of guilt'. Austrians constantly 'portrayed themselves as spectators or as unwilling victims, and evoked their *Persilschein*'.

They wanted to be seen as innocents caught in a world of dark and dangerous forces, and to emerge, whiter than white, armed with their State Treaty, to become a neutral state, politically, economically and morally equipped to gain international respect.

NOTES ON CHAPTER III

1. Die Völkerrechtliche Stellung der Republik Österreich. Motivbericht für einen Vortrag vor dem Kabinetsrat, June 1945.
2. The British Council, Annual Report 1948/49.
3. *The Times*, 25 July 1945.
4. *Four Power Control in Germany and Austria 1945–46*, survey by the Royal Institute of International Affairs, 1956, author's preface.
5. A.J.P. Taylor, 'Europe: Grandeur and Decline', Pelican, 1967, p 325.
6. Hella Pick, *Simon Wiesenthal: A Life in Search of Justice*, Weidenfeld & Nicolson, 1996, p 82.
7. *Austria: A Monthly Report and Review*, September 1947.
8. *Four Power Control in Germany and Austria 1945–46*, op. cit.
9. Oliver Rathkolb, *Gesellschaft und Politik am Beginn der zweiten Republik: Vertrauliche Berichte der US Militär Administration*, Bohlau, 1985, p 343.
10. Hugo Hantsch, quoted in Oliver Rathkolb, *Besatzungspolitik und Besatzungserleben in Österreich von April bis August 1945*, Militärhistorisches Institut, 1995, p 200.
11. Interviews with Cardinal König in Vienna, 1998.
12. Report by the Joint Strategic Survey Committee to the Joint Chiefs of Staff, 5 March 1948.
13. Günter Bischof, 'Prag liegt westlich von Berlin: Internationale Krisen in 1948' in *Die Bevormundete Nation: Österreich und die Alliierten 1945–55*, Haymon Verlag, 1988.
14. Viktor Ergert, *50 Jahre Rundfunk in Österreich, Band II*, Residenzverlag, 1975, p 153.
15. Ergert, *50 Jahre Rundfunk in Österreich, Band I 1945–55*, op. cit., p 39.
16. George Clare, *Berlin Days, 1946–47*, Macmillan, 1989, p 3.
17. Clare, *Berlin Days, 1946–47*, op. cit., p 207.
18. Clare, *Berlin Days, 1946–47*, op. cit., p 208.
19. Clare, *Berlin Days, 1946–47*, op. cit., p 210.
20. Interview, 1998.

1. *(above)* Adolf Hitler's annexation of Austria in 1938 met with the jubilation of at least one third of the country's population, who gave him a hero's welcome when he came triumphant to Vienna to inspect his newly acquired 'Ostmark' domains.

2. *(below)* In 1945, Austrians in search of food and shelter in war-damaged Vienna painted themselves as Hitler's first victims and looked to the US, the Soviet Union, Britain and France to absolve them from any guilt for the Holocaust.

3. Karl Renner was named Austria's federal Chancellor only days after the last Wehrmacht forces had surrendered in Vienna. He proclaimed the new post-war 'Second Republic' in the presence of the Soviet occupation forces.

4. The portrayal of Austria as a victim served the needs of each of the allied occupiers. Under the banner 'Never Forget' a 1946 communist party organised exhibition in Vienna declared Austria as a nation liberated from 'the German fascist yoke'. Nevertheless the exhibition was also a rare attempt in Vienna to portray the realities of the Holocaust.

5. Four-power jeep patrols representing the joint military government of the US, Soviet Union, Britain and France became a familiar sight in Vienna, more reassuring than menacing.

6. Post-war Vienna's gloom and sinister seediness were well-represented in Carol Reed's film *The Third Man,* in which Harry Lime (Orson Welles) personifies the corruption and unease gripping the city during the four-power occupation.

7. *(above)* On May 15th 1955 Chancellor Alois Figl was propelled on th the balcony of the Belvedere Palace by the Foreign Ministers of the four powers that had occupied Austria since the war. This was a Red Letter Day for Austria when the Chancellor was proudly able to wave the State Treaty that finally set the country free.

8. *(below)* Great rejoicing in Vienna and throughout the whole country resulted from Figl's proclamation, *Austria is Free.*

IV

The Occupation Ends – Neutrality Begins

For the Austrian nation, the four signatures on the State Treaty – the US, Soviet, French and British Foreign Ministers – formalised an achievement of paramount historic importance. 'In modern history, the conclusion of the State treaty in 1955 was a unique event: an agreement by the superpowers about another state; an agreement which, rather than causing damage to the state, would be of considerable benefit to it,'[1] wrote the British historian, Hugh Seton Watson.

But the treaty also marked a milestone in the chequered history of the second half of the twentieth century in its wider geopolitical parameters. After more than a decade of confrontation, during a few weeks in 1955 the wartime allies achieved a semblance of common purpose sufficient to secure agreement on the terms of their withdrawal from Austria and the restoration of full sovereignty to the country. In 1955, 'one second of world history moved in our favour. And we made good use of it,'[2] wrote one of Austria's most experienced journalists.

Austrians felt that the true day of liberation had come at last. Bells rang out throughout the country. The signing ceremony was held in Vienna's Schloss Belvedere; the festivities that night in Schloss Schönbrunn suggested to many of the foreign observers that Austria had momentarily recaptured some of its old glory – even if, as the *Neue Zürcher Zeitung* observed, Schönbrunn's 120 kitchens were no longer in working order, so that the elaborate party feast had to be prepared elsewhere in the city and brought out to Schönbrunn in lorry-loads.

For the first time since 1945, the Foreign Ministers of the four victorious nations in the war against Hitler's Germany had achieved a joint agreement, and had appeared side-by-side before a world audience. The Soviet Foreign Minister Molotov was visibly pleased that, for once, he was able to savour the rare experience of spontaneous popular acclaim outside an iron curtain country.

In St Stephen's, British Foreign Secretary Harold Macmillan and his French opposite number Antoine Pinay attended a mass of thanksgiving led by the Austrian Primate, Cardinal Innitzer. In 1938, the same Cardinal had welcomed the Anschluss with a 'Heil Hitler'. In many ways this controversial prelate personified the vagaries and changing attitudes in Austria during recent decades.

In Moscow, *Pravda* set the tone for the Communist camp when it proclaimed that 'the solution to the Austrian question is a success for the peace-loving policy of the Soviet Union, which continually undertakes new steps in the interests of detente'.[3] Such assertions were to prove hollow enough when only a few months later Soviet tanks moved into Budapest to suppress the Hungarian uprising.

Only the West German Chancellor, Konrad Adenauer, introduced a disturbing sour note into the day's proceedings, and launched a series of unhappy exchanges that continued until differences were finally set aside in 1957. One of the main reasons was German anger over the fate of 'German assets' in Eastern Austria, industries built or operated by the Nazis and taken over by the Soviet Union after 1945. Under the terms of the State Treaty, Germany would not be able to recover these. Instead, Austria was allowed to 'buy them back' by compensating the Soviet Union with oil deliveries and industrial goods.

West Germany's senior diplomat in Vienna, Carl-Hermann Mueller-Graaf, was instructed by Bonn to stay away from the grand reception at Schönbrunn, and the Bonn government sent protest notes to Vienna and to its NATO allies. Germany's interests, Adenauer claimed, had been sacrificed. The *Frankfurter Allgemeine* pontificated that Vienna should be reminded 'of its moral duties as a neutral. Ten years after the end of the war, a new injustice had been created.'[4] In Bavaria, the *Süd Deutsche Zeitung* adopted a very different tone. Austria was too insignificant, it implied, for the Federal Republic to mobilise protest against it. It was not worth 'using canon to attack a sparrow'.

Among German politicians there was also intense speculation – unfounded as it emerged – as to whether the Soviet Union would seek to exploit Austria's neutrality as a precedent to impose a similar peace settlement on Germany. Discussions in the German Foreign Office and among Germany's political parties in 1955 revealed 'a mainly negative assessment of neutrality in general – and above all against the background of Europe's division into blocs as well as of the specific example of Austria'.[5]

— * —

A number of Adenauer's advisors were so concerned that the Soviet Union intended to use the Austrian example to press again for a unified and neutral Germany that they tried to persuade Henry Luce, owner of the influential magazines, *Time*, *Life*, and *Fortune* to engage in a campaign against the State Treaty, and especially against an Austrian commitment to neutrality. The editors in New York rejected this advice. 'No question – neutralism is a Soviet trump card, but I doubt it is an ace of spades. We must watch, we must report, we must synthesise for our readers; but I don't think it would be a good idea to get angry. Boy oh Boy, this is a Cold War crisis that sure is not a wolf's crisis.'[6]

The *Time* editors were closer to the mark than they realised when they expressed doubts about a Soviet strategy to impose the Austrian model on a unified Germany. Only a handful of people were aware that Adenauer had received secret assurances that the Soviet Union, under its new leader Krushchev, had abandoned Stalin's long-term quest for a united but neutral and disarmed Germany.

Molotov had used Austria's Vice-Chancellor Schärf as messenger. While Schärf was in Moscow for the end round of the State Treaty negotiations, Molotov had indicated that the Soviet Union did not intend to draw a parallel between Austria and Germany. The Kremlin had concluded that even though neutrality might work for a small country like Austria, it could not be the solution for a country the size of Germany. There was no realistic way of guaranteeing that such a commitment would be respected; and should the Soviet Union go to war if neutrality was breached? 'With respect to a small country, it is feasible to nail down its neutral status in treaty form. A small country cannot afford to treat such a commitment as a disposable piece of paper. But, when we look at a unified Germany with a population of 60–70 million people, what could we do if its government suddenly decided to give up its neutrality? Should we go to war over such a matter? Certainly not; that is why a neutral status is no solution for a large state.'[7]

Molotov's message of reassurance to Adenauer was kept a closely guarded secret for many years. But even had the Soviet position been more widely known in 1955, political analysts would probably still have pondered anxiously the Kremlin's intentions in Germany and Austria.

There is always a narrow dividing line between neutrality and neutralism. But given Adenauer's latent fears about the repercussions of the State Treaty on a settlement for Germany, it is surprising that the German Chancellor at one point side-stepped the issue of German unification. In 1958, Adenauer himself threw out feelers to secure backing for an Austrian-type solution for East Germany.

Willy Brandt describes in his memoirs how Adenauer broached this idea for sanitising the German Democratic Republic, first with the Soviet Ambassador in Bonn and later with Soviet Deputy Prime Minister Anastas Mikoyan. This, Brandt notes, would have presupposed recognition of the East German border. The Berlin Wall had not yet been built, and Mikoyan ignored Adenauer's proposals. However, Ernst Reuter, as Mayor of Berlin, had 'also hoped that something of benefit to Berlin and Germany could come of a solution for Vienna and Austria. But I [Brandt] thought he was over-optimistic. The geographical position and economic and political potential involved meant that there could be no simple comparisons, particularly not at the end of the fifties.'[8]

— * —

It is a delusion to think that the 1955 State Treaty ceremonies generated much foreign interest in Austria's domestic politics. Instead interest centred on the implications of the Treaty for East-West relations. John Foster Dulles later confessed that even for the well-informed pundits of the US administration, Krushchev's motives in agreeing to an Austrian settlement remained obscure.

While the West puzzled over Soviet motives, the Austrian public erred if it believed that with the achievement of the Treaty they had gained complete control over their affairs, and would now be free to focus on economic and social progress. There was much work to be done on reconciling the economy of Eastern Austria, where the Russian presence had taken a heavy toll, with the rest of the country where the West had encouraged rapid progress.

However, even though the superpowers were leaving Austria, the country was committed under the State Treaty to substantial annual oil deliveries to the Soviet Union, and had also undertaken to compensate Western oil firms for the loss of their Austrian enterprises. Even though the Austrian economy made rapid progress, these quasi-reparations were regarded as a heavy burden. Much of Austria's diplomacy was devoted to cajoling Moscow into reducing its appetite for Austrian oil. At the same time, the country's relations with the US were adversely affected by long-drawn-out delays in reaching a settlement with US oil companies over their pre-war properties in Austria.

After 1955, superpower manipulation of Austria was not as intense as it had been during the occupation. But for years to come, both the Atlantic alliance and the Soviet Union attached to Austria an importance in their strategic calculations far above the station of such a small country. The Soviet Union evidently preferred a militarily weak Austria as a buffer between the two military alliances, and possibly also saw it as a role model, if not for Germany then at least for a neutral Yugoslavia.

Soviet interest in a neutral buffer on the borders of the Communist bloc protected the country from Warsaw Pact incursion during the Hungarian uprising in 1956, and again during the Warsaw Pact invasion of Czechoslovakia in 1968. On both occasions, Austria, acting out of concern for human rights, gave temporary asylum to many tens of thousands of refugees and made no secret of its deep disapproval of Warsaw Pact actions.

But even though the Soviet Union refrained from invasion, it had no scruples about infiltrating Austria's trade unions, its youth organisations and other key institutions. For several years after 1955 there was concern in Western capitals that Austria, instead of adopting a Swiss-style neutrality, might succumb to Soviet pressure and become effectively neutered. The Soviets, for their part, remained deeply suspicious that the US was manoeuvering to turn Austria into an outpost for Western interests in Central Europe. There was a measure of truth in both views: for at least a decade after the occupation ended, the two superpowers used subversion as well as diplomatic and economic pressure to influence Austria's behaviour. The Russians worked through the Communist-dominated World Federation of Trade Unions (WFTU), and the World Peace Council, as well as Austria's shrinking Communist Party in efforts to destabilise the Austrian government. Austria, aware that Western diplomats suspected them of being far too susceptible to Soviet influence, risked offending the Russians by closing down the Vienna headquarters of WFTU in 1956, but waited until 1984 before deciding that the World Peace Congress must move its headquarters elsewhere.

As counterpoint, America's CIA and Radio Free Europe each played a highly active role in Austria during the post-Treaty era. Western media were used as conduits, and the CIA-backed Congress for Cultural Freedom, which financed journals such as *Preuves* in France and *Encounter* in the UK, backed *Forum* in Austria to promote pro-Western ideas. The CIA also worked hard to infiltrate the Communist-backed World Youth Festival in Vienna in 1959, which the Austrian government allowed to be staged as an affirmation of its ability to run such an event without succumbing to external pressure.

— * —

Looking back on this period, Austrian leaders acknowledge that the transition from occupation to the full exercise of sovereignty was full of potential pitfalls, and that the elaboration of its own, somewhat lopsided brand of neutrality was a haphazard process.

The State Treaty ranks as a confidence-building measure in the fractious climate of East-West relations. Even so, the rosy glow and the promise of peaceful co-existence that surrounded the signing ceremonies was deceptive. All the governments involved, including Austria's own, had their private doubts that the accord really marked the beginning of the end of the Cold War. They were well aware that the profound underlying differences between the two superpower camps had not been resolved.

None of this could have stopped the foreign and domestic media from interpreting the Treaty in a positive light as the augury of a happier era in East-West relations. Outside the inner circles of government there were many only too ready to be deceived by the spectacle of unity between the four wartime allies. Political analysts were all along far more doubtful, if not downright negative. They were soon proved right: the spirit of jubilation was indeed deceptive. The handshakes in Vienna had only marked a truce in the Cold War, an event that allowed both sides to regroup, to strengthen their alliances, and to draw still firmer lines between the NATO and the Warsaw Pact zones of influence: hostilities would continue with Austria, soon to proclaim its neutrality, still subject to the conflicting pressures of the two armed camps.

Fortunately East-West tensions did not interfere with the smooth ratification of the Treaty in the five capitals – Washington, Moscow, London, Paris and Vienna – or with the rapid dismantling of the occupation. The last occupation contingent – a 20-man British force – left Austrian territory on 25 October 1955, and on the following day, true to the promise which the four powers had extracted from Austria, the Austrian parliament adopted the motion that committed Austria to 'lasting' neutrality. It also prohibited military alliances and the establishment of foreign military bases on Austrian territory.

The parliamentary debate on neutrality was an historic occasion. It could – and should –have been used to urge the Austrian nation to end self-deception and take a more honest look at its recent history. But Chancellor Raab shied away from any attempt to exhort Austrians to accept their share of responsibility for the Nazi era. He treated the past 17 years – from the Anschluss to the end of the war, then on to the end of the occupation – as a seamless uncomfortable whole: 'a 17-year period during which Austria had been deprived of its sovereignty and independence. Now they knew what freedom meant.'[9]

Raab was more forthright about future prospects. Using language that conveyed reassurance to the West – but inevitably caused misgivings in Moscow – he delivered a purpose-designed definition of Austria's concept of neutrality. The country would be neutral between the military blocs. But there would be no neutrality in the realm of economic ties, of ideology, or of human rights. 'Our military neutrality carries no obligations with respect to economic or cultural ties.'

Raab's language made plain that Austria counted itself as a Western democracy, and that its government intended to play an active role in promoting democratic values in neighbouring states. Austria, while it admired the Swiss model – it was the one that the Soviet Union envisaged for Austria – had no intention of remaining on the sidelines of international affairs. It would join the UN – admission was secured on 14 December 1955 – and other international institutions, and would aim to play an active role in international life.

With considerable political courage, Raab promised that Austria, as a free and democratic nation, was committed to respect human rights and would continue to give asylum to all political refugees.

Almost the only jarring note during the parliamentary debate came from the extreme right wing with its rump of former Nazis, the 14 members of the Union of Independents. They refused to vote for the neutrality resolution, not because they were opposed to a neutral status for Austria, but because the party claimed that Austria had not been given a free choice in the adoption of neutrality. The party argued – and for once they were surely not so far off the mark – that neutrality had been imposed on Austria as the price of independence, and that the country lacked the military means to defend its neutrality.

The expansion of Austria's military forces was constrained by the terms of the State Treaty and by its limited financial resources. It was inevitable that for all practical purposes Austria would constitute a military vacuum in the heart of Europe.

Many political analysts believed that this new situation in Austria posed more of a threat to NATO interests than to the Warsaw Pact. The Soviet withdrawal from Eastern Austria made little difference to the Soviet Union's military disposition in Eastern Europe: under the terms of the Warsaw Pact Treaty, Soviet forces were deployed in Hungary – its border only 40km from Vienna – and in Czechoslovakia. The terrain was relatively flat; in any East-West confrontation, Warsaw Pact forces could make a relatively unimpeded return to Vienna, and move on to attack NATO forces in Bavaria or Italy. The NATO alliance, on the other hand, had to contend with much more difficult terrain. The US, British and French occupation zones in Western and Southern Austria encompassed high alpine mountain ranges. Withdrawal meant that NATO's northern flank in Germany was now cut off by difficult mountainous terrain from its southern, Italian, flank. In the event of East-West hostilities in Central Europe, NATO would inevitably be at a disadvantage.

— * —

Less than two weeks after the end of the occupation, on 5 November 1955, Austria was able to crown the momentous events of the past six months with the festive reopening of the Vienna State Opera. Bombed in 1945, the last performance there had, aptly, been of Wagner's *Götterdämmerung*. Now that Austria was once again independent, a star-studded cast performed Beethoven's *Fidelio* as a hymn of praise to the enduring qualities of freedom.

In a gesture that was not echoed by other foreign ministers, Dulles came back to Vienna for the event, treating it as a social occasion and avoiding policy discussions with the Austrian government. This did not signify American indifference to the concerns of NATO's high command. The military had all along predicted a dangerous military vacuum in the wake of a Western withdrawal from Austria. Dulles had only lifted his objections to the State Treaty after West Germany had been securely anchored to NATO and any prospect of German neutrality could be ruled out. The NATO allies now had the assurance of being able to maintain their military bases in the Federal Republic.

Even after the State Treaty, the US remained uncertain of Soviet intentions towards Austria. This led the administration to refuse all proposals to offer a formal guarantee of Austria's sovereignty. General Eisenhower's preferred option in 1955 was to strengthen Austria economically and militarily as a safeguard against its collapse into Soviet hands. Without American economic support, in particular the promotion of investment under the European Recovery Programme (ERP) after 1955, Austria would not have risen so dramatically in the European prosperity league. And later, without political encouragement from President Kennedy, Bruno Kreisky, for all his drive and sweeping views on foreign affairs, would not have gained such a forceful voice in an international community unaccustomed to paying much attention to the views of small countries.

However, the Americans always stopped short of providing a formal guarantee of 'its [Austria's] territory or neutrality except within the framework of the United Nations'.[10] The US and its allies never wavered on this, and remained largely unresponsive when a deeply worried Austria sought US security guarantees during the Hungarian uprising in 1956. True, there were some vague reassurances, the kind of clichés that the UN Security Council later developed to a fine art: the US State Department said that any violation of Austrian territory or neutrality by Warsaw Pact forces would constitute a 'grave threat to peace'. Austria's Ambassador in Washington, Karl Gruber, was reassured by senior US officials that 'they [the Russians] would not get away with this' if they followed their suppression of the Hungarian uprising with an attempt to reoccupy their former zone in Austria.[11] The *Washington Post*, having got wind of this exchange, carried an article headlined: 'Would-be threat to Peace: US warns Russia not to violate Austria's borders or its neutrality'.

But at the highest levels between Washington and Moscow, a somewhat different tune was played. The former US High Commissioner in Austria, Llewellyn Thompson, was adamant that 'it would be extremely foolish even to start a discussion' about guarantees with the Austrians.[12]

Preoccupied by the Suez crisis and the fighting in Egypt, Eisenhower conceded that NATO was in no position to intervene in Hungary – 'Hungary was as inaccessible to us as Tibet,'[13] Eisenhower was quoted as remarking. US intelligence sources have since confirmed that messages were sent by the White House to the Kremlin in 1956 to the effect that Hungary was accepted as falling within the Soviet zone of influence. This in effect gave Moscow the green light to suppress the Hungarian uprising. Given the US position, NATO could hardly be expected to act in support of Austria in the event of Soviet incursions from Hungary into the neighbouring territory. Nevertheless, NATO plainly calculated that its hands-off posture could not be sustained if Warsaw Pact forces penetrated deep into Austria and, moving westwards, became a threat to NATO forces in Germany or Italy. The implications were clear: NATO would intervene to protect its own direct interests, but would not intervene to guarantee Austria's territorial integrity for its own sake. Fortunately, none of this was ever put to the test.

— * —

It would only be natural to assume that Austrian neutrality would be interpreted to mean that the superpowers were barred from discussing military co-operation with the Austrian government. This was not the case. Eisenhower had all along taken the position that the US was not precluded from giving limited military assistance to Austria. The Americans were relieved that 'Austrian political leaders have interpreted their neutrality to mean that Austria is free to cooperate with the West in political, economic and cultural fields and to accept outside assistance in the establishment of its armed forces. The US has encouraged Austria to adopt and maintain this interpretation of neutrality to ensure Austria's Western orientation and minimise the adverse influence on Austria and other nations of Soviet pressure to broaden Austria's neutrality.'[14] Austria evidently agreed that its commitment to remain outside the military alliances could be interpreted with flexibility. In a foolhardy move, Vienna even advanced tentative ideas for loose military links with NATO. This was immediately rebuffed by the US as politically dangerous. Incompatible with the terms of Austria's neutrality and an obvious provocation to the Soviet Union, the idea was dropped. The notion of joining NATO was revived, amidst much domestic Austrian controversy, after 1997 when the international context had radically changed, and when Hungary, Poland and the Czech Republic were becoming members. But the proposal caused so much political controversy, with public opinion seemingly wedded to the neutrality concept, that the Austrian government remained reluctant to make a membership application.

Back in 1955, even though the US had no truck with talk of NATO links with Austria, Eisenhower was far from averse to military aid to the country. He offered Austria substantial supplies of military equipment designed to help the rapid build-up of an effective, though small, defence force. Such US aid was handled discreetly. Even now it is not widely known that during the two years after conclusion of the State Treaty the US gave Austria approximately $70 million[15] of military aid to create a modern force of 60,000 men. The US occupation forces left behind some of their military equipment, and necessarily created a dependency on US spare parts. The Americans also established close liaison with the Austrian military. Their motives were far from altruistic. The US wanted to encourage creation of an Austrian army that would be strong enough to interpose itself as a temporary shield against Warsaw Pact forces in the event of a Soviet thrust towards Germany.

The British were initially far more cautious about co-ordination with Austria's armed forces. They were concerned about Austria's reluctance to take uncomfortable decisions, and thought that its *Schlamperei* was tantamount to unreliability. Foreign Office papers of the period show that the UK questioned whether Austria could sustain its pro-Western variant of neutrality. The UK could not rule out that Austria might still end up as a Soviet satellite. Austria's unqualified willingness to give asylum to the flood of refugees from Hungary in 1956 persuaded the UK, at least temporarily, to revise its judgment. 'Aided by the internal stresses within the Soviet Empire, and spurred by a very real sympathy with the miseries of the Hungarian people, Austria has converted a dangerous lack of direction in her policy into a positive concept of neutrality which has been seen to have attractions in the satellite lands,' Britain's Ambassador in Vienna reported to London. Yet he still saw a danger that 'Austrian neutrality might well be only the first step to satellisation, unless a coherent and independent foreign policy could be evolved.'

— * —

It may seem paradoxical that the Hungarian uprising helped to legitimise Austria's neutral status, while simultaneously identifying the country so clearly as a country with Western values and institutions. But so it surely proved. The human and political fallout from those unhappy events so close to Austria's borders – and still more the Soviet intervention in Czechoslovakia twelve years later – confirmed the durability of Austria's neutrality and political sympathies as no other event since 1955. When Austria opened its frontiers to the flood of refugees fleeing from the Warsaw Pact's suppression of the Hungarian uprising, this imposed a challenging test to the limits of Soviet respect for its sovereignty. The Austrian move was an emphatic assertion of a political philosophy which held that military neutrality was no bar to a commitment to Western human rights values.

The Soviet Union was not amused by Austrian actions. The Kremlin suspected the Austrians of plotting with Western capitals to undermine Communist hegemony over Eastern Europe. The chief Soviet representative at the United Nations accused the Americans of using Austria as a base to aid Hungarian insurgents. Radio Moscow repeatedly asserted that Austria was using the Red Cross to smuggle arms into Hungary. The Soviet news agency Tass declared that the Western media were exploiting the Hungarian refugee problem in Austria to propagate black propaganda against Russia and against the Hungarian regime. Tass correspondents, having visited some of the refugee camps, wrote that 'a growing number of Hungarian citizens had come to understand the falsehoods of Western propaganda',[16] and were prepared to return home to Hungary.

There was a great deal more Soviet huffing and puffing against Austria and its friends. Far more serious than verbal threats, Soviet tanks in Hungary were on the borders with Austria, only 60km from Vienna. In the light of intelligence reports, the Austrian government believed it had good grounds for fearing that Soviet forces might violate Austrian territory. Austria was jittery, even at the highest levels. But the government held fast to its human rights commitments – and won itself world-wide plaudits.

The gamble paid off. Krushchev was unwilling to risk a military showdown with Austria over its refugee intake, fearing that this might yet provoke the US into action. The Soviet leader preferred an independent Austria, interposed between NATO and the Warsaw Pact, to the satisfaction of teaching Austria a military lesson about the limits of active neutrality.

So Austria maintained its open door policy unimpeded, opening schools, hotels, holiday homes to Hungarian refugees as temporary shelter. But all this required more than political daring and good-will. Austria was in need of money, food and equipment to care for the refugees, and above all it wanted the assurance that other countries were prepared to provide permanent asylum for the greater part of the refugees. Throughout November 1956, during the worst fighting in Hungary and the greatest influx of refugees, Austria made almost daily appeals to the West for help with its humanitarian task. During the Cold War, just as much as later, Austria rejected the idea of becoming a country of permanent asylum. Dictated by geography, its vocation was to act as a transit post for refugees.

In the West, there was unreserved praise for 'Austria, the land of asylum'. But the practical response was slow in coming.

The Swiss press was particularly assiduous in comparing Austria's actions with Berne's reluctance to help the refugees from Hungary. The *Neue Zürcher Zeitung* described how Kreisky, as State Secretary in the Austrian Foreign Ministry, had ruled that all Hungarians should be allowed across the border without any reservation, while 'most other West European countries imposed conditions which resulted in considerable delays in admitting refugees'.[17]

Austria truly shamed its Western neighbours: by the third week of November, Austria had taken in over 70,000 refugees (and the figure continued to mount rapidly to a total of over 180,000), while Switzerland had only admitted 4000. Eventually 170,000 were able to move on to other countries, while 10,000, still a considerable number for a small country, were absorbed in Austria.

With Austria in the limelight for its generosity towards the refugees from Hungary, Vice-President Richard Nixon was dispatched to Vienna just before Christmas 1956. He was the highest-ranking American politician to visit the country for decades. He went to refugee camps, insisted on going to the border with Hungary, where he watched refugees crossing at the dead of night, and held talks with Austria's leaders. *Pravda* described the visit as a 'fresh example of gross [US] interference in the internal affairs of other countries',[18] and said that the US had damaged Austrian neutrality. Nixon, undeterred, accepted Austrian pleas for more help in resettling the Hungarians. He persuaded Washington to double the quota for Hungarian refugees, and to decide on a substantial increase in US economic aid for Austria.

The Hungarian refugee action gave Austria a further important bonus. It provoked a rare expression of appreciation from the World Jewish Congress (WJC), a body which has otherwise maintained a stridently critical attitude towards Austria. Nahum Goldmann, WJC President, came to Vienna to thank Austria for its care and concern for the Jews among the refugees from Hungary. Goldmann was so intent on emphasising Austrian generosity towards the Hungarians that he did not, on this occasion, raise the unresolved matter of claims against the Austrian state, which the WJC was masterminding on behalf of Austrian Jews who had lost their lives or properties, or both, during the Nazi era.

With the exception of a brief period in 1945 and 1946, Austria had regularly side-stepped the restitution issue. Its attitude did not change after 1955, even though the State Treaty obliged Austria to address the matter. Shortly before Raab's first official visit to Washington in May 1958, Kreisky warned, in an internal memorandum, that Austria's reluctance to act on restitution would damage its relations with the US. Influential Jewish circles, he said, were pointing out that Austria had received $1.5 billion in US aid, and yet was unwilling to provide $5 million compensation to Jewish victims. 'The State Department cannot understand why Austria was willing to risk the goodwill it had earned itself with its asylum policy during the Hungarian crisis.'[19]

The US administration made a half-hearted attempt to call Austria to order during Raab's official visit, when Dulles urged Austria to find the

$5 million to compensate the 30,000 claimants. It would have provided each victim with the paltry sum of $170.

Goldmann insisted to Raab that such a sum was much too small. Raab countered that, on the contrary, the demand was too high. During a meeting with its representatives, Raab informed the WJC that Austria could not pay more, that it was tired of these claims, and that in any event the Bonn government, as the successor to the Nazi regime, was the proper address for Jewish claims. Nevertheless, a few months later, the State Department reached agreement with the Austrian government that Austria would offer $6 million. This was again turned down by the WJC as inadequate. This was the end of the exchange, the end of an opportunity for at least a partial settlement of the restitution issue; it was a deepening of distrust between Austria and the WJC, a further flight by Austrian leaders from its obligations to grasp the nettle of the Nazi era in Austria.

By way of concrete pressure on Austria to deal with compensation, the Americans had put various Marshall payments to Austria on hold. But as the Austrians soon realised, the Americans were more concerned with delays in compensation to US and British oil companies for enterprises they had owned in Austria before the war than with settlement of the Jewish claims. An accord with the oil companies was reached in 1961, while the Jewish claims continued to fester. In the aftermath of 1956, Austria appeared to assume that its open-door posture during the Hungarian uprising would distract foreign observers from criticising its reluctance to accept responsibility for the persecution of its Jewish population after the Anschluss.

If not downright dishonest, this was certainly false logic, and deserved to fail – as indeed it did. The stratagem did not succeed in 1956, or during Raab's visit to the US in 1958, and failed again after 1968, when Austria showed the same generosity to Czechoslovak refugees as it had to the Hungarians a dozen years earlier.

— * —

In the wider context of Austria's international standing, its actions during the Hungarian uprising brought welcome dividends. Austria's political maturity had come to blossom more rapidly than had been anticipated when the State Treaty was signed, and its leaders were made welcome in the UN and in world capitals. Western nations concluded that Austria had set an honourable example as an outpost of the free world. The Soviet Union was obviously less enthusiastic, and accused Austria of betraying its neutrality commitments. But its bark proved worse than its bite, and steps were soon taken by Moscow and Vienna to normalise relations. Anastas Mikoyan, a senior member of the Soviet Politburo, went to Vienna in April 1957, and though he spoke sternly on his arrival a dose of Richard Strauss's *Der Rosenkavalier* and of the

Spanish Riding School, and some homely words from Foreign Minister Leopold Figl charmed Mikoyan into declaring that 'Mozart will be victorious over NATO and the Warsaw Pact'. As he left Austria, Mikoyan delivered a friendly farewell: 'Auf wiedersehen friends'.

A year later, on an official visit to Moscow, Raab received an exceptionally warm welcome from the Soviet Union, and secured important economic concessions. But pleasing one side often meant displeasing the other. The Austrian Chancellor caused deep misgivings in Washington by offering the Russians his country's profuse thanks for Soviet acceptance of the State Treaty. In the West, his words were interpreted as if Austria held that the Soviet Union alone had been responsible for its successful conclusion. Once again, the US worried that Austria might after all turn out to be unreliable, and could not be counted 'one of us' with a neutral sheen. Had Austria turned to become a pro-Soviet neutralist?

A National Security Council paper pointed to 'a number of developments which, by their juxtaposition, seemed as if they indicate a trend toward an expansion of Austrian neutrality policy into neutralism and a tendency to equate the US and the Soviet Union on moral and political planes. The major incidents were: Austrian prohibition of over-flights to Lebanon (during the Lebanon crisis), excessively friendly remarks about the Soviet Union by Chancellor Raab in Moscow, Austrian abstention on the Chinese moratorium in the United Nations and the visit of the Austrian Defence Minister to Moscow.'[20]

It was as if Austrian neutrality was balanced on a seesaw. During the Hungarian uprising, its neutrality had tilted westwards, and the Russians felt betrayed. Now it seemed to be tilting towards the Soviet camp, and the Americans were suspicious. The big challenge for Austria was to secure a form of neutrality that would win the trust of both superpowers simultaneously.

Chancellor Raab decided that the solution might be to turn Vienna, alongside with Geneva, into a second European capital of the UN. If it was established that Austria was ideally placed to serve as international meeting ground, where even the superpowers could conduct their diplomacy, then Austria's *bona fides* and its neutrality could be seen beyond suspicion.

Moreover, Vienna, used as a major international venue, would be able to reaffirm its faded Habsburg glories as Europe's pre-eminent diplomatic capital. This would be a stimulus to national pride, and could also provide a welcome bonus for the city's economy. The upshot was a decision to initiate the project for Vienna to become a UN city. The high costs involved meant that the project remained on the drawing boards until Kreisky, as Chancellor, gave the go-ahead, and construction was finally completed in 1979.

Initially the idea of Vienna as a UN city also caused considerable misgivings in Washington and London, not to mention Switzerland which wanted Geneva to retain its stature as Europe's only UN city. However, in September 1958 the International Atomic Energy Agency (IAEE) became the first member of the UN 'family' to break the Geneva stranglehold and establish its headquarters in Vienna.

This was an important watershed not just for Vienna but for the country as a whole. It did not have the high profile of the State Treaty. But the IAEE's arrival on the Viennese scene was the beginning of a gradual process of internationalisation for Vienna. It meant that the capital could reinvent itself, becoming again a major diplomatic centre where East and West – and North and South – could meet to conduct peacetime business, to negotiate international agreements, to ruminate in cafes, and to enjoy Austrian *Gemütlichkeit*.

Raab may have sensed all this. But it was Kreisky who understood that, properly exploited, Vienna as a 'UN capital' could provide the essential underpinning for a policy of active neutrality and the assertion of Austria's identity. The way was open – though it would be slow and tortuous – to develop a contemporary image for Austria: to build Kreisky's 'Austrian Model'.

NOTES ON CHAPTER IV

1. Hugh Seton Watson, in *Europäische Rundschau*, no 30/2, p 163.
2. Hugo Portisch.
3. *Pravda*, 16 May 1955.
4. *Frankfurter Allgemeine*, 18 May 1955.
5. *Österreich & Deutschlands Grösse: Ein schlampiges Verhältnis*, Deutsches Unbehagen an der Neutralität Österreich's, 1955 and 1990, p 87.
6. C.D. Jackson (one of President Eisenhower's advisors) to Henry Luce, quoted in Oliver Rathkolb, *Washington Ruft Wien*, Bohlau Verlag, 1985, p 267.
7. Hugo Portisch and Sepp Riff, *Österreich II: Der lange Weg zur Freiheit*, Kremayr & Scheriau, 1986, p 507.
8. Willy Brandt, *My Life in Politics*, Hamish Hamilton, 1992, p 37.
9. Portisch and Riff, *Österreich II: Der lange Weg zur Freiheit*, op. cit, 1986, p 421.
10. State Department telegram to the US Embassy, Vienna, 28 April 1955.
11. Hugo Portisch, *Österreich II: Jahre des Aufbruch's*, p 48.
12. Rathkolb, *Washington Ruft Wien*, op. cit., p 276.
13. Rathkolb, *Washington Ruft Wien*, op. cit., p 273.
14. NSC 5603, US Policy towards Austria, 23 March 1956.
15. Rathkolb, *Washington Ruft Wien*, op. cit., p 37, footnote.
16. Tass, 26 November 1956.
17. *Neue Zürcher Zeitung*, 23 November 1956.
18. *Pravda*, 13 December 1956.
19. Kreisky and Waldbrunner, 21 April 1958, taken from Rathkolb, *Washington Ruft Wien*, op. cit., p 229.
20. Rathkolb, *Washington Ruft Wien*, op. cit., p 168.

V

Bruno Kreisky – Not Yet Chancellor

The prologue to the era of Kreisky's Chancellorship, between 1970 and 1983, had an inauspicious beginning. There was no end in sight to the Cold War in 1959 when Kreisky was promoted to become Austria's Foreign Minister in Chancellor Raab's third coalition government. During his first three years in that office, Kreisky's efforts to establish himself as a significant player in the international community were made all the more difficult because the Cuban crisis had cast a dark pall over the diplomatic scene. In 1962, during the crisis, the US and the Soviet Union had locked horns in a struggle that brought them to the verge of nuclear war.

Inevitably, the pursuit of good relations with the US and the Soviet Union had to be the cornerstone of Austria's foreign policy. It required imaginative juggling and the creation of an image of Austria that satisfied both superpowers. Kreisky had few illusions about the constraints which the Cold War imposed on Austria's foreign policy options. He had been a firm advocate of Austrian neutrality, ahead of mainstream opinion in the Social Democratic Party; but until he became Foreign Minister he always took Sweden and Switzerland as his models. From 1959 onwards, Kreisky argued that Austria must not remain a passive onlooker. Austria must practise an active form of neutrality.

In a foreign policy declaration soon after he took charge of the Foreign Ministry he made clear that his first priority would be to enlarge Austria's potential as a meeting ground between East and West. 'If we are to be in a position to play any kind of role, then it is because at a time of great power confrontation, the handful of neutral states can perform useful functions. Even if we cannot provide a bridge, we can at least on occasion provide a point of contact.'[1]

If successful navigation between the power blocs was of prime importance, Kreisky also set himself three specific foreign policy tasks: to find a solution to the bitter dispute with Italy over South Tirol; to create links with the EEC; to build closer ties with Eastern European Communist countries. He was convinced that Austria must use UN institutions to build a favourable image of itself.

It is surely significant that Kreisky at no stage – no more as Chancellor than as Foreign Minister – thought it important for Austria's world standing to face up to the Nazi era honestly, or to handle the restitution issue as vigorously as Germany. He saw himself as a victim, forced to emigrate to Sweden, and could not bring himself to accept that Austrian society should assume collective responsibility for past actions.

Kreisky judged, correctly, that his political career would advance more rapidly if he joined the consensus that preferred to draw a line under the Nazi past. Like most other national figures, he felt that national reconciliation and nation-building were more important than a grand inquisition and the banning of Nazis from public positions. Moreover, as a Jew who was never comfortable in that identity, he was willing to compromise to great lengths in order to prove to himself, as much as to others, that his first and only public loyalty was to Austria. Years later he was to write that 'We closed our eyes to reality. I have never denied that.'[2] He preferred to deal with the issue of coming to terms with the past by helping people to find their way back to 'democratic morality'. But for a man who was so intent on creating a positive image of Austria to the outside world, the attempt to side-step recent history was a remarkably short-sighted decision, which made the task of his political successors much more difficult. Even before Kurt Waldheim had emerged to personify the dark areas of Austria's past, Kreisky should have understood that inclusiveness – the integration of former Nazi party members into public life – could only delay, and never prevent, the reckoning with the past that Austria would ultimately be forced to make.

There was little need for Kreisky to introduce himself to foreign governments when he became Foreign Minister after the 1959 general election in Austria. As State Secretary for Foreign Affairs since 1953, Kreisky had been involved in the State Treaty negotiations and subsequent foreign policy decisions. Foreign governments had long counted him as one of Austria's influential decision-makers. They realised that he was ambitious, energetic and had a creative, independent mind. They expressed no surprise that a Jew was rising as a political star in Austria. Intellectually he belonged to the West. A US State Department policy paper, written only days after Kreisky became Foreign Minister portrayed him as a 'convinced anti-communist... strongly pro-Western'. He 'advocates close economic ties with the West, but takes a strict interpretation of Austria's declared policy of military neutrality'.[3] In Western eyes, this should have made him 'safe'. But the Eisenhower administration asked itself whether Kreisky's ambition to put his stamp on international affairs might not also make him over-eager to reach out to the Russians at the expense of Western interests.

The administration realised that Kreisky had a great belief in personal diplomacy. He also held the view that military neutrality must not be made to imply inactivity on the diplomatic stage. Eisenhower and his advisors feared that the hyperactive forty-eight-year-old Foreign Minister might seek short-cuts to detente and meddle in affairs which they regarded as far beyond the scope of a small, neutral country. They suspected that Kreisky would bend over backwards to champion detente, even if it was at the expense of vital Western interests. They wanted no private diplomatic initiatives.

President Kennedy was more astute in his assessment of Kreisky's personality. He seems to have understood that Kreisky was trying to give neutrality a constructive direction, and that he could be trusted, and his pronounced pro-Western stance usefully exploited in international contacts.

Soviet leader Krushchev was always reluctant to trust Kreisky, even though he was friendly enough in personal contact with him. He had learned to see Kreisky as a fixture at high-level meetings between Austria and the Soviet Union. He had appreciated Kreisky's understanding of Soviet concerns at the State Treaty negotiations, and afterwards told the Austrian that to the Kremlin he had become a symbol of continuity in a sea of change. Kreisky rashly interpreted this as an encouragement to cultivate personal dialogue with the Soviet leader. At the close of his first visit to Moscow as Foreign Minister in October 1959, Kreisky stressed that the Soviet leaders had not criticised him even after he had said that Austria's military neutrality did not require ideological neutrality. 'During our exchanges this posture did not draw any strictures from the Soviet leadership.'[4]

But even if the Soviet leader kept silent on that occasion, soon afterwards, during a state visit to Austria in July 1960, Krushchev alarmed the Austrian public with warnings against overstepping the Kremlin's understanding of what constituted the bounds of neutrality, making it clear that joining the EEC would not be acceptable; nor would the assumption that neutrality allowed Austria to remain indifferent to America's Cold

War policies: 'The fight for peace concerns all peoples; even the neutrals would be drawn into the catastrophe if war breaks out. Austria cannot remain outside if foreign powers build military bases on its borders.'[5] Austria would have to prove its neutrality by supporting the Soviet Union's 'peace offensive', a campaign that included attacks against 'revanchist Germany' as well as against America's role in the Cold War.

Krushchev dashed Austria's hopes of exploiting his visit to portray itself as a venue for superpower conciliation. Western analysts concluded that Krushchev had used his Vienna visit simply as a platform for Soviet propaganda. Many Western diplomats, including the Americans, boycotted official functions, and both Washington and Bonn delivered protest notes, complaining that Krushchev's remarks were tantamount to a violation of Austrian neutrality.

The German Chancellor, Konrad Adenauer, was equally hard to convince of Austria's credentials as a neutral state. He approved of Kreisky, but questioned Austria's character as a nation and its record of shirking responsibility. Soon after Kreisky's appointment, he told an Austrian visitor that the country's new Foreign Minister was 'a good man. I have been saying this for a long time.'[6] Yet Adenauer was still asserting in 1960 that 'Austria's post-war attitudes prove that they are impossible people. After all they must be held at least as responsible for National Socialism as the Germans, and behaved more enthusiastically [towards the Nazis] in 1938 than the Germans... The Austrians are incapable of learning from history, as their attitude on the restitution issue demonstrates. The Federal German Republic has already paid out 4 billion Marks; Austria not one Groschen.'[7]

—— * ——

Kreisky's six-year stint as a senior Foreign Ministry official had probably made him better known abroad than in his own backyard in Austria. Though he had been an active member of the Austrian Social Democratic Party since his teens, he had only been elected to the party's executive in 1955, becoming a member of parliament in 1956.

Even in 1959, with the greater visibility that he had as Foreign Minister, Kreisky still lacked a large power-base, and had an uphill struggle to win over his own party's rank-and-file, and still more the country at large, to his vision of Austria as a social democracy securely anchored in a stable Europe. He was distrusted by the ruling Austrian People's Party to such an extent that it fought hard to prevent his renomination as Foreign Minister after the general election in 1962. The People's Party had again emerged as the senior coalition partner, but formation of the new government was delayed for weeks until it was finally agreed that the Social Democratic Party's man could retain the Foreign Ministry portfolio. His friend Willy Brandt always believed in

Kreisky's effectiveness as an ambassador for Austria. 'My good friend from the days of exile is a stickler for political honesty. There is no doubt that he increasingly succeeded in regaining for Vienna something of the diplomatic glamour of years gone by.'[8]

Kreisky won a tightly fought party election to become the Social Democrat chairman only after the party had been soundly defeated at the 1966 general election, which enabled the People's Party, for the first time, to rule alone. It took four years in opposition before the Social Democrats made their comeback in 1970, and Kreisky, now its undisputed leader, was able to launch his 13-year era in power as Austria's Chancellor.

Kreisky's design for Austria had taken shape during the State Treaty negotiations, but was firmed up during his almost seven years as Foreign Minister, and became the foundation of his subsequent policies as Chancellor. From the outset, he was emphatic about the interdependence of domestic stability and external security. This required, on the one hand, social peace based on full employment and a generous education and welfare system, and on the other hand a settlement in Europe with a stable balance of power between East and West. The formula was admirable; its implementation was problematical. While Austrian governments had a free hand with respect to domestic policies, fulfilment of the other part of the Kreisky equation was largely dependant on other, far more powerful, countries. Conditioned both by his strong personality and by the intimacy of Austrian politics, where individuals can stamp their mark on public affairs, Kreisky often misjudged the extent to which personal diplomacy could make a real difference where the vital interests of the superpowers were at stake.

His attempts, beginning in 1958, to bring about negotiations on the status of Berlin is one example of his tendency to overestimate the powers of personal persuasion. Berlin was, as always, in the eye of the storm of the Cold War, and had become the touchstone of East-West relations. The Soviet Union's goal was demilitarisation of Berlin, its integration into the German Democratic Republic, and international recognition for the East German state. This was anathema to the West. Adenauer was determined to strengthen the Federal Republic's links with NATO, and remained wedded to the quest for German unification. He had the unqualified support of his Western allies in resisting any change to the four-power status of Berlin.

Kreisky knew that the stakes were high when he decided to try and act as peacemaker in Berlin. He over-reached himself. The saga began late in 1958, when he was still State Secretary. It continued during the first year of his term as Foreign Minister. Kreisky was convinced that three of the key players, Adenauer, Krushchev and his fellow Social Democrat Willy Brandt, then still Mayor of Berlin, liked and trusted him. He was of the view that Berlin held the key to breaking the East-West deadlock over Germany. During a lecture in West Berlin, he proposed a special status for a unified, demilitarised Berlin under UN guarantee. His plan closely reflected Soviet ideas. He followed this up by sounding out the Russians as to whether they were prepared to talk with Brandt. Kreisky always maintained that Brandt had urged him to take this initiative. Brandt's version suggests otherwise.

Either way, Kreisky was both surprised and gratified when Krushchev indicated that he himself would attend any meeting with Brandt that could be arranged. Early in 1959, Kreisky was able to tell Brandt during a brief stopover in Vienna that he would soon receive an invitation to meet the Soviet leader in East Berlin. Brandt informed Adenauer and the Americans. Adenauer's response was to advise him to use his own judgment on whether to accept or decline. This reply led Brandt to speculate that Adenauer was already aware of Kreisky's intervention. 'Kreisky had always been encouraged in his contacts [with Moscow] by State Secretary Hans Globke and Adenauer himself and no contacts could have existed that might have been concealed from the German government.'[9] Adenauer probably felt that Kreisky's initiative could prove helpful. The German Chancellor referred to it later as a useful attempt at unofficial mediation. One of Adenauer's senior aides wrote in his memoirs that 'Adenauer thought of Bruno Kreisky, who had once before assumed an unofficial but useful mediator's role in the relationship between the Federal Republic and the Soviet Union'.[10]

However the Americans were not amused by Kreisky's Berlin initiative. According to Brandt, the US envoy in Berlin, Bernard Gufler, 'made an unusually sharp protest', and warned him in the strongest terms against the meeting in East Berlin. If he went, the Americans might withdraw from Berlin. Besides, there was no guarantee that Brandt would be allowed to return to West Berlin, the American envoy hinted. The Austrians, when they heard of this, thought that Gufler had not consulted Washington, and were not surprised when he was replaced in Berlin shortly afterwards. But whether or not Gufler acted on instructions from Washington, the upshot was that Brandt declined the invitation to meet Krushchev. 'My friend Kreisky, who was in an awkward position in his relations with the Russians, was greatly disappointed; he had taken too much upon himself.'[11] Kreisky felt badly let down, and put a great deal of effort into apologising to Krushchev for having suggested that he could deliver Brandt to negotiations on the future of Berlin. The apologies were accepted.

The Russians evidently still believed that Kreisky could help to engineer direct talks with Brandt, and introduced slight modifications to their earlier proposals for Berlin. Foreign Minister Andrei Gromyko gave Kreisky a new position paper. It was passed on to a senior member of

Germany's Social Democratic Party, Egon Bahr, who came to Vienna to discuss it. 'But the hawks in Berlin again won the day,'[12] the Austrian diplomat Hans Thalberg wrote in his memoirs. Moreover, the German media had obtained wind of Kreisky's involvement and *Der Spiegel* accused the Austrian Foreign Minister of appeasement. Adenauer kept his distance. As for Brandt, this was clearly one of the occasions when he harboured serious misgivings about Kreisky's political judgement. But it did little to disturb the relationship. The two men remained close personal friends, and through their collaboration in the Socialist International they often came to promote joint foreign policy initiatives.

The Americans thought the Berlin episode had justified their reservations about Kreisky. It also reinforced their fears that he was a soft target for the Russians: he should have understood that the Soviet plan for Berlin, however modified, was a non-starter for the Atlantic Alliance.

A year or so later, as Adenauer developed new ideas for a German settlement, he was tempted to use Kreisky to sound out the Russians, but changed his mind, apparently because of the Austrian's close personal relations with Brandt. 'Adenauer initially thought of using Austria's Foreign Minister Kreisky... But the close links between Kreisky and Berlin's Mayor Willy Brandt led Adenauer to the reluctant conclusion that it would be unwise to pursue this idea any further.'[13]

The Russians, for their part, tried to use Kreisky for a second time to act as unofficial mediator with the Germans. In the summer of 1960, Gromyko, during bilateral talks in Vienna, handed over a memorandum outlining Soviet ideas for a German peace treaty. Kreisky passed the document on to Adenauer, but this time he made clear to the Chancellor and to Brandt that he was not prepared to act as mediator. Besides, Kreisky believed that 'Krushchev intended to wait until the Spring, until after the inauguration of the new American President'[14] before initiating meaningful negotiations on a German settlement.

— * —

After John Kennedy assumed the US presidency in 1961, Vienna was chosen as the venue for the first – and as it turned out the only – summit with Krushchev. Though it seemed to confirm Vienna's suitability as a diplomatic venue, its positive qualities as a host city were overshadowed by the failure of the US-Soviet encounter. Austria mounted a handsome banquet in honour of the two leaders. But beyond courtesy calls there was more contact with their wives than with the two superpower leaders and their advisors. Jackie Kennedy wanted communion with horses, and spent time enthusiastically at the Spanish Riding School; Nina Krushchev preferred a taste of Vienna's cultural life: an exhibition of Paul Cézanne paintings and a concert given by the Vienna Philharmonic

Orchestra, where the Soviet violinist David Oistrakh played the Brahms violin concerto.

The 1000-odd foreign journalists in search of diplomatic morsels from the summit far exceeded the number of diplomats involved in the meeting. Media interest focussed almost exclusively on US-Soviet relations. Acres of copy were written. As so often happens at these high-level meetings, little attention was paid to the host country beyond interest in its hotel and restaurant facilities and communication links to the home base.

The miscalculations that marked the Kennedy-Krushchev summit led, a few weeks later, to the most concrete manifestation of East-West division, the erection of the Berlin Wall in September 1961.

And then, just over a year later, with the Cuban missile crisis, the Cold War almost turned hot.

— * —

The deployment of Soviet missiles in Cuba was closely linked to the East-West struggle over Berlin: it was part of Krushchev's long-standing aim to change the strategic balance and to force an Allied retreat from the city. And as the two nuclear superpowers grappled with each other over Cuba, the world had to watch helplessly from the edge of the abyss.

Kreisky had no wish to be a silent bystander. Encouraged by Soviet hints of a possible solution, he decided to act as their sounding board, and publicly proposed that the US should offer to withdraw its nuclear missiles from Turkey as part of a deal under which the Soviet Union took its missiles out of Cuba. Krushchev liked the idea. But Kennedy, though he reflected on it long and hard, rejected the 'Cuba-Turkey' trade-off. Kreisky's vanity led him to suggest in his memoirs that he had initiated the idea of such a deal, and that this had given the superpowers a formula capable of resolving the stand-off. He describes how Kennedy's crisis council responded to his suggestion: 'Kennedy's inner circle was discussing a proposal I had launched to exchange Jupiter missiles in Turkey against Soviet missiles in Cuba. This suggestion was to become an important negotiating element in the exchanges between Krushchev and Kennedy to end the Cuban missile crisis.'[15] Kreisky had an exaggerated view of his importance. In reality, Moscow and Washington had each, separately, considered the Cuba-Turkey trade-off well before Kreisky had advanced it in a speech in Berlin.

However, the tape recordings of Kennedy's crisis management team also show that on the tensest day of the crisis, on 27 October, Llewellyn Thompson, the former Ambassador in Vienna, speculated that Krushchev had come to back the trade-off idea because 'he may have picked up a statement which Kreisky, the Austrian Foreign Minister made the day before yesterday, and which he, Krushchev may think was inspired by us – in which he raised the question of the Turkish bases'. An unidentified member of the crisis team interjected that 'the Russians may have got Kreisky to do it, too'.[16] But whether or not Kreisky acted at the Soviets' behest, he had voiced an obvious proposition which influential American commentators like Walter Lippmann were also advocating. The Kennedy tapes certainly demonstrate that Kreisky was coming to be seen as a figure of substance on the international stage – though not important enough to play an active role as intermediary between the superpowers.

— * —

After the Cuban missile crisis the arms race continued unabated and the Vietnam war intensified. In the divided Europe, the Cold War entered a prolonged phase of stalemate. Gordon Brook-Shepherd, one of the few Western journalists to have reported on Austria consistently for much of the post-war period, argues that after the Hungarian uprising Austria seemed 'to slide into limbo' with 'top diplomatists and newspapermen replaced one by one by a level of representation more suitable to the needs of a small Central European republic of 7 million people'.[17]

Had Kreisky still been alive when Brook-Shepherd wrote this he would have had to concede that foreign media interest in Austria greatly diminished after 1955, and that Austria's domestic politics – other than the unresolved conflict over South Tirol which carried major interest in Italy – aroused few passions abroad. But he would, rightly, have disagreed with the proposition that Austria was slumbering while the dogs of war were barking outside. Quite apart from the constant effort to sustain the trust of the superpowers, Kreisky set himself a wide agenda during his period as Foreign Minister: it included Tirol, European economic integration, relations with Eastern Europe, co-operation with the UN and promotion of Vienna as a centre for UN activities.

The outside world only began to take notice of Kreisky's interest in the Middle East and the Third World after he became Chancellor in 1970; but that does not mean that he ignored these matters while he was Foreign Minister. During his first visit to Egypt in 1964, President Nasser evidently saw him as a man he could trust to act as intermediary with Israel, and used him to convey delicate messages to Jerusalem. Two years later, when the Social Democrats were defeated at the polls and Kreisky was out of a ministerial job, Nasser tried to encourage Kreisky to seek the UN Secretary-General's post. Kreisky rejected that advice, arguing that the Russians would never consent to an Austrian in that post. His rationale? That the United Nations was the last court of appeal over violations of the State Treaty.

Of all the issues that Austrian governments had to address after the signing of the State Treaty, Italy's disputed sovereignty over South Tirol was probably the most challenging, the most tenacious, the most poisonous. It was a raw wound of nationalism. Domestic politics and foreign policy interests were jumbled together in an explosive mix of population shifts, terrorism and deep animosity between Austria and Italy. In 1967, at a crucial point during Austria's endeavours to negotiate an association agreement with the EEC, Italy exercised its veto as a reprisal for Austria's insistence on internationalising the Tirol dispute.

The US was also drawn into the dispute, with Italy and Austria at various times seeking to enlist American support. The Italians had more political ammunition than the Austrians: they did not scruple to remind the US administration that '6 million Americans of Italian extraction would retaliate if the US "double-crossed" them'.[18] In 1959, after Kreisky sought to persuade the US to mediate in the affair, he was brusquely advised that this was a matter between Austria and Italy, and that the US had no desire to mediate. A US State Department note suggested that the Austrian government was making capital out of the South Tirol dispute for its own domestic political advantage. 'We didn't want to get caught up in this thing that had nothing for us at all. It would make one side or the other mad…'[19]

The twists and turns of the efforts to settle the South Tirol dispute produced acres of report and commentary, not only in the Italian and the Austrian media but also among Austria's other neighbours, who were justifiably uneasy about unresolved ethnic disputes in Central and Southern Europe. When Kreisky took the issue to the UN first in September 1959, and again in September 1960, countries that had probably never heard of Tirol were obliged to familiarise themselves with the problem – and in the process take a crash course in Austrian politics.

The South Tirol dispute was a result of the First World War. Italian troops occupied the area at the end of the war, and in the post-war settlement Italy, which claimed it, was awarded sovereignty. Self-determination was rejected, and the border with Austria was set at the Brenner Pass. The 200,000 Tiroleans who lived there found themselves separated by an international frontier from the rest of Tirol. The partition caused bitter resentment and bedevilled relations between Italy and Austria. As a gesture of defiance, Tirol declared itself independent in 1919. Two years later, Tiroleans organised a poll in which 98.6 per cent of the population voted to join Germany – an expression of pro-German sentiment in an important province of Austria which was brushed under the table in the post-1945 drive to assert the durability of Austrian nationhood.

After the Anschluss, the Tirol dispute lay dormant. Hitler did not want to quarrel with Mussolini over South Tirol. 80 per cent of the Tirolean population of South Tirol left, most of them rejoining their families in the other part of the Tirol. Tiroleans did not give up their quest for reunification. In 1945, they expected that Austrian sovereignty over South Tirol would either be restored, or that the region would be given autonomy. The first option was rejected; the second was incorporated into a 1946 treaty between Italy and Austria, and given still greater legitimacy as an annex to the new Italian constitution, adopted in 1948. The South Tiroleans who had emigrated after 1938 returned, thanks to the promise of full autonomy. But Italy had played a nasty trick: in the new constitution, the province of South Tirol was joined to the neighbouring province of Trentino, and together they formed an administrative region in which there were twice as many Italians as Tiroleans. The Italians had betrayed their promise of autonomy for South Tirol. The bitterness grew deeper and terrorism spread.

After the State Treaty, the Austrian government intensified demands on Italy to settle Tirolean claims. Italy refused, claiming that this was an internal matter. More Italians were settled in the province to outnumber the Tiroleans and create facts on the ground. Determined to prove that South Tirol was an international dispute between two sovereign states, Kreisky went to the UN General Assembly in September 1959 and called on the UN to involve itself in the dispute on the grounds that the quarrel was turning into a threat to European security.

Kreisky's initiative failed; The General Assembly fell into line behind Italy's contention that South Tirol was a purely internal matter, outside the UN jurisdiction. But it proved a useful occasion for the new Austrian Foreign Minister to launch himself on the world stage.

Terrorist incidents in South Tirol multiplied. In the autumn of 1960, Kreisky again went to the General Assembly. The roll-call of world leaders attending this session was exceptional, and Kreisky again exploited the opportunity to demonstrate that Austria had now developed into a fully integrated member of the international community. He had an impressive audience: Eisenhower and Krushchev were there locked in bitter dispute over the nuclear arms race; Tito, Nehru, Castro, Sadat and Sukarno were there to signal their determination to break free from the repercussions of the Cold War. A year later these third world leaders were to launch the Non-aligned Movement. They had not forgotten the impression that Kreisky had made as an independent-minded crusader. It was no accident that Austria became the first neutral country to be offered observer status with the Non-aligned Movement.

But the immediate outcome of Kreisky's efforts to internationalise the Tirol dispute was the adoption of a UN resolution calling on Austria and Italy to settle their differences. It took another nine years, an escalation of terrorism, several treason trials, and Italy's blocking of Austrian negotiations with the EEC before a new autonomy agreement, acceptable to all parties, was finally reached in 1969 – by Kurt Waldheim, who had become Foreign Minister in succession to Kreisky in 1966, after the People's Party emerged from general elections as the overall winner and had formed a government without the participation of the Social Democrats.

— * —

Kreisky was on a skiing holiday in Austria when the European Free Trade Association agreement with Brussels was finalised in January 1960. As Foreign Minister, he signed for Austrian inclusion in the EFTA pact during an interlude between ski runs in Kitzbühl. Even so, this was no casual act. Way back during the occupation, Austria's leaders had already recognised the importance of close economic co-operation in Europe. In 1948, Austria had joined other Marshall aid recipients to become a member of the Organisation for European Economic Cooperation (OEEC), formed by the US to administer the aid. The Soviet Union disapproved, but could not block Austrian membership.

After the State Treaty, Austria's commitment to neutrality gave the Soviet Union a forceful weapon to deter Austrian aspirations for closer links with the EEC. The Kremlin voiced few reservations about Austrian membership of EFTA, because the new seven-member organisation set itself no political goals. But the Soviet tune changed radically after Austria began to show interest in a bilateral association agreement with the EEC which had come into existence in 1957. The Kremlin used the neutrality argument as a sledgehammer to warn Austria against links with an institution that had set itself the goal of political, and not just economic, integration. Time and again, the Soviet Union demonstrated that it still found it difficult to countenance Austria as an independent agent and allow the country to take its own decisions with respect to its economic interests.

Warnings were delivered both publicly and behind closed doors by the Soviet leaders, by diplomats and the media. The Russians ignored Austria's contention that the State Treaty itself only prohibited military alliances. Instead the Kremlin countered that German membership of the EEC disqualified Austria from any links with it. It claimed that all EEC countries were members of NATO and reminded Austria of the State Treaty clause prohibiting political and economic union with Germany.

During an exchange with Austrian Chancellor Gorbach in 1961, Soviet Ambassador Avilov argued that the Treaty article about union with Germany, together with Austrian neutrality, was designed to maintain political equilibrium in Central Europe. Even though Austria had not mooted full membership of the EEC, the Soviet diplomat argued as if the country was seeking an arrangement tantamount to Anschluss with Germany. The Russian asserted that this would create problems for the strategic balance in Europe, and run counter to Austrian neutrality. It would be a violation of the State Treaty. Behind the legalistic arguments, there was a further Soviet concern: Austria's economy would undoubtedly benefit from an association agreement with the EEC, and the Soviet Union feared that Austria's growing prosperity would trigger political repercussions in Hungary and Czechoslovakia.

The Soviet press, echoing as usual the official line, carried stark warnings to Austria. *Pravda* attacked Austria in the same breath as America's nuclear arsenals, and insisted that the EEC was an extension of the West's military machine. Radio Moscow argued that 'the EEC was pursuing the same arms race as the Third Reich'.[20] When Kreisky visited Moscow again in 1962, Krushchev went out of his way to warn Austria against further flirtation with Brussels. The Soviet leader described the EEC as a 'Holy alliance engaged in the fight against the Eastern bloc', and told Kreisky not to approach the EEC. 'It would be a blow against neutrality. Austria would be in the anti-Soviet bloc; it would be a second Anschluss, a violation of the State Treaty.'[21]

Political analysts always believed that a key aspect of the Soviet Union's political objections to Austrian links with the EEC related to the belief that the balance of Austria's trade would shift towards the West, away from the Communist bloc. This had the potential to create envy and resentment among Austria's eastern neighbours and cause instability in the Communist camp.

An Austrian in Vienna summed it up this way: 'During the inter-war period, Austria was the poor relation, and the Czechs and Hungarians were prosperous. Now they are the poor relation and Austria the prosperous. Yet nothing has changed in Czechoslovakia and Hungary – except that they are governed differently!'[22]

The Austrian government persevered with its overtures to Brussels, even though public opinion in Austria was affected by the Soviet warnings. People were afraid of losing their country's label of neutrality. As Foreign Minister, Kreisky was always conscious of the need to safeguard Austria's neutrality and was circumspect in his negotiations with Brussels. But he calculated that sooner or later the EFTA countries and the EEC would have to have institutional links. The Social Democrats may have lost one or two crucial seats in the 1966 general election, because of grass-roots concern that the pro-EEC policy constituted a violation of neutrality.

But after the People's Party's election victory in 1966, the new government pressed even harder for association negotiations with the EEC. Soviet President Podgorny, during an official visit to Vienna in November 1966, warned that the Soviet Union was no nearer accepting such a development now than it had been earlier under Krushchev's leadership. 'As Austria's friends, we have the right to declare quite openly that an arrangement with the EEC, in whatever form, would involve Austria in political as well as in economic commitments… This would violate the State Treaty and deviate Austria from the well-trodden path of neutrality.'[23]

The Americans also cautioned, though much less stridently, against Austria's identification with the EEC as a possible violation of its neutrality. The French left no doubt that they were strongly opposed to Austrian overtures to Brussels. They were prepared, they warned, to use their veto. They took their cue from the Soviet Union. No amount of Austrian protestation that the country would insist on neutrality safeguards in any association agreement with the EEC appeared to convince France that anything beyond a trade agreement should be envisaged. President de Gaulle was convinced that EEC links with Austria would cause unwanted tensions on the borders of the Communist bloc. During an official visit to Vienna in September 1968, the French Prime Minister, Georges Pompidou, bluntly rejected pleas for France to lift its objections to Austrian negotiations with Brussels. Austria must not do anything that might disturb the political balance in Europe, he warned.

Italy did not need geopolitical reasons to thwart Austria's endeavours in Brussels. Throughout the 1960s, Rome's relations with Austria was based on the narrowest of parameters: the rival claims on South Tirol. The EEC lent itself as an ideal instrument for a tit-for-tat policy. The Italian veto was maintained until 1969. In the end, it was Kreisky – in 1972, after he had already been Chancellor for two years – who was able to conclude a first agreement with Brussels. It was a trade accord, far less ambitious than had originally been envisaged. It took a further 17 years, the disintegration of the Soviet Union, and a more nebulous perception of neutrality, before Austria, in 1989, was finally enabled to enter into membership negotiations with Brussels. And it was 1994 when the country finally achieved its ambition and joined the EU as a full member.

— * —

Kreisky's commitment to Western values only reinforced his endeavours to improve relations with Yugoslavia and the Communist bloc countries. This was a characteristic of his period as Foreign Minister just as much as of his time as Chancellor. There was much repair work to be done with the pro-Moscow Communist leadership of Eastern Europe after Austria's open door asylum policy during the 1956 Hungarian uprising. There were many bilateral visits, and Kreisky also used the UN as a forum to emphasise Austria's attractions as a good neighbour to the Communist bloc. Much of it was calculated to prove to the Soviet Union that Austria was not intent on selling out to the West.

The government was not alone in pursuing its 'Ostpolitik'. Austria's Primate, Cardinal König has never shared the view that Roman Catholic Church leaders should steer clear of other faiths, or of non-believers: 'Dialogue is essential to achieve mutual respect and understanding'.[24] He applied this approach both to his dealings with Austria's Social Democratic politicians – including Kreisky, who became a close friend – and to contacts with the Communist world.

This remarkable prelate, of an open and enquiring mind, embarked on an 'Ostpolitik' initiative all his own, without prior consultation with the Austrian authorities or with the Vatican. It began with visits to the Polish Primate, Cardinal Wiszcynski, in 1958. At that time, the Vatican was still rigorously opposed to contact with Communist regimes. At the risk of offending Pope Pius XII, both Cardinals thought otherwise, and were convinced that the bishops should talk to the Communists. With Kreisky's connivance, Roman Catholic literature was smuggled in. 'The Poles were astonished to see me. The priests thought we had forgotten them. Just to talk with them was a moral help to them,' Cardinal König recalled. It was the first of several visits, which helped to persuade a great many Poles to take a more benign view of post-war Austria.

König's activities in Eastern Europe were by no means confined to Poland. After Pope John appointed him to a new Vatican commission for 'non-believers', he paid frequent visits behind the iron curtain, most of all to Budapest to befriend Cardinal Mindszenty in his refuge in the US Embassy. Those conversations eventually helped to persuade Mindszenty to leave Hungary in 1971 and to spend his last days in a monastery in Austria.

Communist countries turned a blind eye to König's visits because he was discreet, never publicly talked politics, and gave no media interviews. Always modest in describing his achievements, the Cardinal nevertheless recognised that his visits were appreciated by people who sensed that he meant well and was not trying to exploit them. His presence helped to portray a more positive picture of Austria as a neutral country with an objective approach to the Communist bloc. 'People understood that my visits helped to ease the Church presence. I had the advantage of coming from a neutral country, and people also understood that I was not trying to exploit them and was only trying to establish links that the outside world could respect...'[25]

— * —

Austria's neutrality was tested to its limits in 1968 when Warsaw Pact forces intervened in Czechoslovakia. It came as no great surprise. Waldheim, who had been made Foreign Minister after the 1966 election, had come away from an official visit to Moscow in June 1968, convinced that the 'Prague Spring' would not be allowed to continue unbridled. He had stopped off in Prague, and warned Dubcek against attempting to turn Czechoslovakia into a neutral state.

But during that summer, Austria, remaining true to the same human rights instincts that had guided its actions in 1956, turned a blind eye to the thousands of Czech tourists who poured into the country bearing goods and chattels that suggested they had more than a holiday on their minds. On that August night when the Soviet tanks poured into Prague, there were over 60,000 Czechs in Austria, and they were allowed to remain. But should the borders be kept open for more refugees?

Chancellor Klaus and Waldheim were far more cautious than their predecessors had been in 1956. They worried that Austria was once again at the mercy of the superpowers: would the Soviet Union violate Austrian territory? Was NATO prepared to defend Austria? Waldheim advised against reinforcing Austrian border forces, but became alarmed and changed his mind after a series of Soviet over-flights.

In the midst of widespread nervousness, there was the curious case of the – temporary – decision to stop issuing Austrian visas to would-be Czech refugees. The Austrian Ambassador in Prague, Dr Rudolf Kirchschläger, objected so strongly to the instruction from Vienna that he refused to comply. After a couple of days, the order was lifted, Austria again became a model country of asylum, and welcomed 96,000 Czech refugees. The Waldheim version of the temporary border closure amounts to the assertion that he acted on orders from the Interior Minister, who apparently feared that passports stolen from the Prague Embassy might be used to infiltrate Soviet agents into Austria. Kirchschläger's tale is different. He disclosed several years later that he had been unable to find the relevant files that had led to the visa prohibition, but that Waldheim had assured him that 'he had not known at the time that the order had been issued'.[26]

There is a third version, long rumoured in Vienna but which gained much wider currency when allegations of war crimes were launched against Waldheim. This account suggests that the Soviet Union was threatening to expose the truth about Waldheim's wartime record, and pressured Waldheim to halt the issuing of visas. Not surprisingly, Waldheim has gone to great lengths to deny this. Whether the Russians really had material for blackmailing Waldheim has never been proved. But as the files about this unfortunate incident have mysteriously gone missing, the suspicion surely lingers that the ever-servile Waldheim, pleading that he was 'just obeying orders', might indeed have been acting under hidden Soviet pressure.

There was nothing hidden about the Soviet Union's fusillade of objections and warnings in response to the outpouring of Austrian sympathy for Czechoslovakia's plight. It prompted an anxious Austrian government to go out of its way to emphasise its political neutrality. Austria went so far towards the Kremlin's version of events as to stress that this was a purely 'internal affair' between Communist countries. Clearly Austria was trying to distance itself as much as possible from the superpower struggle.

But Austria was clearly not indifferent to the Czechoslovak crisis. From the opposition benches, Kreisky was outspoken in condemning the Warsaw Pact intervention in Czechoslovakia. Events had shown, he declared, that Communist dictatorships were not prepared to tolerate attempts to secure greater freedoms. In 1968, Kreisky felt free to speak his mind as leader of the principal opposition party.

— * —

The end to the cosy relationship between Austria's two biggest parties came less than a year after the twentieth anniversary of the State Treaty. The longest and most stable coalition between Conservatives and Social Democrats in Europe had undoubtedly provided appropriate political stability for the successful launch of Austria's 'economic miracle' that had produced a striking improvement in living standards. It had laid the basis for the notable economic upswing during the Kreisky era of the 1970s.

The rigid coalition system, under which all important decisions were taken by a small bipartisan committee, had reduced parliament to little more than a transmission belt. But the coalition was underpinned by unusually close relations between unions and employers. This had provided an unbroken spell of peace and wage restraint on the labour front. But these factors also created a frustrating climate of political stagnation and economic immobility, which was to return to Austria after the Kreisky era and the restoration of coalition government.

In 1966, outside observers were agreed that the break-up of the postwar series of coalition governments marked a major departure in Austrian politics. *The Times* said it was too soon to judge 'whether this abrupt change will pave the way for the solution of the structural economic problems of the country, or will create intolerable domestic political tensions... In a country where the memories of the civil war of 1934 are still vivid, where the danger of economic domination by neighbouring Germany is real, and where the geographical position on the edge of the free world is precarious, radical political changes are rare and fraught with danger... However Dr Bruno Kreisky is clearly the brain of the party [the opposition Social Democrats] and possibly the most outstanding thinker in Austria today. He is inextricably linked with the question whether Austria will emerge as an economically more viable and politically more stable country from the new experiment in Parliamentary democracy.'[27]

When Austria's President, Franz Jonas, arrived in London in May 1966, he became the first Austrian head of state to visit the UK since 1918. Jonas was judged as a conscientious head of state, while the UK tended to see Kreisky as a 'vain Cassandra'. British officials groped for interesting material about Austria to highlight in speeches written for the Queen and her ministers. Beyond emphasising that the State Treaty had

9. *(above)* Tens of thousands of Hungarian refugees streamed into Austria during the Hungarian Uprising of 1956, sorely testing Austria's self-proclaimed neutrality after the country had opened its borders to the refugees.

10. *(below)* Richard Nixon – then US Vice-President – came on a fact-finding mission and met with some of the Hungarian refugees in their temporary homes, following Austrian pleas for help to resettle them.

11. Soviet Prime Minister Andrei Kosygin and Foreign Minister Andrei Gromyko hosted a Kremlin reception for Kurt Waldheim when, as Austrian Foreign Minister, he visited Moscow in March 1968. Emerging from its post-war shell Austria in the 1960s again saw a role for itself in international diplomacy.

12. Austrian President Jonas' state visit to Britain in 1966 when Queen Elizabeth gave the unassuming head of state a warm reception, was part of Austria's drive to raise its profile. But there was still a long way to go - even London's Lord Mayor, in a speech of welcome, confused Austria with Australia.

13. When the Soviet and American leaders met in Vienna for the 1979 signing of the Start II, the barely-aware Leonid Brezhnev could not be deterred from embracing a reluctant Jimmy Carter.

14. Vienna's 'UN city' - opened in 1979 - was intended to become a rival to Geneva as the centre of the UN's bureaucracy in Europe. The opening ceremony, including performances by Austria's state opera ballet, was intended to express the country's joy at being recognised as a centre of diplomacy again.

15. *(above)* In October 1973, a furious Israeli Prime Minister, Golda Meir, swooped into Vienna to confront Chancellor Bruno Kreisky over his hostility towards Israel and his apparent softness on terrorism. She later complained she was not even offered a glass of water during her brief visit.
16. *(below)* Chancellor Bruno Kreisky persuaded Egypt's President Anwar Sadat and Israeli Prime Minister Shimon Peres to meet in Austria in 1978, with German Chancellor Will Brandt in attendance, to lend support. Kreisky gloried in the full flow of Austrian (and his own) diplomacy.

proved itself as a success, they could think of nothing more momentous than to highlight the indirect link with the UK through Austrian membership of EFTA, and to praise Austria's cultural achievements, its tourism and its obvious prosperity. Even then, well informed people who should certainly have known better tended to confuse Austria with Australia. There was great embarrassment when the Lord Mayor of London at an official luncheon in Jonas's honour repeatedly referred to Australia.

The *Daily Telegraph* set out to educate the UK. In an editorial, the conservative daily said that Jonas was the representative of a country 'that has become a stabilising factor in Central Europe. Neutral Austria, free, democratic and inseparable from the Western world, provides through human and cultural contacts, a confrontation for her Eastern neighbours... Both government and opposition are fully aware that it was cooperation between the two great parties and not the struggle of one class or group against the other, that helped Austria in the first post-war decade to regain freedom, sovereignty, economic independence. The step from coalition to parliamentary confrontation means a return to basic democratic rules. How this challenge will be met will be a test of Austria's political maturity.'[28]

There was no need to worry. The end of the grand coalition did not mean the end of cross-party political collaboration or, for that matter, of cosy political cronyism. The *Proporz* system – an Austrian form of nepotism – continued undisturbed, so that as ever key posts in the public service, and to a considerable extent even in the private sector, were divided between the two leading parties.

In the wake of their election defeat, and only after internal differences were resolved, the Social Democrats elected Kreisky as their leader. He became a textbook opposition leader, and used his four years in that position to refine his political aims, and plot the way to electoral victory.

But even though Chancellor Klaus and opposition leader Kreisky ably demonstrated that there was life after coalition, they failed to pass another essential test of political maturity: how to master Austria's recent past. Like their predecessors, they were more concerned with rebuilding the national identity than with objective truth or with punishment of Nazi behaviour.

There was one man amongst them who refused to let sleeping dogs lie. He was Simon Wiesenthal, and he had beavered away in Vienna collecting data on Nazi penetration in Austria. At first he tried quietly to alert Austrian leaders to his findings that Austria's civil service and judiciary was still peppered with former Nazis, that denazification had been shockingly inadequate, and that only a few Nazi criminals had been brought to trial. When he saw that his arguments fell on deaf ears, Wiesenthal drew up a detailed document to illustrate 'the guilt and atonement of the Nazi perpetrators from Austria'.

While Austrians had constituted under ten per cent of the Third Reich's population, there was 'extensive proof that Austrians were responsible for the deaths of three million Jews (out of the estimated six million who were killed)'. Yet there had been far fewer war crimes trials in Austria than in Germany. The Austrian judiciary, Wiesenthal argued, was riddled with former Nazis who were deliberately impeding the course of justice. He urged judicial reform and the exclusion of former Nazis from jury service. And he told Klaus that 'This is not just a domestic Austrian problem... An observant world is following the conduct of the trials, and Austria's international standing is at stake.' During his trips abroad, Wiesenthal said, he was frequently confronted by 'painful questions about the sad situation in Austria. Rightly so, my questioners always stress the international implications of Austria's behaviour. Only rapid and energetic measures can re-establish Austria's already weakened international standing. Only an unequivocal attitude by the representatives of our country can reawaken the public conscience; only the unqualified commitment to justice can silence those who are pressing for a general amnesty for all Nazi crimes. If this problem is not resolved, Austria will be guilty of leaving an empty space in history, and this will leave a stigma for all time.'

Klaus and Kreisky chose to ignore Wiesenthal's testimony, and opted for inaction. That was surely a great mistake. Wiesenthal's predictions that Austria's image would carry a world-wide stigma proved to be correct: not the successes of the Kreisky era; not Austria's economic prosperity or its accession to the EU; not its importance as an international meeting ground; not even the lead that Chancellor Vranitzky gave after 1989 in awakening Austrian consciences, or the testimony of Jewish survivors pointing to help given to them by individual Austrians. None of this has prevented international ambivalence towards Austria and perceptions of Austrians as an antisemitic people reluctant to face the truth about their behaviour during the Nazi era.

NOTES ON CHAPTER V

1 *Forum*, September 1957.
2 Bruno Kreisky, *Im Strom der Politik*, Siedelr, Kremayr & Scheriau, 1988, p 45.
3 Oliver Rathkolb, 'Bruno Kreisky: Perspectives of Top-level US Foreign Policy Decision-makers, 1959–83' in *The Kreisky Era in Austria*, Transaction Publishers, 1994, p 131.
4 Bruno Kreisky press conference, Moscow, 14 October 1959.
5 Krushchev press conference, Vienna, 30 June 1960.
6 Kreisky, *Im Strom der Politik*, op. cit., p 29.

7 Kreisky, *Im Strom der Politik*, op. cit., p 29.
8 Willy Brandt, *People and Politics*, HarperCollins, 1978, p 102.
9 Brandt, *People and Politics*, op. cit., p 102.
10 Hans Globke, *Konrad Adenauer und seine Zeit*, Deutsche Verlaganstalt Stuttgart, 1976, p 671.
11 Willy Brandt, *My Life in Politics*, Hamish Hamilton, 1992, p 41.
12 Hans Thalberg, *Von der Kunst Österreicher zu sein*, Bohlau Verlag, 1984, p 256.
13 Globke, *Konrad Adenauer und seine Zeit*, op. cit. p 670.
14 Brandt, *People and Politics*, op. cit., p 101.
15 Kreisky, *Im Strom der Politik*, op. cit., p 122.
16 Ernest R. Mays & Philip D. Zelikow (ed.), *The Kennedy Tapes: Inside the White House during the Cuban Missile Crisis*, Harvard University Press, 1997, p 502.
17 Gordon Brook-Shepherd, *The Austrians*, HarperCollins, 1997, p 417.
18 Oliver Rathkolb, *Washington Ruft Wien*, Vienna, 1997, p 159.
19 Rathkolb, *Washington Ruft Wien*, op. cit., p 162.
20 Radio Moscow, 6 October 1961.
21 Hans Thalberg, *Von der Kunst Österreicher zu sein*, Bohlau Verlag, 1984, p 285.
22 Ibid., p 285.
23 Podgorny radio declaration, Vienna, 20 November 1966.
24 Interviews with Cardinal König, 1998.
25 Interview with Cardinal König, 1998.
26 Kirchschläger press conference, Vienna 20 May 1974.
27 *The Times*, 15 May 1966.
28 *Daily Telegraph*, 17 May 1966.

VI

Beyond the Corridors of Power

Cultural Icons as Opinion-formers

It was 1946: they were a small group of Harvard students and academics; they had a few thousand dollars and the opportunity to use the dilapidated baroque Schloss Leopoldskron on the outskirts of Salzburg. Few of them had seen, but all knew about, war-shattered Europe, and this spurred them on to draw up a still ill-defined project for bringing European and American students together to learn about each other and exchange ideas about the architecture of the post-war world.

Almost everyone they approached for help said it was a madcap idea: the notion was premature. Salzburg was under American occupation. The US army would not allow students from other countries, or even from other zones in Austria, to attend. Food was short. There were bound to be unhappy clashes between participants from the countries of the wartime alliance and some of the Austrians and Germans who would be present.

But an Austrian-born Harvard academic, Clemens Heller, and two of his friends persevered, and during six weeks in the summer of 1947 an American Studies seminar was held at Schloss Leopoldskron. The oldest among the participants were in their thirties; the youngest only twenty-one or twenty-two. They ate potatoes and macaroni, and drank Coca-Cola; they slept in bare rooms on narrow army cots covered with rough sheets made of flax. The gardens were running wild, but nothing could spoil the view of the adjoining man-made lake and the mountain range beyond. 'We were all young. We had in one way or another been in the war, and there was a line-up of victors and vanquished that was very sharply perceived,' recalled the economist Karl Kaysen. 'The hostilities were greatest between the Scandinavians and the French on the one side, and the Germans and the Austrians on the other. The Brits and the Americans were out of it; we had never been occupied; we never had to deal with that feeling.'[1]

Walt Rostow, the political scientist, bought a pair of Lederhosen from a German participant, a former Luftwaffe pilot, only to discover later that they were from German army surplus and had seen service with Rommel's army. He didn't wear them – not because of their provenance, but because they were uncomfortable for tennis.

There were palpable tensions at the 1947 Salzburg Seminar, but they eased after an evening when students from each of the countries represented at the Seminar read poems of their choice. The atmosphere was heavily charged, especially poignant when the Americans, the last to read, opted for Walt Whitman's 'Reconciliation'.

The reading was given outside, on the terrace overlooking the lake. Elspeth Rostow – in 1947 newly married to Walt, and at Salzburg to teach foreign policy – still remembers how badly they were bitten by mosquitoes and how they went indoors scratching at their itching skin, but elated by the poetry. After the reading 'there was a greater sense of humanity than I had perceived earlier, and I saw that next morning people had begun to become more comfortable with each other'.

The US occupation authorities had a less romantic view of the bonding activities at Schloss Leopoldskron. The American founders of the Salzburg Seminar were thought to be too left-wing to be trusted; some were suspected of fellow-travelling, and the gatherings at Leopoldskron became an East-West battle ground between the students and the military government. For a while the Americans refused to give a visa to Heller, the moving spirit behind the gathering.

Eventually the US military revised their views, and recognised the usefulness of the Seminar and the idealism of its founders. Ever since, the institution has been supported by the US government, and though it raises most of its funds privately it has also had government help. Most of the founders became distinguished establishment figures in mainstream America, but regularly returned for teaching stints at Salzburg.

Fifty years after those first blissful summer days at Leopoldskron, the Rostows, Karl Kaysen and several other of the original participants were back at Schloss Leopoldskron to celebrate the anniversary of a remarkable enterprise dedicated to the strengthening of international understanding. Ever since that long-ago blissful post-war experience, an impressive string of distinguished foreign academics, politicians, lawyers, bankers, artists, musicians, journalists – even royals – have come to Schloss Leopoldskron to lead an almost seamless series of discussions with successive generations of students. The themes have broadened, with American Studies now occupying a much smaller place, and European, transatlantic, technological and global issues moved to the forefront.

The notion of victor and vanquished has long since been eradicated. The Salzburg Seminar has become an established institution, which the Austrian government and the Salzburg authorities enthusiastically support, for good reason. It has exposed Austrians and foreigners to each other in the best kind of intellectual and physical surroundings. Mutual prejudices have been shed as faculty members have learned about and from each other, have spent time in a now handsomely refurbished Schloss Leopoldskron, and have shared in the splendours of music-making in Salzburg. Austrians have been able to explain themselves and to discuss the subjects that make them most uncomfortable – such as antisemitism or the resurgence of right-wing extremism.

Nothing could illustrate that better than a January evening in Schloss Leopoldskron in 1996. A high-powered seminar to discuss the 'New World Order' after the Cold War was in session. An influential group from around the world participated, and the discussions were challenging and of remarkable quality. It was snowing. Outside on the frozen lake, groups of skaters were gliding under a full moon – an animated Breughel painting.

Indoors, everybody was sitting in the semi-dark, the great hall lit up by a brightly-burning fire. Eva Nowotny, at the time Austria's Ambassador to France, had a keen audience as she described Austria's domestic political scene, warts and all. There were awkward questions, especially about the burgeoning Haider phenomenon, and Nowotny made no attempt to minimise the significance of his growing support from the Austrian electorate. But she also put it in the context of a country firmly committed to the EU, and argued that Austria's integration into the fabric of Western values had gone beyond the point where it could be derailed by an ambitious populist nationalist. The jury, however, remained out, even then. Informal exchanges like this could help, but did not put an end to all doubts about Austria's credentials as a fully sanitised nation.

— * —

It is worth focussing attention on the Salzburg Seminar because it is always surprising how little awareness there is in Austria of this institution, and of its extraordinary usefulness in bridge-building between Austria and the outside world. The local government of Salzburg lends active support, and senior Austrian diplomats, like Nowotny and Peter Jankowitsch, serve on the Seminar's board, while a good many other Austrian experts have participated in sessions. But on the whole, it seems that there are far more people in the US, UK and France who know about the activities at Schloss Leopoldskron than within Austria itself. This is all the more surprising since Schloss Leopoldskron itself is so well-known to aficionados of the Salzburg Festival, and has an even bigger claim to fame as a point of pilgrimage for lovers of *The Sound of Music*, which was shot there. Foreign tourists, if they know nothing else about Salzburg, will come looking for a glimpse of that terrace where Julie Andrews at last found her Count and set off with her lover and his children, singing as they crossed the mountains fleeing from the Nazis.

But for all that, it is the Salzburg Festival that has a much more tangible connection with the house and its grounds. Max Reinhardt, one of the Festival's founders – the other two geniuses behind the Festival were Richard Strauss and Hugo von Hofmannsthal – bought the eighteenth century Schloss in 1918, and lived there after he was forced to leave Berlin in 1933. It was there that many of the Salzburg Festival operas were planned. The most famous musicians and singers of the inter-war period rehearsed there. To this day, the rooms still seem to reverberate with the voices of Elizabeth Schumann or Lotte Lehman, and the presence of Richard Strauss, Arturo Toscanini and so many virtuosi of the world of opera and classical music.

During the years before the Anschluss in 1938 perverted the character of the Festival, Reinhardt and his collaborators succeeded in establishing Salzburg as the most prestigious of all the international music festivals on the calendar. After Hitler came to power in Germany in 1933, they felt that the Festival should also be used to serve a political purpose as a 'bastion of freedom close to the German border, and as a refuge for the artistic elites driven out of Nazi Germany'.[2]

Toscanini, a frequent presence between 1934 and 1938, was particularly insistent that the Festival must establish itself as an anti-fascist, anti-Nazi showcase for the performing arts. Festival audiences had little interest in such political statements. They loved its exceptional musical standards, and enjoyed its cosmopolitan character. Salzburg was a fixture on the annual summer high society circuit. One American critic called the Festival 'Hollywood on the Salzach', and noted that it had become 'the home of stars and snobs'.

Toscanini created consternation with the Festival plans for the 1938 season when he announced his withdrawal weeks before Hitler's troops marched in, to be welcomed by a solid phalanx of Salzburg's citizens cheering them on with German flags and shouts of 'Heil Hitler'. Later it became the only Austrian city to stage a public book-burning of the works of Jewish authors.

As in Germany, so also in Austria, the Nazis banned the performance of 'degenerate' music and theatre. Göring decreed that the Salzburg Festival was to be a celebration of the German soul. No more *Faust* or *Jederman*, and certainly no more Jewish composers or musicians. Reinhardt,

Bruno Walter, Toscanini and many other prominent artists were either excluded because they were Jews or because they were principled enough to stay away in protest against the Nazi regime. But there were many exceptions – for example Karl Böhm and Wilhelm Furtwängler – who were prepared to compromise for the privilege of being allowed to perform.

The Vienna Philharmonic Orchestra, which regularly played in Salzburg, was told to dismiss all Jewish musicians after the Anschluss. Suitably Aryan replacements were quickly engaged, and the orchestra fulfilled all its commitments in Salzburg in 1938 and 1939, and continued to play regularly at the behest of the Nazi authorities throughout the war in Salzburg, Vienna and in Germany.

Foreign music critics who covered the 1938 Festival disliked its 'aryanisation', but seemed more concerned by the lax dress code and the extensive beer drinking among the spectators brought in by the Nazis from Bavaria. They missed the elegance of past festivals.

Nazi functionaries now took control of the Festival, a bust of Goebbels was put up, and anyone suspected of being of Jewish extraction was dismissed. The Nazis used music for propaganda purposes. Mozart's operas, a staple at the Salzburg Festival, were recruited to call Austria's youth to arms. 'In Mozart's name we call the young to arms,' declared Austria's Nazi Governor, Baldur von Schirach.[3]

Hitler, accompanied by Martin Bormann and Albert Speer, came to the premiere of *Don Giovanni* to open the 1939 Festival. They were feted with endless salvoes of 'Bravo' and Nazi salutes. The Vienna Philharmonic Orchestra, which would normally have played throughout the Festival, was abruptly ordered to go instead to Nürnberg to perform Wagner's *Meistersinger*.

The Nazis were determined to maintain the annual Salzburg Festival during the war and 'restore its German character', as Göring put it. Programmes were narrowed to concentrate on Beethoven, Richard Strauss, Mozart, Wagner, Brahms. High-ranking Nazi visitors who came to Festival performances were accommodated at Schloss Leopoldskron, which had been sanitised of all traces of Reinhardt. Many of the great names of the music world who had been regulars in Salzburg or Vienna were missing – as well as Toscanini and Walter, there was Vladimir Horowitz, all of whom had emigrated to the US. Böhm and Clemens Krauss, however, had no scruples about working in Salzburg under the Nazis, insisting that they were safeguarding the Festival's traditions. Krauss remained director until 1944. Böhm went to Vienna in 1942, to be head of the State Opera. Both men were able to attract the best singers available in Germany and the German-occupied territories. They included Hans Hotter, Erich Kunz, Anton Dermota, Irmgard Seefried, Hilde Güden and several other young artists whose fame spread after the war. Their willingness to perform under the Nazis attracted little attention. But Böhm's and Krauss's collaboration with the Nazis was far more problematical. Like Austrian-born Herbert von Karajan, who had joined the Nazi Party as early as 1933, and Germany's Elizabeth Schwarzkopf, who justified Party membership as a passport to performance similar to trade union membership,[4] their records were closely examined before the two conductors were allowed to perform again after the war's end.

— * —

The four occupation powers in Austria did not attempt to define a common cultural policy for the country. The gulf between the Soviet concept of culture as a propaganda tool and the Western belief in freedom of speech was unbridgeable, even during the euphoria of victory. But the absence of a common attitude to the restoration of Austria's cultural life also meant that there was little co-operation in handling the sensitive matter of denazification in the performing arts.

Salzburg was under US occupation. The Americans were keen to revitalise the Festival as a way of demonstrating America's commitment to Austria's cultural regeneration. They tried but failed to persuade Toscanini, Walter or Yehudi Menuhin to participate in the first post-war festival. Obliged to rely on the talent available to them inside Austria, the Americans gave no clear directives about the engagement of artists who had compromised themselves with the Nazis. Festival administrators were left guessing about American intentions, and there was much agonising over the acceptability of several outstanding musicians whose record under the Nazis was considered controversial. The Festival succeeded in opening its doors in 1945, using many singers who had also been prepared to perform under the Nazis.

The Americans made an unsatisfactory attempt to operate the same points system for the performing arts, which the three other occupying powers were also haphazardly administering. Artists had to complete questionnaires about their wartime activities, and these were used to score penalty points to determine whether they should be put onto black, grey or white lists. Three penalty points were sufficient for the black list. But there were no clear criteria for defining pro-Nazi transgressions. Most of the artists in question were popular figures in Austria. Austrians, already convinced that the country as a whole had been victimised by the Nazis, wanted to see and hear their favourites on the stage. Whitewash was liberally applied: it sufficed to argue that those who had flirted with the Nazis had done so only in order to be able to perform and remain true to their art. Henry Alter, an Austrian emigré, noted in November 1945 that 90 per cent of Austria's artists would have had to be disqualified from performing if the Allies insisted on the observation of strict denazification procedures. Tacitly the Allies accepted the argument that 'European artists had always felt free to accept honours and compliments from governments without necessarily feeling that they owe them loyalty, or were required to have a political conscience'.[5]

The Americans soon discarded the points system as unworkable, and were agreeably relieved when responsibility for denazification was handed over to the Austrian authorities in the autumn of 1945. A commission set up by Felix Hurdes, the Minister for Education, made it an aim to secure clearance for significant figures in the performing arts. The Allies had retained veto rights. But the commission encountered only minimal resistance from them. Karajan was allowed back to the Salzburg podium in 1946, Furtwängler in 1947, Böhm in 1948.

During the ten-year occupation, the foreigners among the Festival audiences were largely made up of occupation personnel. But gradually the range of artists from abroad increased. When the State Treaty was finally signed in May 1955, Salzburg was ready to resume its international character and regain its world prominence. The glory days soon returned, with Salzburg again engaging all that was excellent in musical talent, and attracting wealthy music lovers from around the world, most of whom treated the Festival as it had been treated before the war, as a happening apart, somehow disembodied from mainstream Austria. The politics of denazification did not preoccupy the visitors. If politicking had to rear its ugly head in Salzburg, then it was usually confined to the internal artistic and financial disputes and scandals that regularly engulf the Festival. In that area passions always run high. It is all good knock-about stuff: the rivalries between conductors, arguments about programming, innovation and traditionalism; the prominence or neglect of the festival's straight theatre section; ticket pricing and subsidies etc. Even Festival Director Gerard Mortier's threat to leave Salzburg in protest against the Freedom Party's entry into government in January 2000 was more theatrical than political. After several dramatic press statements, Mortier changed his mind and decided after all to work out his contract. For those directly affected by these controversies, such matter are, understandably, of consuming importance. For the outside observer there is both bemusement and amusement.

Inevitably there have been exceptions among Salzburg Festival devotees – and not only among Austrian emigrés – who feel that Austria's Nazi record so blemishes the country that they cannot return to Salzburg to enjoy the Festival offerings. Absences were especially marked in 1990, when Kurt Waldheim, as Austrian head of state, was invited to open the proceedings. There is an unwritten understanding that Austrian presidents are entitled to officiate at the opening of the Festival at least once during their period in office. But at a time when Waldheim was already comprehensively shunned by the international community, it surely made little sense to honour him at a Festival that prides itself on its international appeal.

Salzburg was again suffering from cancellations in 2000, when many regulars decided against visiting a country with Jörg Haider's party serving in Austria's coalition government.

Salzburg may have felt that it had already made amends in 1988, on the fiftieth anniversary of the Anschluss, when it dedicated that summer's Festival to Jewish artists and intellectuals who had suffered under the Nazis. To mark the occasion, Salzburg also published an account of the Festivals in 1937 and 1938 which highlighted the contrast between Toscanini's commitment to the free expression of the arts and the impact of the Nazi *diktat* after the Anschluss. The brochure also listed post-war Festival activities, emphasising that the programming had included numerous Jewish authors and composers.

This move to atone for the past may have soothed bad consciences in Salzburg, but there was probably too much self-justification to mollify its numerous critics abroad, who felt that the Festival had still not adequately acknowledged the extent to which it had allowed itself to be manipulated by the Nazis and had betrayed first principles of artistic integrity. But for all those who stay away, there are many more who battle annually for tickets. In increasing numbers, they are also coming to the newly created Mozart concert week in January and two short festival seasons at Easter and at Whitsun. They come to Salzburg to listen and enjoy, to see and to be seen. They meet their friends from across the world.

Pampered by Salzburg and its surroundings, these foreign audiences gain a distorted picture of Austria. It is a world apart. The tendency is to see it as a becalmed country, prosperous, complacent, perhaps unprincipled, its people fond of good food and rustic dress, living up to its reputation as 'an island of the blessed'.

The Salzburg Festival is good for Austria's prestige, but it encourages a glorified and therefore misleading image of the country. In terms of prompting outsiders to take an intelligent interest in Austria's post-war evolution, I suspect that the Salzburg Seminar can claim to have done rather better than the Festival.

Austria itself obviously takes pride in the prestige of the Festival. The country's tourist industry is a major beneficiary. But none of this is enough to prevent debate, often very heated, as to whether such an elitist institution deserves to receive high public subsidies. This, often rancorous, debate bears a not inconsiderable resemblance to the arguments about the massive state subsidies and lottery grants to the Covent Garden Opera House in the UK.

— * —

While taxpayers' money for Salzburg remains controversial, the Vienna Philharmonic Orchestra and the Vienna State Opera are virtually sacrosanct. These institutions shape the national identity to an extent which is not present in other countries. The symbolic importance of the Burgtheater, the national state theatre, is less pronounced. Its work is little known outside the German-speaking world, even though its programmes encompass both world classics and new innovative writing. At home and abroad the State Opera and the Philharmonic are established as Austria's flagships in the performing arts. They are hugely important in shaping the Austrian image in countries that might otherwise be dismissive of Austrian determination to project itself as a cosmopolitan society and one of the world's cultural centres.

An orchestra is always more mobile than an opera company, and the Philharmonic is a frequent presence in leading concert halls abroad. Foreign tours by the Vienna State Opera are rarer. But a visit to the Opera in Vienna is regarded as a tourist high-point. Concierges at Vienna's leading hotels maintain a highly profitable trade in scarce opera tickets. No official visit to Vienna is complete without a government-sponsored evening at the Opera. The annual Opera Ball is the key event of the winter season. It has attracted considerable attention abroad since one of the Ball's regulars, the construction industry magnate, Richard Lügner, began to wave his chequebook in the direction of well-known figures, including the Duchess of York, to encourage them to join his party.

The Philharmonic is master of its universe. It is a self-governing association of musicians which celebrated its one-hundred-and-fiftieth anniversary in 1992. It works closely with the Opera, providing the orchestra for most of its performances. Unlike the Opera, the Orchestra receives no direct state subsidies. But as with the Opera, the Philharmonic is regarded as a national treasure, and is projected abroad as well as at home as an export that helps to define the Austrian character. Clemens Hellsberg, chronicler of the Philharmonic's history, called his book *Democracy of the Kings*. The title reflects more than pride in its self-governing statutes. The orchestra considers itself pre-eminent in the world of music.

Hellsberg's book acknowledges the ousting of 12 Jews from the orchestra after the Anschluss and the banning of Jewish composers such as Gustav Mahler from its programmes. He notes that the orchestra included 50 Nazi Party members among its players at the end of the war, and describes how special pleading – the need to maintain musical standards – enabled the orchestra to escape denazification and hold on to 20 of its 'illegals' – the musicians in their midst who had joined the Nazi party voluntarily even before 1938. Dismissals were limited to five musicians, whose record of co-operation with the Nazis was too obvious to be ignored. Players who lost their place in 1938 were not encouraged to return. The book is emphatic that there were no Nazi war criminals in the orchestra's ranks. Hellsberg's account also prides itself that the 'banned' composers were again performed immediately after the war –

though it took several years before Mahler's genius was again properly honoured and his music regularly performed by the Philharmonic.

As in Salzburg, so in Vienna: During the early period of the four-power occupation, the Western Allies were keen to boost public morale – and give pleasure to the music-loving members of their own forces – by encouraging the Philharmonic to perform. But in 1945 and 1946 they were still keen to keep the Nazis out of public life. A projected concert tour to the UK, Switzerland and France in April 1946 had to be postponed because of visa problems. Both the Americans and the Russians also vetoed concerts in Vienna because Herbert von Karajan, who was to conduct, remained under a cloud for his Nazi Party membership. In the following Spring, the Philharmonic was allowed to tour France and Switzerland, but only on condition that none of the musicians who had been Nazi Party members participated.

By the summer of 1947, the Cold War had already diverted the Allies from their preoccupation with denazification, and the orchestra was able to make a triumphant reappearance in the UK, greatly helped by Walter's decision to make a come-back as their conductor. His readiness to forgive the past helped the orchestra to overcome any lingering resistance to its return to international concert platforms. Walter enthused that their concert-giving had conjured up once again a positive picture of Austria. 'Do you know what you have achieved during these weeks? You have made history,' he said to the orchestra. 'You have heard and have read in the press how your concerts have been judged, and what they think of Vienna; that they sympathise with a city and a people in difficult circumstances; that Vienna remains a city whose culture and musical life evokes the greatest admiration, and that you have reinforced that reputation.'[6] When the State Opera, together with the Philharmonic, came to London a few weeks later there were some protests – not caused by Nazi associations, but because the British Musicians' Union worried about loss of work for themselves.

George VI, the Prime Minister, Clement Attlee, and the Foreign Minister, Ernest Bevin, were not deterred. They came to a gala performance. On the stage to introduce an extraordinarily talented ensemble of singers stood Richard Tauber, the Jewish tenor who had been forced to emigrate from Austria in 1938. Buckingham Palace was advised by the Foreign Office that the occasion offered an excellent opportunity to confirm a formal end of the state of war with Austria.

The critics reviewing the Opera performances were ecstatic. Pointing to the efforts of the British Musicians' Union to halt the season, they were caustic in dismissing their claims: British performers could not have competed successfully against the excellence of the Austrians.[7]

In 1948, the Vienna Philharmonic secured a clean bill of health in the UK from an unexpected source. That year the orchestra was brought to the UK under the auspices of a young impresario, Victor Hochhauser, who felt no compunction about associating with them, even though he was an orthodox Jew whose grandfather had been Chief Rabbi of Hungary and who had lost family in the Holocaust. At the urging of Yehudi Menuhin, Hochhauser even invited Wilhelm Furtwängler to conduct during the London season, but only after he had agreed to reinstate Jewish members of the pre-war orchestra for the duration of the London season. Walter and Joseph Krips also conducted, while Menuhin and Kathleen Ferrier were among the soloists during this glittering London concert tour, one of many to follow.

The Philharmonic has always prided itself on its image as an Ambassador for Austria, at no time more so than during the orchestra's first post-war appearances in Vienna, Salzburg and above all abroad, when they carried the message that Austria and its cultural heritage remained intact. The annual New Year's concert, transmitted to countless countries, has been used to reinforce the image of a country enthralled by its old-world insouciance and devoted to its musical traditions.

This diverts critical attention away from the country's relationship with the Nazis. It also points to a dichotomy between the continuity of Austria's cultural traditions and its behaviour in the political arena. It is tempting to put Austria's musical accomplishments into one sphere, leaving Austrian behaviour during the Hitler era and its aftermath in another. But the two are surely intertwined. Hellsberg remains acutely conscious that the Philharmonic has not been able to shed its 'Nazi Orchestra' image conclusively, not without good reason: for example, in 1953 the orchestra elected Helmut Wobisch, a former high-ranking member of the SS, as its business manager.

It has become a rarity for outsiders to recall that the Philharmonic has a tainted record. However, on the Orchestra's one-hundred-and-fiftieth birthday, *The Times* commented that 'there are dark reasons why this orchestra is hated by some people; it is because of the repeated incidence of antisemitism in its history'.[8] The *New York Times* was also briefly provoked into discussing the part played by musicians in the promotion of Nazi culture. Its music critic insisted that 'Fifty years after Hitler came to power, tales about musicians during the Nazi period still have the power to shock. In the 1930s for example, Karl Böhm would offer the Nazi salute at concerts... and in 1936 he even paid homage to the Führer in a written message: 'Nazism has set musicians a goal and a task which it is worthwhile to apply all our talent and strength, namely the service of the German people and its cultural strength'.[9] But such strictures were uncommon. The editors of the *New Grove Dictionary*, the definitive musical reference encyclopedia, paid no attention in its first post-war edition to the Nazi affiliations of Austrian or German musicians. Even when the Waldheim controversy was at its peak, relatively few of the Philharmonic's admirers in the US or elsewhere turned their wrath on the Orchestra, or on the State Opera, or were greatly influenced by the crass antisemitic record of the two institutions.

Aside from the quality of the music-making itself, recent foreign interest in the Vienna Philharmonic has focussed much more on the orchestra's reluctance to admit women members than on its Nazi past. Where once the orchestra had argued that the need to maintain standards justified retention of Nazi musicians, it now insists that the absence of women was never grounded in a boycott of the female sex, but only in the failure to identify suitably able women on a par with the existing members of the orchestra. Quality above everything! Even though the principle of equality has now been accepted, the hurdles against women remain virtually insuperable.

— * —

During the Orchestra's one-hundred-and-fiftieth anniversary celebrations, little attention was paid in Austria or abroad to a handful of pages in Hellsberg's long book which addressed the Philharmonic's association with the Nazis. Interest in the Orchestra's behaviour came only later, in 1995, when the Director of the Vienna State Opera, Ioan Holender chose to mark the fiftieth anniversary of Austria's Second Republic with a dramatic acknowledgment of the shame that Austria's musical establishment deserved to bear both for its behaviour under the Nazis and also after the war, when it failed to make amends, and even continued to honour Nazi collaborators.

The massive Opera House, one of Vienna's most prominent landmarks, had been largely destroyed during a US bombing raid just weeks before the end of the war. Its rebuilding became a priority project, with no costs spared. It took until 1955 to restore it to its former glory. At one point, the Austrian government had intended to combine the reopening of the Opera with the achievement of the Treaty. But the final stage of the State Treaty was concluded so fast that the restoration of the Opera House could not be completed in time. The festive opening gala of the reconstructed Opera House, with a performance of Beethoven's ode to freedom, *Fidelio*, took place on 5 November 1955. A veil was drawn over the fact that the work had been performed at Hitler's behest just two weeks after the Anschluss in 1938 to celebrate that event. Hermann Göring had been guest of honour on that occasion.

In 1955 the guest-list was very different. Austria's head of state and its government were joined by a distinguished international audience that included the Swiss President, the US Secretary of State, Greta Garbo, Igor Stravinsky, Oskar Kokoschka, Jean Cocteau and Le Corbusier. But the occasion had dubious undertones. The iron curtain in the new Opera House was the work of Rudolph Hermann Eisenmenger, an artist, who had played a prominent role under the Nazis and introduced a characteristic Nazi theme to the new curtain's design. Another sour note was struck by the fact that the Vienna Philharmonic played under the baton of Böhm, Opera Director during the last three years of the war, reappointed to the post in 1954 in spite of his controversial behaviour under the Nazis.

Under the Nazis, Böhm had allowed the Opera to be used as a flagship for 'Aryan' culture. After 1945, an official order was in force, banning him from conducting until 1949. But this was not strictly enforced, and Böhm conducted in Graz in 1947 and in Salzburg in 1948. At the reopening of the State Opera it was ironic that Toscanini and Walter, who had fought so tenaciously against Nazi penetration of Austria's cultural life, were in the audience while Böhm was in charge of the performance.

Böhm's musical ability was unquestioned, but his political record obviously left much to be desired: he was, after all, the man who drove Walter away before the war. Even on this November day in 1955, when Austria was reaffirming its independence, one of the people who had embraced the cultural Anschluss with Hitler's Reich was acting the role of master of ceremonies.

The reopening of the Vienna State Opera, supreme though the performance was, counts in the annals of Austria's post-war history less as a musical event than as a social, political and cultural landmark. At home and abroad it was seen as the symbolic act that sealed the restoration of the Austrian nation and the recovery of political freedom. But under Böhm's baton, the opera's resumption of 'business as usual' also helped to perpetuate Austria's 'big lie' about the Nazi era.

— * —

Holender, Director of the State Opera since 1991, is very conscious of the special place which the institution occupies. He was well aware that he could and would make an important impact when he decided to mark the fiftieth anniversary of the Second Republic in 1995 with a concert and exhibition that would frankly acknowledge the Opera's – and by implication also the whole Austrian nation's – compromises with Naziism. Holender is a firm convert to the idea that culture is an important instrument of political education. In Austria it has to be used to create awareness in the past and to demonstrate to the world that the country is capable of making amends by creating a healthier cultural environment.

Holender is a Romanian of Jewish-Hungarian extraction, and some of Vienna's intellectual elite questions his motives in promoting the Opera as an instrument of political morality. His critics argue that he is pandering to the post-Waldheim mood in the Austrian government, which has called for acknowledgement of Austrian responsibility for antisemitic crimes during the Nazi era. Such criticism does not do him justice. Holender is certainly no saint, but his actions reflect a degree of integrity, which I, like many others, have found convincing.

The Republic's fiftieth anniversary commemoration was eloquent. Entitled 'A House remembers after 50 years', the gala programme was made up entirely of music by composers banned under the Nazis. He wanted to have music 'that might not have been heard for a thousand years if the Nazis had remained in power'.[10] The artists included Placido Domingo, José Carreras, Edita Gruberova and many other stars who frequently sing in Vienna. Even so, the musical and emotional high point of the concert was the appearance on the stage of a small elderly man, Karel Berman, the sole survivor of an ensemble which had bravely provided musical distraction for fellow inmates at Theresienstadt concentration camp. Berman reduced the House to silent tears with two haunting melodies composed by his dead comrades.

Interspersed with the musical performances, one of Austria's leading actors, Klaus Maria Brandauer, read from Nazi texts, illustrating both the brutality and the absurdity of Nazi attitudes to Jewish composers, and the Nazi appropriation of Mozart and other icons of the musical world to promote their propaganda. The extracts were selected by Oliver Rathkolb, one of Austria's leading historians, whose expertise on the Nazis' misuse of culture has earned him the compliment of being called 'the Wiesenthal of Austria's cultural life'. In the programme notes, Rathkolb pointed to the 'absurdities of Nazi censorship, to which living and dead composers were sacrificed'.[11] But he also underlined that anti-semitic polemics were rife in Austria's musical world even before 1938, and that the Nazis found fertile ground to extend their campaign against the Jewish members of that world.

During the interval, the audience found itself confronted in one of the foyers with a well-documented exhibition of antisemitic measures enforced by the Opera during the Nazi era. In the galleries where opera-goers normally gossip idly and comment on the dress code while they wait for the performance to resume, they were shocked into looking at their past: into the way musicians had allowed themselves to be used to pervert traditions and promote the inculcation of teutonic culture in Austria. Reaching up almost to the height of the grand staircase from the foyer, a video-installation in the shape of two revolving columns had been erected with the names of more than 3000 Jewish intellectuals and artists who had either perished in the camps or been forced to leave the country. They left an intellectual vacuum which cannot be filled. A small number of writers and actors had chosen to come back of their own volition after the war. But the Austrian government itself did little to encourage or facilitate the return of these emigrés – though it has always been quick to claim credit whenever an ex-Austrian won a Nobel Prize or other international honours.

The performances and the exhibition at the Opera that night on 27 April 1995 were impressive, and played on the conscience. And yet the event might not have had its dramatic – and hopefully lasting – impact had it not been for the daring and controversial speech that Ioan Holender chose to deliver to this hand-picked audience of Austria's political and intellectual elite, of senior diplomats accredited to Austria, and of foreign journalists specially invited to Vienna for the event.

It was an astonishingly frank indictment of Austria's propensity to self-pity and to myth-making. He exposed how the Opera had readily shed its Jewish contacts before the war – 40 of them had been dismissed in 1938, and none had been invited to return after the war. He railed against the hypocrisy of the Second Republic's founders for claiming that Austria had been Hitler's victim and the turning of a blind eye to Nazi collaborators like Böhm. The strictures applied as much to the Vienna Philharmonic as to the State Opera, and indeed were directed at a much wider audience.

The gala was shown on Austrian television. It was also interpreted abroad as an act of courage by the high-profile Director of the prestigious Opera, and as a sign that Austrian society, almost five years after Chancellor Vranitzky had at last publicly recognised the necessity of facing up to the truth, was slowly awakening from its long sleep of self-delusion. 'Holender's programme helped to deny the attempt to pretend that the past wasn't real, to recognise how much of the human spirit it distorted and destroyed,' the influential American journalist Flora Lewis wrote in the *International Herald Tribune*. She recalled how the Austrians had clung to the Allied endorsement of its 'victim' status as 'an excuse for self-pity and for refusing to acknowledge their country's role in the war, which was used almost ever since. But this year a line has been drawn at last, and appropriately a high point was made... at the Opera with absolute clarity... It was an extraordinary meeting, the House was jammed and the audience carried away.' Although the Opera had been reopened in 1955, 'only now has it regained honesty in its pride'.[12]

Simon Wiesenthal, still intent on eliminating the vestiges of Naziism in Austria, was greatly encouraged by the positive reaction that Holender provoked at home and abroad. In a letter to the Opera chief that Wiesenthal also passed on to friends in the US he said that survivors had waited 50 years for the performance that Holender had initiated. He interpreted the evening as 'a turn in official interpretation and attitudes'.[13]

Three years later, Holender again went on the offensive, this time in co-operation with the government and with the President of the Austrian parliament, Heinz Fischer. By now it had been decided to mark 5 May annually as Day of Remembrance for the use of force and racism in memory of the victims of National Socialism ('Gedenktag gegen Gewalt und Rassismus im Gedenken an die Opfer des Nationalsozialismus').

Holender, who had seen the Russian composer Grigori Frid's one-act opera *The Diary of Anne Frank* in Germany, persuaded Fischer that a performance in the Austrian parliament would be a worthy way of provoking remembrance of dark events.

Linked to this 'external' performance, Holender staged an exhibition of 'degenerate' (*entartete*) music in the Opera in the former Gobelin Hall, now renamed Gustav Mahler Hall. Mahler was the Opera's most distinguished Director, and after the war the Philharmonic had been slow to reinstate his music in its repertoire. Now Holender made sure that audiences would have a constant reminder of Mahler's achievements. A portrait of Mahler, controversial in style but no longer in subject, by the Austrian emigré R.B. Kitaj is now on display in the Mahler Saal. Half a century after the end of World War II, the Vienna State Opera is seeking to come to terms with its past when it was a ready stage for Nazi propaganda. Performance of the Anne Frank opera was widely interpreted as a symbolic gesture of atonement.

A year later, on 4 May 1999, the Day of Remembrance was marked with the performance of another harrowing operatic composition, Udo Zimmermann's *Weisse Rose*. This was about Sophie Scholl and her brother Hans, two German students who were executed in 1943 after being caught distributing anti-Nazi leaflets. Again the whole panoply of the Austrian state was present in the rarely opened Reichsratssitzungssaal of the Austrian parliament to hear members of the Opera sing the agonised cries of the two doomed young people, asserting to their last moments the right to freedom.

Not content to be the moving spirit behind such evocations of Nazi evil, Holender has also set about replacing the Opera's 'Nazi' iron curtain. Under the motto 'looking to the future', and turning the Opera into a 'museum of the future', an overhang now covers the controversial iron curtain. The overhang is to be changed annually, with the design entrusted to artists selected by a respected jury. The first temporary curtain, for the season 1998–9, was commissioned from the American artist Kara Walker. The original curtain will be bared each summer as a museum exhibit, while the Opera is not in residence. Holender insists, 'If one leads an institution of this importance, it isn't enough to bring great singers to the stage. One also has to articulate the great issues of the day'.

The Opera has cleansed itself. Under his influence it may even have accelerated a more widespread rethinking of Austria's cultural life. But has the Opera, with its unique standing in Austria, also succeeded in asserting itself as a role model for Austria itself? Doubtless, Holender's call to Austria's conscience deserves to stand among those outstanding moments in a nation's history when its moral stature is called to account. Whether the country as a whole has yet fully responded to the challenge is less certain.

NOTES ON CHAPTER VI

1. Fiftieth anniversary celebrations of the Salzburg Seminar, 28 June 1997.
2. Clemens Hellsberg, *Demokratie der König*, Kremayr & Scheriau, 1992, p 481.
3. Baldur von Schirach, speech, 1941.
4. *New York Times*, letter from Elizabeth Schwartzkopf, 22 March 1983.
5. Stephen Gallup, *Geschichte der Salzburger Festspiele*, Kremayr & Scheriau, 1989, p 183.
6. Hellsberg, *Demokratie der Könige*, op. cit., p 513.
7. Hellsberg, *Demokratie der Könige*, op. cit., p 512–13.
8. *The Times*, 25 March 1992.
9. *New York Times*, 27 August 1983.
10. Interview with Ioan Holender, 14 October 1998.
11. '27 April 1995: A House Remembers', programme notes, introduction by Oliver Rathkolb, p 6.
12. *International Herald Tribune*, 4 May 1995.
13. Letter from Simon Wiesenthal to Ioan Holender, May 1955.

VII

Chancellor Kreisky – A Post-imperial Emperor

Bruno Kreisky never lacked belief in his ability to move mountains. But even in the flush of success on that election day, 1 March 1970, he did not imagine that it marked the overture to a 13-year reign as Chancellor, during which he would lead *homus alpinus* to join mainstream Europe and preside over a politically stable and economically prosperous country that was respected, even envied, by the world's major powers. Few political leaders become icons in their own time; but the 'Kreisky era' became common parlance even before Kreisky retired from active political life. Moreover, the full employment policies which he championed rapidly entered international nomenclature as 'Austrokeynesianism'.

During visits to Austria, I had many close-ups of Kreisky as Chancellor. Observing him in action, and the response he secured from his audiences, it was obvious that he possessed a large measure of that intangible gift: charisma. He knew it, and he used it to the full – except on occasions when rational behaviour was overwhelmed by impetuous, explosive temperament: his vindictiveness towards Simon Wiesenthal; his careless talk about Israel; or his destructive drive against his one-time 'favourite son', Hannes Androsch, in the later stages of their relationship, are among the most blatant examples of Kreisky's loss of self-discipline.

But for most of the time, a first class intellect combined with well-defined goals for promoting his country's interests allowed Kreisky to exploit Austria's strategically sensitive place on the European map to elevate its international stature well beyond the the country's insignificant size. He always believed that Austria's growing importance as a 'classic meeting ground for international diplomacy was a major factor in Austria's national security'.[1] It was also very clear to Kreisky that Austria's considerable tourist attractions – its mountains and its lakes, its architecture, its music-making – added up to much more than a major source of foreign currency, and would prove an invaluable aid in the creation of a favourable image for Austria.

'Kreisky was too large for his country' was a refrain that foreign leaders voiced while he was in power, and which men like Helmut Schmidt or Denis Healey, and even Carter, comment upon when asked to assess the Kreisky factor in post-war politics. He always suffered from the handicap that 'the national power-base was missing, while Austria's neutrality also denied Kreisky any voice in the military and economic councils of the West'.[2] He largely made up for this by applying his finely honed political antennae – by what Schmidt best described as Kreisky's *Fingerspitzengefühl* ('political antennae') to exploit the nuances of East-West power politics. Henry Kissinger expressed a similar view.

In his account of the 1972 Salzburg meeting between President Nixon and Kreisky, Kissinger writes of Austria's 'shrewd and perceptive Chancellor, who had parlayed his country's formal neutrality into a position of influence beyond its strength, often by interpreting the motives of competing countries to each other. That he could bring off this balancing act was a tribute to his tact, intelligence and his instincts for the scope – and the limits – of indiscretion. He was much travelled; his comments on trends and personalities were invariably illuminating. He had a great sense of humour and far more geopolitical insight than many leaders from more powerful countries... One of the asymetries of history is the lack of correspondence between the abilities of some leaders and the powers of their country... Nixon remarked later that he wished Kreisky could change places with some of the Socialist leaders in larger European countries whose insight and sturdiness he rated less highly.'[3]

— * —

As Chancellor, Kreisky personified Austria. He relished this role. Until the Kurt Waldheim debacle, he was not just the best-known, but almost the only Austrian politician to cut a figure outside his own country, with Hannes Androsch, Finance Minister for over ten years of the Kreisky era, the only other Austrian political figure to achieve extensive recognition among his peers abroad. Kreisky did not like this kind of competition from one of his lieutenants. The rivalry for international endorsement contributed in no small measure to the bitter break between them.

During his long apprenticeship in foreign affairs, followed by four years in opposition as leader of the Social Democrats, Kreisky had turned himself into a wily tactician as well as a clever strategist. In 1970, as head of government, he had at last secured the pivotal position that enabled him to push towards his intertwined goals of a modernised, outward-looking Austria, and of international respect secured through maximising the Austrian contribution to conflict resolution and East-West detente.

Prosperity and stability was a *sine qua non* for Kreisky. He was haunted by memories of Austria during the 1930s, with its mass unemployment, social unrest and its disastrous political consequences. As Chancellor, full employment coupled to a generous social welfare system had to be his top priority, even if this could only be achieved at the cost of high budget deficits. Austria's national identity had to be strengthened so as to convince, once and for all, both the nation's own people and the world that it had lost all hankering after ideas of the greater German nation. The UK and France had to be disabused of the notion that the Austrians were no more than a milder, more relaxed version of the German people, of whom there was no need to be afraid. Germany had to accept that Austria could never again be seen as its spearhead into Central Europe, and discard any lingering ideas that Austria was an artificial construct, that the country would eventually return to the German fold. He always acknowledged that among his parents' contemporaries there had been a widespread belief in the existence of a pan-German cultural community spanning Austria as well as Germany. But for Kreisky, this model was a closed chapter.

Kreisky never deluded himself into thinking that Austria could rely on its armed forces for its defence. Austria's security had to depend on political tools – on making the country useful to large and small powers alike as a well-serviced, secure and agreeable meeting ground; on enhancing Austria's presence in the UN; and not least, on turning himself personally into a diplomatic sounding-board whose experience and counsel could win the respect of world leaders.

※

Kreisky was already fifty-nine years old when he became Chancellor. Yet he fought the election campaign in 1970 not merely by urging the need for change away from a domination of the political scene by the People's Party, but more significantly by stressing the importance of generational change. He promised a 'New Austria', for a younger Austrian. He argued for modernisation, and for the country to 'Europeanise' its outlook. Tony Blair would hardly have thought of using Kreisky as a model for his election campaign in 1997. Yet the coincidence of theme is striking. The big difference is that Blair personified generational change, while Kreisky in 1970, though stressing the need for rejuvenation, was already past middle age and still too deeply caught up in the traumas of the Anschluss and its aftermath to be able to shed many of the protective, partly out-moded, layers of political behaviour that Austria had built up in the early post-war years. It would take a big stretch of the imagination to describe the Kreisky era as revolutionary. It is more accurate to see it as a period of gradual change, in which care was taken to avoid abrupt or harsh decisions that risked ruffling Austrian *Gemütlichkeit* or denting Austrian attachment to convention. Kreisky's injection of radical, youthful talent was strictly limited.

His belief in political and social consensus as the essential precondition for stability in Austria was as profound as that of any of his predecessors. Though Kreisky became only the second Austrian Chancellor able to dispense with coalition government, he continued to respect the *Proporz* system, with its guaranteed participation of the two main political parties in virtually every facet of Austria's governance. Under this system, the two main parties have for decades divided key posts in both the public and private sectors between their own supporters. This has created an elite network inhibiting non-party members from gaining positions of power and influence on merit alone. Though some insiders claim that the system has already been diluted, and that ability, even without party membership, is increasingly rewarded, its removal has become an important political issue which Haider's Freedom Party is exploiting with considerable success.

The 1970 election did not produce an absolute majority for Kreisky's Social Democrats. Its singular importance lay in the fact that the People's Party not only lost the overall majority it had enjoyed since 1966 but also ceased to have the largest number of seats, as it had in every election since the war. The tide had turned – and has not been reversed to this day. Beginning in 1970, and since then with each successive election until 1999, the Social Democrats won the right to lead the Austrian government – a record unmatched in any other Western democracy. In 1971, and again in 1975 and 1979, Kreisky secured absolute majorities. Since then, the Social Democrats have remained the largest party in parliament, but have won a diminishing number of seats, and had to form coalition governments.

In 1999, though still emerging top of the polls, the Social Democrats were unable to form a coalition government, and had to give way to the controversial People's Party-Freedom Party coalition. For only the second time since 1945, the Social Democrats were out of office.

Back in 1970, the outcome of Austrian election was startling enough to attract considerable international attention. Foreign observers concluded far too readily that Kreisky's success was evidence that antisemitism in Austria was dead, that majority support for a Jewish politician demonstrated that Austria had cleansed itself of racial prejudice. But closer observers of the Austrian scene knew that Kreisky's success had little bearing on the Jewish factor. What had been decisive was his charisma and his instinctive understanding of how to appeal to younger voters without antagonising older ones. He knew how to convince the grassroots that he would at one and the same time assure continuity and modernise the party, bringing it closer to the Scandinavian and West German models of social democracy.

After his victory in 1970, Kreisky was confronted with a choice between returning to the old pattern of coalition or risking a minority government, with the People's Party in opposition, relying on the support of the right-wing Freedom Party for survival. Never an enthusiast for power-sharing, Kreisky opted for the second option.

Carefully hidden from public view, the Social Democratic Party's relationship with the Freedom Party goes back to the late 1950s when the party's neo-Nazi character was still very pronounced. Throwing moral scruples to the wind, the Social Democrats, as part of a strategy of dislodging the People's Party from its parliamentary majority, had provided token help to the Freedom Party in 1959, and made a substantial campaign finance contribution in 1963. Kreisky had built up good personal relations with Friedrich Peter, the Freedom Party's leader.

When Kreisky announced his minority government, the German weekly *Der Spiegel* alleged that the Social Democrats had bought itself an insurance policy: by undertaking to cover the Freedom Party's election campaign debts, the Social Democrats were alleged to have secured a promise that the Freedom Party would vote with the Social Democrats. Kreisky fiercely denied that any campaign contribution had been made to the Freedom Party. But *Der Spiegel* was not far wrong in its central contention that he was prepared to help the Freedom Party make parliamentary progress in return for support.

Kreisky had no scruples about accepting that a political, if not a financial, price had to be paid to secure the survival of his minority government. He proposed an understanding with the Freedom Party, offering it a number of sensitive public service posts and a commitment to electoral reform that would work to the small party's advantage.

The promise was kept. Electoral reform was implemented. But the unwritten alliance with the Freedom Party came to grief over the 1971 budget, and Kreisky called an election. This time the Social Democratic Party secured its first overall majority. It was no longer dependent on the Freedom Party's good-will, although Kreisky retained close contact with its leadership.

During the period of the Social Democrat minority government, surprisingly little attention was paid, except in *Der Spiegel*, to Kreisky's flirtation with the Freedom Party, even though it was an open secret that former Nazis had found a political home there. But then almost nothing had surfaced of the Social Democrats' earlier dealings with the Party. Details of the financial help were only disclosed many years later. Kreisky himself was convinced he was right to make a deal with the Freedom Party. 'Kreisky had no difficulty in overcoming any possible moral scruples he may have had with respect to the neo-Nazi past of the FPO [Freedom Party], since to him that party in the 70s represented primarily the liberal and anti-clerical wing of the middle classes... Kreisky no longer saw any reason for remaining aloof to the FPO [Freedom Party] or regarding it as an outcast in the democratic state.'[4] His belief in inclusiveness overwhelmed any twinge of guilt by association.

When Kreisky formed his first cabinet, he insisted that his aim was to give the Social Democrats a new, preferably youthful, image. Youth was personified by the appointment of the thirty-four-year-old Hannes Androsch as Finance Minister. But the new also included the old: four of the 11 cabinet nominees turned out to have been former members of the Nazi Party, one of them, Hans Öllinger, even being identified as a former member of the murderous Waffen SS, the arm of the SS which had been in the forefront of implementing the 'final solution'. The presence of former Nazis in the Austrian cabinet came to light not because Kreisky volunteered the information, but because the Nazi-hunter Simon Wiesenthal searched his files, discovered their antecedents, and passed all this on to *Der Spiegel*, which promptly published the story. Kreisky was unapologetic, arguing that every citizen had the right to reconsider his or her views, including those held during the Nazi era. Though Öllinger resigned from the government, Kreisky filled the gap by appointing another former Nazi, still leaving himself with a quartet of cabinet ministers who appeared to have more of a past than a future in what was billed as a reformist administration.

Kreisky himself was furious with the embarrassment that Wiesenthal had caused, to the point of deciding that the Nazi-hunter, unlike former Nazis, was beyond redemption and was to be treated as an implacable foe. It was the beginning of a bitter feud between two egocentrics which was to blight both their lives and prompt an avalanche of critical, and therefore unwelcome, foreign attention on the Chancellor.

The confrontation sharpened in 1975, when Wiesenthal published evidence that Friedrich Peter, the Freedom Party leader, had been an SS officer in a unit that had engaged in large-scale civilian killing in Poland and Russia in 1941. Though Wiesenthal accused Peter of failing to disclose his full military record, he stopped short of charging him with war crimes. Wiesenthal had prepared his dossier on Peter during the 1975 election campaign, when rumours circulated that Kreisky would, if he failed to secure a clear majority, invite the Freedom Party to join a coalition as junior partner. In the event, the Social Democrats secured an overall majority and had no need of a partner. But immediately after the election, Wiesenthal made public his information about Peter. Kreisky was incandescent, going well beyond rational argument. He claimed that Wiesenthal was trying to destroy him, and insinuated that the Nazi-hunter had collaborated with the Gestapo during his wartime captivity. He also questioned whether Israel had prompted Wiesenthal to act against him. The impact on Wiesenthal's life was dramatic. He became the target of hate-mail, and was physically threatened. He sued Kreisky for defamation. Kreisky hinted that he might resign in order to be free to fight the case. His popularity in Austria grew. Ordinary people supported his stand. A proverbial taxi-driver encapsulated public opinion on the streets of Vienna: 'We don't like the way Wiesenthal keeps hounding people... even if Herr Peter was guilty, I don't think most Austrians would mind if he became a Minister'.

The accusations made by Wiesenthal gave an ominous impetus to Austria's latent antisemitism. Within 24 hours of being interviewed on television about Peter's SS past, Wiesenthal received over 100 threatening telephone calls, and became the target of a public witch-hunt. Newspapers were flooded with letters demanding an end to this attempt to stir up the past. A Freedom Party member of parliament affirmed unhesitatingly that Peter's SS unit had simply done what good soldiers do: obey orders and perform their duties. There was no justification for allowing the Freedom Party leader's past to harm the image of his party now.

Kreisky and Wiesenthal gave rival press conferences that attracted a larger number of foreign correspondents than had been seen in Vienna since the Kennedy-Krushchev summit in 1961. During an interview with *Der Spiegel*, Kreisky made a remark that Israelis never allowed him to forget, and which many Jews will never forgive: 'If the Jews are a people then they are a wretched people'.[5] When this observation made world headlines, Kreisky insisted that an aside had been distorted and blown out of all proportion: since he did not believe that the Jews constituted a 'people', he would surely not want to label them collectively, he insisted. The Kreisky Archive in Vienna has several large boxes filled with press cuttings from many parts of the globe about the Kreisky-Wiesenthal conflict and its fallout. Austrian embassies were ordered to send weekly media reports to the Chancellor. The envoys frequently prefaced their reports with expressions of regret that there were no positive reactions, and that all comment about Austria remained adverse, or at best confused by the Chancellor's stance.

Why had Kreisky, the much-admired statesman, allowed matters to get out of hand? What kind of a complex did Kreisky have about his own Jewishness that made him lose all self-control? Could he remain in office? What did the antisemitic campaign against Wiesenthal say about the moral health of Austria? How could Kreisky reconcile his assertions that there was no such 'tribe' as a Jewish people with his efforts to inject momentum into the Middle East peace process?

Typically, the *Jerusalem Post* wrote that 'whenever he is reminded of his Jewish origins, he loses his political sense and reasonableness, and tries to prove the remoteness of his links to Judaism'.[6] It was obvious that the explanation of Kreisky's clash with Wiesenthal lay in his awkward relationship to Jewry and the Jewish State. Kreisky always denied this. On the contrary, he warned Israel's Ambassador in Vienna in forceful terms that his dispute with Wiesenthal over Peter was a purely domestic Austrian affair, and that Israel had no right to meddle in this matter.

As the affair thundered on, Kreisky became more and more insistent that the Nazi period in Austria could only be understood in the context of Austria's crisis during the mid-1930s. The majority of young people who turned to the Nazis in 1938 had been victims of the political situation, he argued. Kreisky fiercely denied all suggestions that his Jewish origins required him to adopt pro-Israeli policies. In the end it was Kreisky's own party which concluded that the Chancellor risked political self-destruction unless the polemics and the court proceedings between their Chancellor and Wiesenthal were halted. A compromise was worked out: Wiesenthal withdrew his libel case; a proposal for a parliamentary investigation into the affairs of Wiesenthal's Documentation Centre was dropped; there was no apology, no handshake. The assault on Wiesenthal's *bona fides* left a permanent black mark on Kreisky's reputation, and Wiesenthal had to wait until after Kreisky's death before Austria was prepared to join other countries in honouring him for his life's work.

Even after Kreisky's retirement from active politics, the two were to clash again and again. However their later recriminations did not reach quite the same crescendo as in 1975. It no longer diverted Kreisky from focusing his mind and energy on firming up Austria's 'golden age'. But the effect of the Wiesenthal affair could never be entirely wiped out. Kreisky's reputation abroad suffered – and not just in Israel, where he was distrusted on many other counts, but also in the US and to a lesser extent in the UK and France. Austria's standing was affected as much as, or even more than, Kreisky's personal reputation.

The Austrian public, having readily joined in the persecution of Wiesenthal rather than question Peter's fitness for public office, had once again betrayed its antisemitism. For those who cared about such matters, the Kreisky era shone less brightly after 1975. But as so often happens, *realpolitik* prevailed. Kreisky had made himself useful in the international arena. His country, christened 'blessed island' by no less a figure than Pope Paul VI, was a trouble-free zone on the dividing line between East and West, and was useful enough to make itself a highly desirable neutral meeting ground. Too many powers had an interest in maintaining business as usual with Kreisky's Austria.

— * —

Kreisky liked to portray himself as a radical. On the domestic scene this expressed itself in the measures he implemented to maintain full employment and strengthen the welfare state. Kreisky's bid to reduce Austrian dependence on imported energy supplies by switching to nuclear power was another radical move, and one that ended in defeat: the Zwentendorf nuclear power plant was completed in 1976 but remained unopened and unloved, an example to the environmental lobbies of other countries how a highly motivated protest movement can achieve its goals by democratic means. Opposition to nuclear power led to a referendum on Zwentendorf in 1978, where a normally placid people was moved to defeat the cornerstone of a popular government's energy policy. This did not, however, trigger Kreisky's demise or the fall of the government. On the contrary, buoyed up by expressions of confidence despite the lost referendum, Kreisky was re-elected in 1979 with an even larger Social Democrat majority than in 1975.

In the sphere of foreign affairs, Kreisky as Chancellor always felt himself less bound than in his domestic policies by the need to proceed by consensus in his own back-yard. But there were other constraints: even though years had passed since adoption of the State Treaty, Kreisky, not surprisingly, judged it crucial to retain the confidence of the two superpowers. Given the tensions of the Cold War, this strategy required a delicate balancing act. It is a measure of Kreisky's success that even though he occasionally provoked misgivings in one or other camp, both superpowers continued to value his views on East-West issues. Even when they disagreed, they still respected his foreign policy activism. This was all the more to his credit, since he was so often busy stretching the meaning of active neutrality into unexplored territory. This is aptly illustrated by his championship of the Conference for Security and Cooperation (CSCE) in Europe, right from its early, controversial, stages. At a time when the US was still deriding it as a Soviet device both to legitimise the division of Germany and to secure recognition of the post-war map of Europe, Kreisky already realised that it had far greater promise to help the human rights cause in the Communist bloc than to serve the Kremlin's geopolitical ends. At the risk of being written off as a Soviet poodle, Kreisky acted soon after the 1970 election to warn against delaying tactics in negotiating an accord on European co-operation and security.

Driven by Austrian self-interest, but probably also more perceptive than the Western powers, Kreisky seems to have understood much earlier than his colleagues in Washington or Moscow that the CSCE process had the potential to encourage human rights activists and dissidents in the Soviet bloc, and perhaps even to promote the disintegration of the Soviet system. In July 1970, an Austrian memorandum was sent to the US, Canadian and all European governments in which the Austrian government set out its arguments and proposed Vienna as venue for the CSCE negotiations. Ahead of Mikhail Gorbachev, Kreisky seems to have envisaged that the CSCE document could ultimately be used to build what the Soviet leader always called a 'common European home'.

Austria negotiated actively on the complex document, which took many years of tough bargaining to draft. He continued to lobby Western governments, but for a long time failed to convince Western leaders of the importance of the CSCE negotiations. Kreisky was rebuffed by President Nixon and Henry Kissinger, by British Prime Minister Harold Wilson and by NATO Secretary-General Joseph Luns. But when Gerald Ford became US President, there was a change of attitude to the process, and Kreisky was even asked to assist in defining a consolidated Western European position on the concessions they wanted to secure from the Soviet Union. Foreign diplomats speculated that Kreisky's dream was to host a second 'Congress of Vienna'. That did not materialise. Geneva, and above all Helsinki, became the neutral cities where the principal elements of the accord were negotiated. The document, finalised in 1975, bears Helsinki's imprint.

As agreement on the CSCE document at last drew close, the Soviet Union clamoured for a summit. Kreisky agreed that the time was ripe, and embarked on a campaign to convene a summit of all the participating countries. If there were outstanding points to resolve, it should be done at the summit, he argued. Only French President Giscard D'Estaing concurred. Elsewhere among Western countries he ran into opposition. It was unwise, he was told, to saddle the summit with negotiations or anything other than the finished treaty, a signing ceremony and keynote speeches. Germany's Chancellor Schmidt's reaction was typical. 'The Austrian Chancellor is always a welcome visitor in Bonn. Chancellor Adenauer already cultivated him as a realistic judge of affairs. German-Austrian relations are no longer on the agenda; they were resolved a long time ago... As for the CSCE, West Germany believes that all outstanding issues must be settled before a summit is convened.'[7] Yet even though Western leaders disparaged Kreisky's efforts, there is little doubt that his campaign gave a vital impetus to the negotiations. By the end of August 1975, the vital gaps in the CSCE document had been closed, and a summit could be convened to sign the 'Helsinki Final Act', as the accord has come to be known.

At the summit, Kreisky angered the Soviet Union with provocative words about the freedom of signatory states to choose their own form of government – even if it meant the freedom to break loose from Communism. 'We are prepared to struggle and we welcome CSCE not least because the principles that have been arrived at are such as to allow this global struggle to take peaceful forms. At any rate this is how we interpret the passage from the declaration of principles, which speaks of the right of every participating state to freely chose and develop its political, social, economic and cultural system.'[8]

Kreisky's relations with Presidents Carter and Reagan were tenuous. While insisting on his commitment to human rights, Kreisky, in common with several other Western leaders, was alarmed that Carter's persistent campaign for human rights in the Communist bloc was compounding the difficulties of negotiating with the Soviet Union. He did not endear himself to the Carter White House when he suggested that US activism risked becoming counter-productive. Commenting on Carter's diplomacy, Kreisky warned that 'There are two kinds – the highly visible and audible, which are important; but also those daily contacts, diplomatic and by other means, which don't ever get publicised'.[9] Carter possessed one saving grace where Kreisky was concerned: he had the merit of acting constructively to promote peace in the Middle East.

Reagan, on the other hand, saw few redeeming features in Kreisky. The two men never liked or understood each other. After their first meeting, Kreisky told friends that there had never been another American President with whom he found so little in common. Kreisky did not attempt to hide his concern over Reagan's 'evil empire' concept of the Soviet Union. Even though Reagan recognised that Kreisky was an outspoken anti-communist, they clashed over Reagan's 'Star Wars' proposal to develop an anti-ballistic missile defence system, and over policy towards Poland under martial law. Kreisky asserted that the Polish leader, Marshal Jaruzelski, should be trusted to restore civil rights in Poland. This was anathema to the US administration. Undeterred, Kreisky in 1982 showed his antagonism by criticising the 'Reagan Show' for its policies in Latin America and Turkey. It was only after Kreisky's retirement in 1983, when Reagan's anti-communism began to mellow, that the two men at last found a little common ground.

In his dealings with Moscow, Kreisky was much more circumspect, and was careful not to let down his guard. But in spite of Moscow's ban on Austrian entanglement with the EEC, which remained as absolute as it had been in the 1960s, he persisted with the search for closer links with Brussels. The Kremlin continued to issue repeated warnings, in public and in private, that Austria's overtures to Brussels, if successful, would be open to challenge as a Treaty violation. Soon after Kreisky became Chancellor, *Pravda*, in a characteristic comment, argued that 'it would be dangerous for Austria to negotiate with the EEC'. Germany, the Kremlin claimed, 'would exploit this to increase its economic hold on Austria.

Worse, a decision to join the Common Market would be a political move in violation to its treaty commitments.'[10]

Even though Austria held off with its application for full EU membership until the collapse of the Soviet Union, Kreisky became far more active in pursuit of closer links with Brussels than he had been as Foreign Minister. He refused to be intimidated, and always resisted public comment on Soviet media warnings. If the Soviet Union had anything to say, it should use diplomatic channels. His government beavered away to strengthen EFTA's negotiating hand on a collective approach to Brussels to secure greater access to EEC markets.

Austria was up against a lack of solidarity in EFTA. Soon after the UK joined the EEC in 1972, Austria signed its trade agreement with Brussels, covering manufactured goods. The Soviet Union was suspicious, but made no attempt to intervene. In this limited move towards Brussels Kreisky had called the Kremlin's bluff, and emerged unscathed.

Washington watched all these manoeuvres with a beady eye. Initially the Americans felt that Austria allowed itself to be too easily intimidated by Moscow; but they did not want to intervene on its behalf in Moscow or Brussels. George Ball, one of America's most ardent advocates of European economic integration, said that 'Austria was the victim of Soviet stubbornness', and praised Kreisky for shrugging off Soviet threats by applying for an association agreement with the EEC. As Under-Secretary of State, 'though I initially took a hard line with Austria, I always intended to help them find a solution. After a while they began to understand that I did not wish to damage their interests.'[11]

During the Kreisky era, globalism had not yet emerged as a challenge to the traditional concepts of national governance and international relations. But Kreisky instinctively glimpsed the new trend. The importance he attached to the use of international and cross-border institutions to pursue broad policy aims went beyond Austria's narrow self-interest. The Socialist International always held a special place for him. With the Swedish Prime Minister, Olaf Palme, and the German Chancellor, Willy Brandt, Kreisky formed a triumvirate which he regarded as the virtual embryo of a world government cast in a social democratic mould. Brandt was its spearhead in relations with the Communist bloc; Palme was the pointman for Africa, and Kreisky for the Middle East. As a trio, 'we met now and then in a friendly atmosphere to discuss world events without the pressure of an agenda or of time limits... All three of us led large and influential parties, and we were friends who could discuss anything and had the power to make things happen,' wrote Willy Brandt.[12]

However, Brandt and Palme, unlike Kreisky, were always doubtful that the Socialist International, with its world-wide membership of social democratic parties, was much more than a talking shop. Its impact on international relations was smaller than Kreisky portrayed, according to other prominent social democrats who experienced it in its heyday during the 1970s and 1980s. Kreisky regarded it as his personal fiefdom. He had far less influence over other international institutions, but that only made him more insistent that machinery such as the CSCE process, the East-West arms control negotiations – especially the complex Mutual Balanced Force Reduction (MBFR) negotiations, located in Vienna – the Council of Europe, the EEC, the Non-aligned Movement were all waiting to be used effectively to promote peace, human rights and economic advance. Foremost in Kreisky's thinking were the UN and its agencies. Almost from the outset of Austria's UN membership, Austrian forces became a feature of UN peacekeeping operations. During the Kreisky era, Austrian blue helmets were widely deployed in African and Middle Eastern trouble spots.

In his first appearance as Chancellor at the UN General Assembly in September 1970, Kreisky played for Third World support by promising to devote one per cent of Austria's GNP to development funds. This was more than any other UN member country has ever offered. Kreisky never made good on his undertaking. But Third World countries always felt he was on their side, all the more so since he also championed the idea of a Marshall Aid Plan for developing countries. He argued that the world economy would benefit from a generous injection of aid to the developing world. Nothing came of this. Even so, they counted Austria as a staunch friend, and supported Kreisky's efforts to make Vienna, after New York and Geneva, the third UN capital. To back this endeavour, the Kreisky government went ahead with construction of the 'UNO city' in Vienna's Donaupark. The project had been agreed by the Klaus government, but had been left on the drawing board. It would still take until 1979 to complete, but at least Austria could now demonstrate that the Social Democrats – unlike its predecessor People's Party government, which had baulked at the expense – was willing to use its tax revenues in support of Vienna's claim that it possessed all the right qualities to serve as international meeting ground.

The Americans were hard to convince – not because they thought that Vienna lacked facilities, but on the contrary because they feared that a majority of the UN membership would prefer Austria to New York, and might press for a transfer. But during an official visit to Washington in September 1974, Kreisky overcame US objections. He succeeded in convincing the newly installed President Ford that Austria had no intention of stealing the UN away from New York, where Austria's Kurt Waldheim was Secretary-General.

— * —

Waldheim owed a great deal to Kreisky, although he was no socialist. For a time, while Kreisky was Foreign Minister, Waldheim had been head of mission at the UN. But afterwards, while the Social Democrats were out of office between 1968 and 1970, Waldheim was back in Vienna serving as Foreign Minister in the People's Party government. According to one of his aides, when Kreisky first became Chancellor in 1970 he briefly toyed with the idea of retaining Waldheim as Foreign Minister: Waldheim's servility would have suited Kreisky's intention of taking personal charge of foreign policy. But it made no political sense to put Waldheim into a Social Democratic cabinet, and Kreisky turned to Rudolf Kirchschläger for the job. As consolation prize, he offered Waldheim the London embassy – one of the more desirable diplomatic postings in the Chancellor's gift. But Waldheim turned it down. He wanted to return to the UN. Kreisky was surprised – he had little inkling that Waldheim was already scheming to become UN Secretary-General – but he agreed to send him back to New York.

Before long, Waldheim reported that he believed there was a strong possibility he could be elected to the top post in the UN. Kreisky almost fell from his chair with astonishment: he still assumed that the Soviet Union would veto any Austrian candidate. However, he decided to sound out Soviet diplomats, and was gratified to obtain a positive reaction. This decided him to support Waldheim's candidacy. The Austrian diplomatic corps was mobilised to promote him. To insure against a Chinese veto, the decision was taken to recognise the Peoples' Republic of China ahead of the US and its Western allies.

When the Security Council met in December 1971 to select the new Secretary-General, Waldheim sailed through with the Soviet Union already voting for him in the first round. Years later, the Soviet Foreign Minister, Andrei Gromyko, confided why the Soviet Union had changed its mind over the suitability of an Austrian national to head the UN. In 1966, it would have been out of the question. By 1971, 'more time had passed, and Austria had honoured its commitments under the State Treaty'. Gromyko also alluded to the way Waldheim, as Foreign Minister, had acted during the 1968 events in Czechoslovakia. Austria, the Soviet Minister said, had acted far less provocatively during the Warsaw Pact intervention in Czechoslovakia than it had during the Hungarian uprising in 1956. It is open to speculation whether Gromyko's remark was intended to imply that the Soviet Union had any particular hold over Waldheim.

But undoubtedly the Russians realised, in common with Kreisky, that Waldheim was always prepared to adjust to a servant-master relationship with those who had the power to shape his career. Once elected, Waldheim certainly used his pole-position to promote Austria's bid to be officially designated as the UN's third capital – on condition, recalled one of his UN associates, that Waldheim was always treated with fanfares and accorded multiple honours during his frequent visits to his homeland. Again, Waldheim was planning quietly ahead – this time to use his position as UN Secretary-General to give himself maximum exposure for eventual election to the Austrian Presidency.

Vienna never did manage to match Geneva in importance as a UN centre. The International Atomic Energy Authority (IAEA), the UN Industrial Development Organisation (UNIDO) and a number of smaller UN bodies have made their headquarters in the UNO city. But the large UN bureaucracy in Geneva resisted all attempts to move at least some sections of the secretariat to Vienna. The cost of living was thought to be too high, while centrally located accommodation was less readily available; international civil servants quite simply did not want to be uprooted from established routines.

Even if the UNO city is under-utilised, Kreisky did succeed in making Austria a popular venue for high-profile summits and protracted diplomatic negotiations. President Nixon came to Salzburg in 1971 and 1974. Salzburg was a favourite with President Sadat, who held meetings there with Presidents Nixon and Ford, with Yasser Arafat and other Middle East leaders, and of course with Kreisky.

However, Vienna rather than Salzburg became the main focus for international diplomacy in Austria. The seemingly endless MBFR negotiations to reduce East-West arsenals of conventional forces involved hundreds of security experts from the two military camps. Aspects of the Helsinki Declaration and its follow-up in the CSCE process were negotiated in Vienna. The important negotiations to secure a second Strategic Arms Limitation Treaty (SALT) – one of the few frameworks for superpower contact during this phase of the Cold War – zig-zagged between Helsinki and Vienna and culminated in what was probably the single most important diplomatic event of the Kreisky Era: the 1979 Carter-Brezhnev summit to sign SALT II. As President Carter emerged from Airforce One, he declared that the US and Austria were bound by 'the strong bonds of friendship, mutual respect and our shared devotion to democratic ideals'.[13] Even if that was a mere routine expression of appreciation to the host country, to Austria it still meant a great deal to secure a high public approval rating from the US President.

Kreisky was highly gratified that Vienna had been chosen in preference to Helsinki for the summit. Even if Vienna was only being used as a service station to the superpowers, their presence could be exploited to emphasise Vienna's international vocation. Though both sides were confident that Austria would provide adequate security and communications arrangements, each leader cocooned himself with supplies brought from their own country. 'Almost the only Austrian product that Mr Brezhnev is likely to taste is the water he will use for brushing his teeth,' I wrote as a curtain-raiser for the summit. In addition to doctors and medicines, and hundreds of security personnel, 'President Carter is bringing his own sirloin steaks, and cornflakes for daughter Amy. They are also bringing their armoured cars; Carter a Cadillac, Brezhnev a Rolls Royce in preference to a Soviet-made car.'[14]

It was a mild June week. Close on 2000 journalists had descended on Vienna to cover the last few negotiating hurdles that had to be resolved before the treaty could be signed. Then it was ready. The capital was bathed in sunshine; the air was perfumed with the scent of flowering chestnuts and lilac. The two leaders cut a sharp contrast as they arrived at the Hofburg for the ceremony: Carter, moving easily, with his schoolboyish grin on full display; the ageing Brezhnev, no longer fully aware, glassy-eyed and mummy-like, had to be supported by aides exchanging anxious looks. Kreisky sat proudly in the front row of the Redoutensaal as the two leaders signed the Treaty and made their speeches emphasising the historic nature of the event. Much to Carter's discomfiture, Brezhnev slurred as he haltingly read his speech, and afterwards insisted on a stiffly performed bearhug with Carter.

No high-level meeting can take place in Vienna without a visit to the Opera. As the two leaders took their seats alongside President Kirchschläger there was moderate applause. When the conductor, Karl Böhm, made his entrance, the American correspondents noted that 'there was wild and sustained applause lasting five minutes and by far outshining the welcome given to Carter and Brezhnev'.[15] The Viennese were making their own value statement – not altogether in line with their political leadership's priorities. But no matter. Where Austria's vital interests were concerned, the two leaders had made an important gesture just by being there. Moreover the Americans paid Kreisky the compliment of consulting him for his views on likely Soviet behaviour under a leader who was plainly no longer in full control of his faculties. And Carter had been seen on millions of television screens as he sanctified Vienna as 'the third city of the United Nations', capable of providing 'an especially appropriate setting to pursue the goals of understanding. Historically Vienna has been a crossroads where different cultures and political systems meet.'

Then the President singled out the 1955 State Treaty as 'the first major co-operative agreement' between the US and the Soviet Union, which helped 'to move both nations beyond the hostilities and suspicions of the Cold War era towards stability in Europe and greater cooperation in the pursuit of peace'.

It was always Kreisky's ambition that the Second Republic should be more than a theatre for reconciliation, and that it could itself become an actor in the search for settlement of international disputes. In East-West relations, the superpowers dominated. But in the Middle East, Kreisky was convinced that Austria – or rather he personally – could establish enough diplomatic space to influence both Israel and the Arab World, and nudge both sides forward into a realistic peace process. A just settlement, he believed, would have to involve mutual recognition by Israel and the PLO, Israeli withdrawal from the West Bank and the establishment of a Palestinian state. The Middle East brought out the best in Kreisky's strategic thinking – but also the worst in his egocentric, impulsive character.

NOTES ON CHAPTER VII

1 Bruno Kreisky, *Im Strom der Politik*, Siedelr, Kremayr & Scheriau, 1988, p 239.
2 Gordon Brook-Shepherd, *The Austrians*, HarperCollins, 1996, p 418.
3 Henry Kissinger, *The White House Years*, Simon & Schuster, p 1204.
4 H. Pierre Secher, *Bruno Kreisky: A Political Biography*, Dorrance Publishing 1993, p 43.
5 *Der Spiegel*, 24 November 1995.
6 *Jerusalem Post*, 24 October 1975.
7 *Süddeutsche Zeitung*, 24 June 1975.
8 Kreisky speech at the CSCE summit, August 1975.
9 *International Herald Tribune*, 16 March 1977.
10 *Pravda*, 26 October 1970.
11 George Ball, *The Past has Another Pattern*, Norton, 1982, p 219.
12 Willy Brandt, *My Life in Politics*, Hamish Hamilton, 1992, p 317.
13 White House transcript, 14 June 1979.
14 *Guardian*, 14 June 1979.
15 White House pool report, 15 June 1979.

VIII

Kreisky's Middle East Ventures

Kreisky's involvement with the Middle East is a tangled story; certainly not one that always reflects to his credit: he antagonised Israel, made compromises with terrorists, provoked critics into branding him an antisemitic Jew, sought to reduce America's key role in the Middle East peace process by relying more on the UN, and overestimated the extent to which Europe could influence the search for a settlement. And yet I suspect that when the historians deliver their verdict Kreisky's intervention in Middle Eastern affairs will be seen as a significant contribution to the initiatives that led to the Camp David Accord and paved the way to the acceptance of the PLO as a legitimate partner in Middle East peace negotiations. Kreisky's role in facilitating the exodus of Jews from the Soviet Union will also come to be better appreciated, as will secret diplomacy that helped to free Israeli prisoners in Syrian hands.

While in office, Kreisky's engagement in Middle Eastern affairs was tolerated by the Soviet Union, and welcomed – to varying degrees – by the four US Presidents – Nixon, Ford, Carter and Reagan – who were in office during Kreisky's 13 years as Chancellor. But in Israel, Kreisky came to be regarded with deep suspicion and eventually as an object of hate, accused of betraying Israel's interests because he could not come to terms with his Jewishness. It was less so during Kreisky's first two years as

Chancellor. He had not yet embarked on his campaign of open dialogue with the PLO, and was still fighting a losing battle to have Middle East issues included in the Helsinki Declaration on the Conference on Security and Cooperation in Europe (CSCE). The *Jerusalem Post* was sufficiently positive about Kreisky that it headlined an interview with him in 1972 'Austria-Israel – Relations best ever'. Such sentiments disappeared after he broke the taboo on negotiations with the 'terrorist' PLO. Israeli leaders competed with each other to denigrate him as a Jew who was intent on betraying Israeli interests, and as the representative of an antisemitic nation whose record under the Nazis could not stand up to examination. By 1979, relations had sunk so low that Israel was comparing Kreisky with another Austrian, Hitler. Israelis could not forgive Kreisky for advocating recognition of the PLO, and suggested that this was tantamount to supporting the elimination of Israel.

Even when their attitude became less venomous, Israel's leadership always under-rated Kreisky; he could rarely do things right where Israel was concerned, though occasionally, when it suited them, they used him – most notably when Austria became the principal transit point for emigrating Soviet Jewry. But when Kreisky first broached direct contacts with the PLO it was condemned by Jerusalem and Washington as high treason. He was ahead of his time. Yet with the wisdom of hindsight, Kreisky surely made the right judgement when he advocated direct talks between Israel and the PLO, while also insisting that such negotiations could never get underway without Palestinian recognition of Israel. On the other hand, it remains as difficult now, as it was then, for outside observers to accept that Kreisky was also right to give in to Arab terrorist blackmail, first in September 1973 by closing the Schönau transit camp for Soviet Jewry, and again in 1975 after a murderous attack against OPEC, when he allowed the terrorists and their hostages to leave Vienna.

Schönau proved less of a surrender than was assumed at the time. It only became clear later that the camp's closure did not affect Kreisky's willingness to provide transit facilities for Soviet Jews. Even so, it is hard to accept the logic Kreisky used to justify Austrian surrender to the terrorists: he reasoned that a small state, unlike the major powers, had few options in dealing with terrorist blackmail. It is even harder to understand that Kreisky allowed an angry exchange over the Schönau affair with the Israeli Prime Minister, Golda Meir, to divert him from passing on a warning from Egyptian sources that military action against Israel was imminent. Had Kreisky spoken, Israel might have been less taken by surprise with the Yom Kippur War.

What is certain is that on the two occasions when Austria had to deal with Arab terrorism – Schönau and the OPEC attack – Kreisky laid himself open to the charge of capitulating to terrorism. This inflicted considerable damage to his credibility in Western capitals, made it much harder for him to influence Israeli thinking on the central issue of its relations with the Palestinians, and weakened his hand in pressing for a comprehensive Middle East peace settlement. Kreisky always claimed that his commitment to the preservation of the state of Israel never wavered, even though he had no sympathy for Zionism. Meir, however, believed that his anti-zionism meant that Kreisky also had no qualms about undermining Israel's vital interests. Along with Kreisky's ill-judged remark, made in the context of his bitter confrontation with Simon Wiesenthal, about the 'ugly' Jewish people, this made for a potent brew of mistrust of his Middle Eastern activism in Israel, and among many Jews elsewhere.

Kreisky was suspect as a person, and so was Austria as a nation. It was widely assumed in Israel that Kreisky was moved by personal animus against Israel, and befriended the Arabs not least because he was concerned to secure Austria's oil requirements from the Middle East, and to expand its export markets, including arms sales, to the Arab world. There was some truth in this. Yet unlike most other strands of Kreisky's foreign policy, his intervention in Middle Eastern affairs probably had far less to do with the promotion of Austria's security or its economic interests than with his sense of mission to end the state of war between Israel and the Arab world, and lay a sound foundation for peaceful co-existence in the Middle East. Such a sense of mission would in all likelihood have been fed by the recognition that here was a wonderful opportunity to achieve priceless publicity for neutral Austria. He was also not above enjoying the exquisite irony of the Jewish leader of a former Nazi state taking up the cause of the victims of a Jewish state.

In his memoirs, Kreisky claims that there were three reasons that drove him to his engagement in Middle East affairs: the eviction of Palestinians from Israel, which he compared to his experience of being forced to emigrate from Austria in 1938; his conviction that Israel could only survive under conditions of peaceful co-existence with Arab neighbours; and the logic of massive Western dependence on Middle Eastern oil supplies, which meant that the world could not remain indifferent to Arab interests. He also felt a natural affinity with the Palestinians, often comparing the experience of occupied Austria's ten-year quest for the restoration of full sovereignty to the Palestinian search for a settlement.

As Foreign Minister, Kreisky's 1964 visit to Cairo was his first direct exposure to the Arab world. An Arab summit was in progress in Cairo, where measures against Israel were on the agenda. But President Nasser asked Kreisky to pass on a message to Jerusalem to the effect that there was no intention to try to solve the sensitive dispute over water supplies for Israel's neighbours by force. Kreisky came away persuaded that the aggressive anti-Israel rhetoric he had heard at the summit had little military backbone. On his return to Vienna, he passed this on to the Israeli Ambassador.

Israel's Prime Minister Eshkol was unimpressed. Kreisky's upbeat analysis was attributed to a charm offensive by the wily Nasser. Meir, then Israel's Foreign Minister, also questioned Kreisky's good faith by wondering why an Austrian of Jewish extraction had agreed to go to Egypt for an Arab League summit. There never was any meeting of minds between Meir and Kreisky. The fact that they were both Jewish divided rather than united them. They came from entirely different backgrounds, had been conditioned by different circumstances. Though she eventually recognised his contribution to the cause of Soviet Jewry, during most of her political life she saw him as an enemy of Israel. He, in turn, believed she was beyond reason, that she acted as if she personified 'the Bible, and with the Bible one cannot argue'.[1] He always felt that Meir reacted to his views 'with complete lack of understanding'.[2]

The gulf between them was huge: in Meir's corner the committed zionist, born in Kiev, brought up in the US, and transformed into an Israeli leader, fiercely suspicious of any encroachment on Israel's hard-won independence. In Kreisky's corner, the assimilated, consistently anti-zionist Jew whose first loyalty was to Austria, but who saw himself as a sound and objective judge of Israel's interests. Both had an explosive nature and were adept at personalising and dramatising conflict situations. It had the hallmark of an incendiary relationship.

The two had met at the UN and at meetings of the Socialist International before Kreisky became Chancellor. In 1969, he made his first tentative attempt to have the PLO admitted to membership of the Socialist International. Israel blocked it. One of those present, Israel Gat, who ran the Israeli Labour Party's international department, said that Kreisky, being 'a practical politician, not an adventurer, did not want to have the Socialist International with the PLO in and Israel out'.[3] So he yielded to Israel – but continued to urge the PLO's case for inclusion. Gat did not question Kreisky's good intent towards Israel. He was one of the few among Meir's advisors who tried to convince her that Kreisky was 'not and never had been an enemy of Israel'. Before the Second World War, Kreisky had rejected the Zionist ideal, and had refused to associate himself with the idea of a homeland as a solution for the Jewish people. 'But once Israel had become a fact, Kreisky wanted Israel to exist, to prosper, and to make it as safe as possible.'[4]

Since the Six-Day War, Kreisky had been convinced that Israel must establish contact and talk with the leaders of the Arab world, including the PLO. Austria was too small, and therefore not influential enough, for Kreisky to project himself as a mediator. He saw himself much more as a go-between, or facilitator, using the Socialist International, Austria's neutrality and most of all his network of Middle Eastern connections as his vehicles of persuasion. To that end, Kreisky soon began to exploit his Chancellorship to support various initiatives for encounters between Israelis and Arab groups. This produced little of substance.

— * —

Then, on 28 September 1973, the Schönau crisis erupted. An Arab terrorist unit seized three Soviet Jews and an Austrian customs official travelling on a train carrying the emigrants to the transit camp at Schloss Schönau. After 14 hours of negotiation, the hostages were freed. In return, Kreisky had agreed to close down Schönau, but refused to give them any undertaking to end the transit of Soviet Jews through Austria. He permitted the hostage-takers to be flown out of the country. Kreisky justified his surrender on three counts: by contending that human lives had been at risk, by disclosing that Schönau had been exposed to earlier threats from terrorists, and finally by disclosing that for some time already Israeli agents had infiltrated Schönau and were in virtual control of Schönau, with Austrian personnel often impotent to intervene on behalf of the Jewish emigrés.

There was a related factor, never made explicit by Kreisky because it would only have intensified international censure: he had already for some time been looking for a pretext to close Schönau. His reason? Israeli control over the camp meant that the Soviet Jews were allowed no choice in their ultimate destination, and were being forced to go on to Israel, even though many would have preferred to go elsewhere. Kreisky believed they must be allowed the option of emigrating to other destinations. This required new transit arrangements firmly under Austrian management and control.

Closure of Schönau enabled Austria to open a new transit camp at Wollersdorf. But it took a while for Kreisky's critics to realise that his 'capitulation to terrorism', as it was widely described, had not been as abject as had been assumed, and that it had not been used as a pretext to end Austrian hospitality for Soviet Jewry. Immediately after the seizure of the hostages, Kreisky had proposed that Schönau should be placed under the protection of the UN High Commissioner for Refugees (UNHCR). But this was one of the rare occasions when Kurt Waldheim, as UN Secretary-General, did not comply with one of Kreisky's requests. The UN itself was not prepared to help, and UNHCR, he ruled, had no authority to act with respect to migrants who were in transit to other countries.

Instantly, Austria became a huge news story. Austria, and foremost its Chancellor Kreisky, were splashed all over the front pages and editorial columns of the world's most influential newspapers. Governments and international institutions were issuing strictures. Ordinary people in many countries were bombarding the Chancellor's office with protest telegrams. There were demonstrations outside Austrian embassies and consulates.

But all this attention was no cause for joy in Austria. Kreisky's, and with him Austria's, good name was being questioned, and was in danger of being lost. His reputation suffered not only in Israel but throughout most of the West. Even if not everyone shared the Israeli view that Kreisky was selling out to the Arabs, there was the American and British view that Kreisky had undermined their adamant stand against any kind of dealing with terrorists. Austria had become the first Western democracy to make political concessions to terrorists in order to free hostages. It was certain to encourage more hostage taking, they predicted gloomily. Initial reactions – they improved when it became clear that the closure of Schönau would not affect Austria's willingness to provide transit facilities for Soviet Jews – to Kreisky's handling of the Schönau affair was outright condemnation, and pleas to reverse the decision. Kreisky had betrayed the Jewish migrants, had brought renewed shame on his country, had opened the door to terrorism. Only the Arab world congratulated him as their very own hero, as an honourary Arab. In his memoirs, Kreisky records that the 'closure of Schönau provoked world-wide indignation and protests of a very special kind'.[5]

After a three-hour session, the Israeli cabinet published a communiqué, expressing its 'astonishment' over the 'unjustifiable decision' of the Austrian government. This was bound to lead to 'further blackmail and terrorist action, and added a new element of danger to the transit rights of Jewish emigrants'.[6] Jerusalem's Mayor, Teddy Kollek, who was born in Vienna, said he felt ashamed for Austria.

In London, a much-quoted editorial in the *Observer* said that 'it is astonishing that a reputable government like Austria's should allow itself to be dictated to by a couple of gunmen in a matter of such profound importance as the transit of Soviet Jews to Israel. Faced with the appalling choice, it would surely have been better to risk the loss of 4 innocent lives than to surrender on such a major matter… Chancellor Kreisky's deal not only disgraces his country, it will also, inevitably encourage similar acts of violence in other countries.'[7] Another British commentary was even more critical: 'It is difficult to imagine why the Austrian Chancellor, who is himself a Jew, chose this cowardly way. Could it be that the Russians put diplomatic pressure on him because they would only be too happy to create new complications for the exodus of Jews? Or is Austrian antisemitism once again rearing its ugly head? In the light of Chancellor Kreisky's inexcusable weakness, it is impossible to suppress such suspicions. Austria could only save its honour by cancelling the decision to close Schonau.'[8]

In the US, the closure of Schönau was interpreted as fresh evidence against Austria, in line with the Anschluss and with the country's failure to meet restitution demands or to try war criminals. The *New York Times* headlined its condemnation of the Austrian government's 'capitulation' with the phrase 'Surrender to Terror'. It was 'a grievous error', based 'on a fatal misconception that, if only the Soviet Jews would stop entering Austria, then the murderous Arab terrorists would disappear and Austria could go on enjoying its post-World War II prosperity and peace... But far from winning peace and quiet by surrendering to Arab blackmail, Dr Kreisky is inviting every possible fanatic who can get his hand on a gun to try and duplicate this Austrian success in that country and elsewhere.'[9] By legitimising banditry, Austria had joined the bandits, ran the popular outcry among Jewish communities in the US. Austria had committed a sin against the international community.

Kreisky's office analysed all the media comments, and summarised them in twin columns: on one side the critical ones, on the other the few even half-way positive editorials in the US, France and Germany. The more friendly papers had noted in mitigation of Kreisky's actions that Austria was a small country, voluntarily carrying a large burden by facilitating the transit of Soviet Jews. The international community should show itself more supportive of the responsibilities that Austria had taken on as a country of asylum. President Nixon's reaction was ambivalent. He told a White House press conference that 'The Austrians are in a very difficult position here... Anybody who knows Dr Kreisky's background knows that he is certainly not antisemitic. But Austria is in the eye of a hurricane, and relatively weak militarily, and has made what I am sure is for Mr Kreisky a very painful decision... I recall that at the time of the Hungarian revolution, Austria opened its arms very generously to thousands of refugees, and I know that is the Austrian custom and tradition.' Nevertheless, Nixon urged Kreisky 'to reconsider his decision for this fundamental reason that goes far beyond his country, and even ours, and that is that we simply cannot have governments, large or small, give in to international blackmail by terrorist groups... But naturally I am not going to put my friend, Mr Kreisky, into a position of trying to dictate to him what to do.'[10]

In the US Senate, the reaction against Kreisky's decision over Schönau was overwhelmingly negative. A Senate resolution described the camp's closure as 'an outrage against humanity'. However, Senator Fulbright, the influential chairman of the Senate Foreign Relations Committee, tried to tone down the opprobrium against Kreisky. In a letter to the Chancellor, he referred to Kreisky's 'wisdom and courage', and noted that 'there are few people in the world today who are able to resist such pressure'.[11]

But Kreisky was able to resist pressure from all quarters, most signally from Meir, to reconsider the closure of Schönau. She visited him in Vienna after a dramatic appearance at the Council of Europe, where she declared that 'in Vienna for the first time a government has come to an understanding, an agreement with terrorists. A basic principle of the freedom of movement of peoples has been put under question, at any rate for Jews, and this is a great victory for terrorism and for terrorists.' In fairness, Meir added that Israel was 'most grateful to the Austrian government for all that it has done for tens of thousands of Jews who have gone through Austria from Poland, Romania, and the Soviet Union'.[12]

Once installed in Kreisky's imposing office, Meir, left alone with the Chancellor, informed him that his capitulation to terrorists was unacceptable and that the closure of Schönau could not be allowed to stand. Kreisky responded with 'something I simply couldn't accept,' Meir wrote later. He said that 'You and I belong to different worlds'.[13] Their mutual sparring degenerated from a dialogue between the deaf to a bitter quarrel between the deaf. Meir continued to argue, but made no progress, and stormed out, looking very wild, and announced that she would not attend the joint press conference with Kreisky which had been planned. She had no intention of sharing a platform with him. She went straight back to her plane, and on arrival in Israel asserted that she had been so badly received in Vienna, that she had not even been offered a glass of water.

The Austrians retorted that her mood had been such that they had no chance to offer her anything to drink – or to eat. But Meir's complaint was quoted throughout the world as a devastating commentary on Austria's heartlessness. Kreisky became a byword for shabby treatment of a Jewish leader.

Far worse, the bad atmosphere between Kreisky and Meir contributed to the fact that he did not pass on Egyptian hints of an imminent attack on Israel which he received a day after the Israeli Prime Minister's visit. President Sadat had sent his Tourism Minister, Ismail Fahmi, to congratulate Kreisky on his handling of the Schönau incident. During their conversation, Fahmi casually mentioned that 'there will be war'. Kreisky was unsure whether he said 'before Christmas' or 'before the end of the year'. He 'thought it was a little strange for him to tell me that, even if I was regarded as a friend of Egypt'.[14] Kreisky failed to pass the information on to the Israelis. In the event, the Yom Kippur War broke out three days after the meeting with Fahmi. Whether Israel would have paid more attention to a warning from Kreisky than to other signs of war preparations against them is obviously open to doubt.

Henry Kissinger has described how Israel's Ambassador in Washington, Simcha Dinitz, came to his office on the last day of September in a very worried state. Kissinger assumed he was worried about Syrian tank movements on the border with the Golan Heights. But it was not so. Schönau and Austria was the Israeli diplomat's main concern. Dinitz insisted on talking about Schönau, focusing all his 'attention during the crucial week before the [Yom Kippur] war on Austria, not on Egypt or Syria'.[15]

During the war, the Schönau saga receded from world attention. It took several weeks before it was realised that Kreisky had never intended to close the doors on the emigrants from the Soviet Union. Meir accepted that she had been premature in her condemnation. Her spokesman, Meron Medzini, conceded that the Israeli Prime Minister may have been 'a little hasty in her judgement'. She realised that 'far from halting the influx of Soviet Jewry, four weeks after the Schonau terrorist attack, the emigrants from Russia reached the highest monthly quota recorded'. But, 'as a temperamental woman, she had seen it as a monstrous insult inflicted by an Austrian Chancellor who was a Jew. For her that was unforgivable.'[16]

Austria, however, felt badly misunderstood. At considerable risk from Soviet retaliation, the country had opened its doors to floods of refugees from Hungary in 1956 and from Czechoslovakia in 1968. Austria coveted its reputation as a 'land of asylum'. Kreisky had been sympathetic to the cause of Soviet Jewry from his early days in the Austrian Foreign Ministry. Arie Eliav, a former General Secretary of Israel's Labour Party, who had also served as a diplomat in Moscow and earlier been involved in the smuggling of Jews to Palestine, confirms that in the late 1950s, Kreisky helped Israel to smuggle bibles, prayerbooks and other articles of Jewish faith into the Soviet Union. 'Without the assistance of Kreisky and his colleagues in the Foreign Ministry and the security establishment, we would not have been able to do anything. We also had smaller operations of the same kind for Prague, Warsaw, Bucharest and Budapest. The Austrians gave us the green light. Kreisky not only gave us his blessing. When Jews started coming out, he gave us all necessary assistance. The Austrian government helped get Jews out by all ways, some legal, some illegal. We once gave Kreisky a list of prisoners of Zion. Kreisky intervened and facilitated their departure. This started in the late '50s and continued in the '60s.'[17]

All this took place before the Americans and the Soviets approached Kreisky with the proposal that Austria should provide transit facilities for Soviet Jews. The Soviet Union did not have diplomatic relations with Israel. They could not be flown out directly. The Jewish emigrants were reluctant to transit through Romania, the only Communist bloc country with diplomatic links to Israel. The Netherlands and Norway, two other countries that were approached, declined, fearing Arab terrorist protests. Austria was thought to be safe because of Kreisky's good relations with the Arab world. Kreisky agreed. The number of Soviet – and Eastern European – Jews who passed through Austria between 1968 and 1986 totalled 270,199, with far more than half of them after the 1973 closure of Schönau.

— * —

With the passage of time, Schönau has become a blip on Austria's record as an asylum country. Yet even though Israel later acknowledged that its attacks on Kreisky may not have been wholly warranted he was never able to secure the modicum of trust from Israeli leaders which he needed to drive home the message that dialogue with the PLO was the essential prerequisite to a Middle East peace settlement.

President Sadat found Kreisky impressive from their first meeting in 1974. From that time on, he sought out Kreisky's views, welcomed his efforts to promote dialogue between Israel and the Arabs, and came to Austria quite frequently. They formed a genuine friendship. Kreisky certainly had some influence on Sadat's decision to make his historic visit to Jerusalem. 'There are two Jews who really impress me,' Sadat wrote to one of his intimates. 'One is Henry Kissinger; the other is Bruno Kreisky'. And he added, 'If there are Jews like Kissinger and Kreisky, then there is a chance that Israel can produce a government with a less intransigent posture than Golda Meir's'.

Kreisky came to Egypt in 1974 as leader of the first of three fact-finding missions to the Middle East on behalf of the Socialist International. The missions were Kreisky's brainchild, and he persuaded the Socialist International to accept them during a meeting in London in November 1973. Meir was present together with Britain's Prime Minister, Harold Wilson, German Chancellor, Willy Brandt, Swedish Prime Minister, Olaf Palme, and several other social democratic leaders. Kreisky and Meir, as usual, sparred with each other. But after even the most pro-Israeli among the socialist leaders were won over to Kreisky's arguments, Meir did not attempt to block adoption of the decision to send a mission to all the countries of the Middle East to explore negotiating prospects.

The first fact-finding mission took Kreisky to Syria, Egypt and Israel. In Cairo, at Sadat's insistence, Kreisky had his first meeting with Yasser Arafat. The PLO leader was regarded by the US and its allies as a terrorist, and it was taboo for Western leaders to speak with him. Once again, Kreisky courted criticism, and was accused of kow-towing to terrorism. But Kreisky was not a man to respect taboos when he felt that logic dictated a different course. His initial encounter with Arafat, however, left him unimpressed. He questioned whether the PLO leader had very clear ideas about PLO strategy. Later, the two men formed a much better relationship. Issam Sartawi, Arafat's representative in Europe, became close to Kreisky, and worked with him to promote dialogue with likeminded Israelis.

Kreisky became convinced long ahead of other Western leaders that it was short-sighted and mistaken to dismiss Arafat as a terrorist who therefore had to be disbarred from negotiations. Kreisky preferred to see him as a freedom fighter, and sometimes said that he and Arafat were soul brothers. Arafat has always acknowledged that he owed Kreisky a big debt for helping to make him acceptable as a negotiating partner. Arafat was part of the solution far more than part of the terrorist problem, Kreisky reasoned, and he continually pressed for the PLO's diplomatic recognition.

Kreisky's last port-of-call during the first Socialist International mission was Jerusalem. He gave the Israelis an essentially positive assessment of attitudes in Cairo and Damascus. To his surprise, he was warmly welcomed by his old foe Meir and her colleagues. He also met the opposition Likud leadership. Menachem Begin was 'frosty', with Yitzhak Shamir and Ariel Sharon making no attempt to hide the fact that they saw him as an opponent, even an enemy. In an after-dinner toast, Meir declared that she had overcome her reservations about the Socialist International mission, and appreciated that Kreisky had brought valuable information. Then she made a gesture he had never expected to hear: she publicly apologised for her behaviour over the Schönau affair, and thanked Austria for facilitating the emigration of 200,000 Soviet Jews, and the provision of asylum during their transit.

By now Kreisky was convinced that the national rights of the Palestinians had to be respected, and that the PLO had to be recognised as a party to the negotiations with Israel, but that in return the PLO had to recognise the existence of Israel. President Nixon, on his last overseas trip before Watergate forced him into resignation, stopped off in Salzburg on his way to Moscow and showed qualified support for Kreisky's views on the Middle East.

A couple of weeks later, at the end of June 1974, Meir was succeeded by Yitzak Rabin. He and Kreisky were more at ease with each other. But, like Meir, Rabin could not accept Kreisky's arguments that the Palestinians must be brought into talks, and that the land-for-peace formula should be endorsed by Israel. In 1974, Rabin's approach to peace negotiations had not yet moved towards the flexible positions that were to cost him his life two decades later. But Rabin and the other leaders who joined Harold Wilson at Chequers to hear Kreisky's report on the mission were impressed by the Austrian leader, and most of them agreed with his conclusions and recommendations. Kreisky felt he was beginning to shift European governments away from their pro-Israeli line towards a more even-handed approach to Middle East problems.

Kreisky, seeking to maintain the momentum of his Middle East campaign, went to the UN General Assembly in September 1974 with the same message: Western recognition of the PLO, Arab recognition of Israel. There was considerable applause, but not for both sides of the equation – each camp only endorsed the part it wanted to hear.

The second Socialist International mission to the Middle East, in February 1975, took Kreisky to North Africa, including Libya, where Colonel Gadhafi appeared to be greatly impressed with the Austrian

Chancellor, and spent hours unfolding his version of a third way in politics. Kreisky was mesmerised by him, and wrongly assumed that Gadhafi could be weaned from terrorism and used as a constructive force in the search for a Middle East settlement.

The trio of missions was completed in 1976, when Kreisky went to Saudi Arabia, Jordan and Iraq. In all three countries, he insisted that there could be no progress without recognition of Israel. He was heard politely, but failed to achieve any kind of breakthrough. Afterwards Kreisky presented the Socialist International with a detailed analysis of his observations from the three missions. There was no beating about the bush. The missions had been useful in clarifying positions, but they had achieved very little towards a peace settlement between Israel and the Arab world.

Unkind tongues amongst Socialist leaders portrayed it all as little more than an ego-trip for Kreisky. The missions had given him a higher profile in the international community; they had reinforced his popularity at home; they had helped to bolster his standing in the more moderate parts of the Arab world, and gained him respect in Washington.

In 1975, when the UN General Assembly adopted the controversial resolution which labelled Zionism a form of racism, Austria strongly condemned the move and voted against it. But thanks to Kreisky's networking, the vote did little damage to Austria's standing in the Arab world. Increasingly Kreisky was being treated as a friend, and as the PLO's protector.

— * —

Arab extremists, who considered the PLO too soft, lacked the respect for Austria which the more moderate elements had developed. In December 1975, terrorists again struck in Austria. This time it happened in Vienna and the attack was against a ministerial session of OPEC, which had had its headquarters in Vienna since 1965. Three guards were killed, and 11 oil ministers were among 90 hostages. The terrorist group was led by Carlos 'the Jackal' (Ilich Ramirez Sanchez), and included a Palestinian, a Jordanian and a Lebanese. They called themselves 'Arm of the Arab Revolution', and they had a contract to murder Sheikh Zaki Yamani, the Saudi Oil Minister. He was not amongst the dead, but had been taken hostage.

One of the terrorists' demands was for the Austrians to give them a plane, complete with pilots, so that they and their hostages could fly to the Middle East. They also issued a manifesto which called for the rejection of any peaceful resolution of the Middle East conflict, reiterated a refusal to recognise Israel and demanded support for Palestine resistance. They apologised for 'the difficulties which our action has caused the peace-loving people of Austria'.[18] Within 24 hours, Kreisky yielded to the terrorists' principal demand: a plane was allowed to take off with the terrorists 11 Ministers and 22 other OPEC delegates. As during the Schönau crisis, he had again lost his nerve.

While Carlos, the last member of the terrorist group to leave, prepared to mount the steps up to the plane, the Austrian Interior Minister, Otto Rösch, was photographed shaking the terrorist's hand. The gesture caused considerable caustic mirth at Austria's expense, and was seen as yet more graphic evidence that Austria was a soft touch for terrorism.

In Algiers, the hostages were released after the Saudi government bought off Carlos's contract to kill Yamani. The hostage-takers were allowed to disappear again into the terrorist undergrowth. Austria went through the motions of demanding the return of the terrorists to be tried for their crimes. But Kreisky knew it was an empty gesture.

Israel enjoyed a moment of *Schadenfreude* that Austria, the Arabs' protector, had been hit by Arab gunmen: Austria had still not learned that to give in to terrorists was to invite more terrorism. More to the point, Israel was joined by a wide swathe of commentators across the world who now had new material to fuel criticism of Kreisky as a leader who lacked principle and was making a habit of capitulating to terrorists.

The US administration, however, took a more balanced view on this occasion, and did not join the international chorus of criticism of Kreisky's handling of the OPEC incident. President Ford, himself now actively engaged in Middle East diplomacy, felt that he needed the Austrian Chancellor's help. Just a few months before the hostage-taking, in May 1975, Kreisky had arranged a meeting in Salzburg between Ford and President Sadat, a meeting which belongs to the genealogy of the Camp David accord.

— * —

In 1978, Kreisky again intervened at a key juncture: It was soon after Sadat had made his historic first visit to Jerusalem. With the intention of building trust between the Egyptians and Israelis, Kreisky arranged meetings in Austria first between Sadat and Shimon Peres, leader of the Israeli Labour Party, and afterwards between the Egyptian President and Ezer Weizman, Defence Minister in Begin's Likud government. But Kreisky remained convinced that negotiations for a settlement between Israel and Egypt could only be brought about with the participation of the PLO. Naturally, he realised that Begin was the prime obstacle to contacts with the PLO. In an interview for a Dutch paper, Kreisky had another one of his irrational outbursts, and spoke in derisory tones about Begin, describing him as a little Polish lawyer, a 'Jew from Eastern Europe totally removed from reality... The most hated diplomats today are the Israeli ones... They need another 100 years.'[19] Begin retorted, 'He is known as a man who hates his mother and his father'. Israeli papers described him as a renegade, as a Jew without honour; the *Jerusalem Post* asked why Austrians tolerated him. More to the point, commentators questioned whether Kreisky had not fatally damaged his mediation efforts in the Middle East. Rabin, speaking for the Labour Party opposition, was so outraged by Kreisky's various sins and his continued campaigning for PLO recognition that he weighed in to condemn Kreisky's 'wild, hate-filled attacks against Israel, against the Jewish people and against Israeli personalities'.[20]

But even if the Israelis had trusted Kreisky, he would in any event have been edged out of a central role in the Middle East peace process, now gathering momentum. The Americans were increasingly confident that the timing was right for them to stoke up the process. Jimmy Carter had succeeded Ford as President. In November 1978, Kreisky gave Carter the substance of conversations with two influential PLO advisors. According to Kreisky, the PLO would endorse negotiations between Sadat and Begin, and would accept the existence of Israel, provided the Palestinians were, as a first step, given autonomy on the West Bank and Gaza. Carter's reply was guarded. He found Kreisky's 'report to be quite useful, and I hope you will keep me informed of your assessments of trends in Palestinian thinking. As you know the next phase of Middle East peace negotiations should deal with matters of direct concern to Palestinians, and it will be particularly valuable to me to receive your counsel on how best to encourage a constructive Palestinian role in the peace process.'[21]

Kreisky put less effort into pressurising Sadat to insist on drawing the PLO into the Camp David talks: he had assumed that Sadat would make it a pre-condition that Arafat be there. But Begin was unalterably opposed, and Sadat, setting aside Kreisky's arguments, agreed to come to the US without the participation of the PLO. In the euphoria of the September 1978 Camp David Accord, Kreisky was a voice in the wilderness with his prediction of more obstacles to progress unless the Palestinian problem was finally tackled. He tried to move matters on by facilitating meetings between the US Ambassador in Vienna and one of Arafat's confidantes. He also embarked on a more perilous course to secure US recognition of the PLO.

Soon after the success of Camp David, the US was confronted with the Iran hostage crisis. When the Americans, desperate to free the hostages, asked Kreisky in November 1979 for help, his response was to suggest that Arafat might be the person to handle the matter. He added the proviso that the US would have to deal directly with the PLO.

No doubt it was a mark of the reputation that Kreisky had made for himself on Middle East affairs that Carter assumed the Austrian leader's contacts could be useful in the hostage crisis. Kreisky admitted that he had no personal line to Khomeini. But at his urging two senior US emissaries flew to Vienna to discuss matters further. Kreisky put forward his proposal to use Arafat as an intermediary. Kreisky had assured them that he was not trying to trap the US into a back-door recognition of the PLO, as a 'quid pro quo to get Arafat's intervention with Khomeini'. The Americans however chose to read it differently, as an obvious indication that 'Kreisky wanted the Carter Administration to undertake a "demonstrable action" openly and directly with the PLO, which could be a de facto recognition of the PLO'.[22]

In any event, when the Israelis were informed of Kreisky's proposal, they saw this as further evidence of Kreisky's perfidious behaviour, and said they had no doubt at all that this was just a trap to secure US recognition of the PLO. By the time the Israelis made their views known, Arafat had already agreed to fly to Teheran. But the Americans called a halt and ordered the 'Austrian connection' closed.

Disregarding advice from some of his own colleagues, and well aware that a fresh storm of protest from Israel and its friends would hit him, Kreisky decided to go ahead unilaterally with Austrian recognition of the PLO. In March 1980, Austria became the first Western country to establish formal diplomatic relations with the PLO. Peres immediately protested, arguing that Kreisky's action endangered Israel's existence and security. A senior Israeli diplomat said that Austria 'seemed to have forgotten the sufferings of the Jewish people during the Second World War'.[23]

If Kreisky was merely ahead of his time – and essentially right about the PLO – he was wrong to assume that Colonel Gadhafi would be prepared to distance himself from terrorism. But he understood this too late, only after the Libyan leader had accepted an invitation to Austria and had descended on Vienna in March 1982 with a mammoth delegation of 300. The Libyan leader's arrival coincided with President Reagan's decision to designate Libya an 'outlaw state' and impose an oil embargo and a prohibition on the export of US technology to Libya. Eugene Douglas, Reagan's co-ordinator for refugee matters, issued an official protest which described Austria as 'host country to a terrorist leader and protector of the PLO... This has created a situation which is hardly calculated to improve Austria's image in the United States.'[24]

The Gadhafi visit has left a black mark against Kreisky's place in history. He was already a sick man, his chancellorship waning. Jerusalem described the Austrian welcome extended to Gadhafi as the high-point of Kreisky's anti-Israeli activities. The US administration and other Western governments were equally appalled that he should invite a terrorist 'outlaw' to Vienna. Reagan did meet Kreisky later on, but there was little cordiality between them. For Americans, Austria's international reputation had been further damaged – for some irretrievably. Kreisky knew that he had misjudged Gadhafi and had squandered some of the diplomatic capital he had so painstakingly built up over many years. But this did not deter him from injecting himself forcefully into the debate that raged over Israel's invasion of Southern Lebanon in June 1982. He placed Austria firmly behind the sharpest critics of the Israeli action, describing it as a 'terrible act of aggression', and appealing to the conscience of the world to force Israel to restore Lebanese sovereignty and end the bloodletting it had unleashed. 'Israel is morally bankrupt. Its leaders have shown their true face.'[25] There was much more from Kreisky in similar vein, including accusations that Israel's behaviour was Nazi-like.

Israeli public opinion was of course itself divided over the Lebanon invasion. But inevitably official Israel used Kreisky's anti-invasion pronouncements as further evidence of his deep-seated antagonism towards the Jewish state.

And yet there was another side to all this mutual recrimination. The public exchanges were not allowed to stand in the way of secret Israeli approaches to Kreisky to use his influence to help find 20 Israeli soldiers missing in action in Lebanon. Even the Red Cross had been unable to discover what had happened to them. Arie Eliav, who had become Begin's special representative for the release of prisoners of war in Lebanon, turned to Kreisky. 'With no prior warning I knocked on Kreisky's door. He agreed to help, on one condition: that he would help the Palestinians as well. He said he would do this even though he was dead against Begin, dead against what we were doing in Lebanon. He said: you can work from my office.'[26]

Kreisky brought in one of his own Middle East experts. They were joined by the PLO's representative in Europe, Issam Sartawi (who was killed by Arab extremists in 1983). The trio went to work, meeting with Israeli generals and visiting Egypt and Lebanon, all of it facilitated by Austria. 'Begin knew that Kreisky was helping us,' Eliav confirmed. The mission was partially successful: six Israelis were exchanged for 5000 Palestinians in Israeli hands. In a second exchange, three who had survived and four dead Israelis were exchanged for 200 Syrians.

In contrast to the virulent Austrian campaign against the invasion of Lebanon, Kreisky respected the need for confidentiality in all matters connected to the prisoner exchange negotiation. He never referred to it in public, and never made capital out of it. Though it might have done his image some good in Israel and the US, Kreisky accepted that the negotiations could only have a positive outcome if they were kept out of the public domain.

Kreisky tried a different avenue to restore his stature in Washington. He expressed strong backing for Reagan's Middle East peace initiatives, and busied himself in support of US peace moves among his friends in the Arab world. It was too late: there is little evidence that the Reagan

White House took much account of his activities, even though Senator George McGovern lobbied on his behalf, writing to Vice-President Bush, that it would be 'a great mistake to ignore a man of Chancellor Kreisky's stature'.[27]

In February 1983, Kreisky paid his last official visit to Washington. Reagan was cordial, and announced that he had nominated one of his close personal friends, Helene van Damm, to become the next US Ambassador to Austria, a decision that turned out to be eminently useful for Austria's gossip columnists, but was otherwise of dubious worth. The presidential massaging of Kreisky amounted to little more than the kind of gesture-politicking of which Reagan was such a past master. Kreisky's time as wheeler-dealer in Middle East affairs had been and gone.

Among Kreisky's greatest achievements had been to recognise and promote Western awareness of Sadat's commitment to a negotiated Middle East peace settlement. Then there was Kreisky's persistence in trying to bring the PLO in from the cold, and his belief that Arafat deserved to rank among Arab moderates. His constant theme that the Palestinians must recognise the legitimacy of Israel, but in return must be given a state, or at least autonomy, also count to Kreisky's credit. It is a puzzle why Kreisky never sought much public recognition for Austria's willingness to provide transit facilities for almost 200,000 Soviet Jews – Schönau is remembered as a surrender to Arab terrorists far more than as a symbol of Austria's hospitality to innumerable Jewish migrants.

But the greatest puzzle of all is why Kreisky chose to make himself so criticised and unpopular in Israel: time and again he shouted his frustration with Israel from the roof-tops. His public behaviour undermined his secret diplomacy, and made it largely impossible to act as a go-between, or to sustain influence in Washington. It is by no means unreasonable to conjecture that Kreisky's anti-Israeli rhetoric damaged Austria's standing among American Jews to such an extent that it fired their enthusiasm to exploit the allegations against Kurt Waldheim and to bring Austria's international standing to the lowest point of its post-war history.

NOTES ON CHAPTER VIII

1 Hans Thalberg, *Von der Kunst Österreicher zu sein*, Bohlau Verlag, 1984, p 418.
2 Bruno Kreisky, *Im Strom der Politik*, Siedelr, Kremayr & Scheriau, 1988, p 319.
3 Interview by Eric Silver with Israel Gat, former Director of the Israeli Labour Party's International Department, 1998.
4 Ibid.
5 Kreisky, *Im Strom der Politik*, op. cit., p 323.
6 Associated Press, Jerusalem, 30 September 1993.
7 *Observer*, 30 September 1993.

8 *Sunday Telegraph*, 30 September 1973.
9 *New York Times*, 8 October 1993.
10 President Nixon press conference, 3 October 1973.
11 Letter from Senator Fulbright to Chancellor Kreisky, 8 October 1973.
12 Golda Meir, *My Life*, Weidenfeld & Nicolson, 1975, p 351.
13 Ibid.
14 Interview with Kreisky in 1983, *Jerusalem Post*, 3 August 1990.
15 Henry Kissinger, *Years of Upheaval*, Little,Brown, 1982.
16 Hugo Portisch, *Österreich II: Jahre des Aufbruch's*, pp 377–8.
17 Interview in 1998.
18 Terrorists' communiqué, Vienna, December 1975.
19 Interview with Kreisky by James Dorsey, *Trouw*, September 1978.
20 Oliver Rathkolb, lecture on Austria-Israel relations delivered on Austrian Radio (ORF), May 1998.
21 Carter to Kreisky, 29 January 1979, quoted in Oliver Rathkolb, 'Bruno Kreisky: Perspectives of Top-level US Foreign Policy Decision-makers, 1959–83' in *The Kreisky Era in Austria*, Transaction Publishers, 1994.
22 Robert J. Lipshutz, 'The Hostages: the Austrian connection', quoted in Rathkolb, 'Bruno Kreisky', op. cit.
23 Helga Embacher and Margit Reiter, *Gratwanderungen: Die Beziehungen zwischen Österreich und Israel*, Picus, 1998, p 160.
24 Communiqué, issued in Vienna 24 May 1982.
25 Interview with Kreisky, *Stern*, 28 August 1982.
26 Interview with Arie Eliav.
27 Rathkolb, 'Bruno Kreisky', op. cit, p 21.

IX

The Golden Age of Economic Prosperity

'I almost feel ashamed to mention it to a Briton: but the fact is that in 1977 Austria was exposed to only 86 hours of labour strikes. This year, up to November 1978, we have had a three-week strike in a tire factory employing 450 people, and we'll probably end the year with our normal average of 3000–4000 lost working hours. This represents an annual loss of about six seconds of working time for each Austrian worker. By comparison, most other members of the OECD – Organisation for European Cooperation and Development – reckon with an annual strike rate of 2–3 days per worker.' These words from a leading trade unionist reflected a widely held view.[1] During the 'golden age' of Bruno Kreisky's reign, it would have been churlish to question the slight tone of triumphalism which had crept into this Austrian trade unionist's description of industrial peace and widespread prosperity that his country was enjoying. I was preparing a *Guardian* Survey of Austria, and was interviewing politicians, bankers, employers, trade unionists and the proverbial grass-roots. Everywhere there was the same stress on the commitment to industrial peace, to the welfare state, and to a coherent incomes and prices policy as the basic elements of Austria's remarkable economic record.

If this was true in 1978, it had also been true two decades earlier, and remains broadly true today. Social cohesion, institutionalised through close, formalised consultation and co-operation between government, the employers' federation and the trade union federation – the social partnership – help to explain how Austria has weathered the economic cycle, including the two oil price crises of the 1970s better than most of its Western trading partners.

During the Kreisky era, this mechanism ensured full employment – the Chancellor's absolute priority – together with wage restraint, low inflation, a business-friendly taxation system, substantial infrastructure investment, and a hard and stable currency, shadowing the DM. Austria's trading partners were slow to detect that the consensus on economic policy began to weaken during the second half of the 1970s, when a deep rift developed between Kreisky and his Finance Minister, Hannes Androsch.

Britain's *Financial Times* awarded Austria an 'economic Oscar'; and the *International Herald Tribune* noted that 'by any measure Mr Kreisky's accomplishments have been impressive. During the past decade, compared to average performance elsewhere in Western Europe, Austria wound up with the tenth largest and fastest-growing economy, and the lowest inflation rate.'[2]

It was rare, almost unheard of, that such a combination of economic results could be achieved in tandem with a successful policy of full employment. But this is precisely what happened in Austria during the greater part of the Kreisky era: Austria consistently secured a negligible unemployment rate, by far the lowest of any Western economy, with youth unemployment virtually unknown. Public sector investment also led to significant improvements in Austria's infrastructure. Austria was greatly envied abroad. Notwithstanding the collapse of the post-war fixed exchange rate system in 1973, the oil price shocks of 1973 and 1978, and the 1975 world recession, Austria, they all agreed, was enjoying a golden age.

The glow inevitably dimmed with the realisation that Kreisky had clung for too long to inefficient nationalised industries, that the welfare system was overburdened, and that budget deficits were growing out of control, that internal tensions between Kreisky and Androsch over the direction of economic and financial policy were creating uncertainty. The latter's resignation led to disturbing – if only passing – glitches in the good news version of Austria's economic history. Fortunately Kreisky's successors set about to repair tensions that could have caused lasting damage to the economy and to the social partnership. They firmly held to economic policy by consensus between the key players – industry, the trade unions and the government. By this process, it was possible for Austria to privatise, restructure and modernise key sectors of the economy far more smoothly than some of Europe's larger economies, and to remain in the top league of economic performance among the industrialised democracies. At the approach of the millennium the authoritative *Financial Times* annual survey of Austria was once again able to tell a familiar success story: a 'strong economy and political stability'[3] in a country that had adapted itself well to changing circumstances in world affairs.

Austria's economic successes neither began nor ended with Kreisky's chancellorship. The decisive economic upswing had begun under the previous, conservative government. In 1970, the Austrian economy was already close to the European average. But the world had paid little attention. This changed after Kreisky took charge: his high profile in international diplomacy and his efforts to promote Vienna as a major UN capital stimulated greater interest in the small country's economic achievements. Politicians and pundits constantly came to study and admire, to envy. They dubbed it 'Austrokeynesianism', and later preferred the term 'Austro-monetarism'; and they yearned to replicate this new 'ism' elsewhere. It was seen as an admirable manifestation of a mixed, market-dominated economy, one that produced at one and the same time excellent economic results, social peace and an all-round improvement in living standards.

Western commentators routinely side-stepped Austria's neutral status, and treated the country as a Western free market economy – a perception which, not surprisingly, caused deep misgivings in Moscow and reinforced Soviet resistance to Vienna's eagerness for closer links to the EEC. The nationalised sector – larger than in any other Western economy – prompted little adverse comment among the devotees of private enterprise in OECD countries. When Kreisky came to power, the state controlled directly or indirectly about one third of Austrian industry. From the pre-war era, the Austrian state had inherited public control of the basic utilities, and in 1945 it added a huge industrial and banking empire, including the iron and steel industry, oil refineries, machine tools works and the major banks. Foreign pundits recognised that this had been done for left-wing doctrinal reasons but on sound economic grounds, to prevent the Soviet Union from claiming them as German assets.

Austria's admirers were slow to understand that they were looking at a one-off model, not susceptible to replication elsewhere. While Kreisky often sought to enlist other countries in his foreign policy initiatives, Androsch was always far more reserved. He deliberately avoided any suggestion that Austria's way of managing the economy contained a formula that could be equally successfully applied elsewhere. On one occasion, when French President François Mitterrand declared an intention to follow the Austrian model, Androsch, far from feeling flattered, warned that it could not function under French conditions and could only lead to failure – and so it proved. France was soon forced to reverse its policy. Again, in 1980, when the IMF surprised Androsch during its annual meeting by naming him chairman of its important policy-making Interim Committee, he interpreted it as significant international recognition of Austria's achievements. But he did not encourage the IMF to single out Austria as an economic model for other countries.

Britain's Denis Healey, during his period as Chancellor of the Exchequer, habitually held up Austria as the perfect example of a combination of the welfare state, economic dynamism and social peace. But he was realist enough to recognise that several of the factors that made this possible in Austria did not prevail on Britain's turbulent scene. Austria operated in a different social climate. Class divisions played little role; the income spread was reasonably equitable; the political and intellectual elites knew each other intimately and were accustomed to working with each other across the political divide. Above all Austria was marked by a unique historical baggage that had dictated its devotion to political and social consensus during the early post-war period. The commitment to consensus after 1945 derived from the legacy of insecurity during the inter-war period . Those difficult years were marked by economic collapse and social division which provoked near civil war and street-fighting in Vienna, and opened the possibility of the Anschluss to National Socialism.

— * —

It was almost another decade after the 1955 State Treaty before the country felt self-confident and prosperous enough to dispense with government by grand coalition involving the two major parties. But even then, belief in the need to maintain a coalition of economic interests and nurture an economic and financial policy consensus, far from withering away, grew stronger. It was perceived as the best possible guarantor of rising living standards.

In a major survey of Austria's accomplishments at the end of the 1970s, *The Economist* ruled that Austria was ending the decade 'triumphantly'. Tongue in cheek, the survey's author, Sarah Hogg (later advisor to Prime Minister John Major) wrote that the 'Austrians have two explanations for their economic success: one is that they exported all their economists to Britain and the United States... The other is that it is always easier to keep a small house in order.' She aptly describes the small pond in which Austria's big fish operate: 'In little Austria, policy is made by a cosy circle of people who each tend, like Poo-Bah to combine the roles of Lord-High-Everything else [a reference to Gilbert and Sullivan's *The Mikado*] – speaker of the parliament and president of the trade unions (Mr Anton Benya), prominent opposition politician turned Governor of the Central Bank (Mr Stephan Koren). Out from the tutelage of Austria's young but long-serving Finance Minister, Hannes Androsch, have streamed some of his favoured bureaucrats into key positions, reinforcing the consensus at the apex of Austria's famous triangle of Social

Partnership. This net contains most of the opinion-makers of a population no larger than Greater London's; even the opposition is drawn as much as possible into it... Managing the Austrian economy is not, therefore, the impossible task of reconciling warring groups that thwarts the neat economic theories of the governments of larger economies.

'Not that the business of arriving at consensus is a quiet one; or that the Austrians are a naturally contented lot: a bunch of Viennese will probably be found grumbling at the doors of paradise.'

In any case, there was more to Austria's success than the compactness of its ruling class, *The Economist* assured its readers. Policy-making by consensus only pays off if the policies themselves are sound. Japan had been the only Western industrialised country to exceed Austria's growth rate between 1970 and 1979. During the second half of the 1970s Austria had 'achieved more than almost any other developed economy to employ its people and stifle inflation by a pragmatic selection of economic policies untainted by doctrinaire beliefs'. What made this achievement so 'extraordinary' was the fact that Austria had been able to avoid roaring inflation even though the high growth rate had been secured in the 'old-fashioned Keynesian way by a public sector deficit'. Hogg particularly admired that 'by the end of 1979, Austria actually had a lower inflation rate than any developed economy'.

The answer to the conundrum was to be found in 'the strong currency route' taken by the Finance Minister together with the head of the Central Bank. Instead of opting for 'the classic prescription, IMF-style of a sizeable devaluation and deflation, the pair were highly eclectic in their choice of economic policies, and decided otherwise'. But this only worked because Austria's union leaders agreed to apply a policy of wage restraint and linked increase to improved productivity.

It all seemed too good to be true, and the *Economist* survey ended on a down-beat note, questioning whether the Austria's golden age could last much longer. But last it did, for a while. Three years later, in 1982, the distinguished *Financial Times* commentator Samuel Brittan produced another up-beat verdict on the Austrian economy, and found far more to admire than to criticise in Austria's economic policies. Headlined 'A slightly tarnished miracle', his analysis came to the conclusion that 'by most international yardsticks, Austria is one of the few great success stories of the Western world. Since the late 1960s, its average economic growth rate has been above that of the European OECD countries, and its inflation rate well below them. Many of these success indicators would apply, until recently, to Germany... The feature that distinguishes Austria sharply from her neighbour is, however, its low unemployment. German unemployment is approaching 2 million and represents more than 8 per cent of the labour force. After a year of zero growth, Austria's unemployment is 3–3.5 per cent... The deservedly famous social partnership is often seen outside Austria far too narrowly as a voluntary incomes policy which can be copied elsewhere. It is far more. Above all it is an expression of a desire for unity and reconciliation following two world wars and a strife-torn period in between... The success of the social partnership is to be measured in terms such as the ease of social intercourse among all Austrians; the low class barriers and the habits of compromise and reasonableness. These aspects are more important than the precise economic or institutional forms which, so far from being a rigid model for other countries to follow, are likely to evolve in Austria itself, in the direction of more flexibility in wage and price-setting and greater sensitivity in economic and financial policy.'[4]

From his first day as Chancellor, Kreisky had always been adamant that full employment, underpinned by a sound education system, had to be the top priority for Austria's economic policy-makers. Everything else was secondary. By 1979, when his critics were warning that such an unequivocal approach to economic management was only shoring up future troubles, Kreisky defended himself with the much-quoted dictum 'A few billions [of schillings] of debt are not as bad as hundreds of thousands of unemployed'.[5] The end justified the means. In his book of economic management, featherbedding in the large nationalised sector and budget deficits could be justified without reservation so long as they prevented unemployment.

Shortly before the 1983 election that ended Kreisky's long reign, the Chancellor was still insisting that his policy emphasis on 'jobs, jobs and again jobs' was unassailable because it made unemployment 'inconceivable'.

— * —

The early years of Kreisky's chancellorship were marked by harmonious collaboration with Androsch, who was only thirty-two when he was given the finance portfolio in 1970. An accountant by profession, Androsch had only been in parliament for three years, but had already become the Social Democrats' spokesman on economic affairs. The two men were agreed on policy aims. Androsch was personable, knowledgable, inventive and efficient. He was given a free hand to develop economic policy. He cultivated close links with the pillars of the social partnership and won the all-important trust of the powerful head of the Austrian trade union movement, Anton Benya. His popularity grew.

Kreisky and Androsch became firm friends, often holidaying together, and by no means infrequently settled economic policy issues on the ski slopes of Austria. At home and abroad, Androsch was being described as the emperor's crown prince. This turned out to be illusory. Kreisky could not live with a crown prince, and Austria lost one of its ablest politicians for good.

GUILTY VICTIM

I have followed the bruising Kreisky-Androsch saga from its early stages when they acted in partnership, to their bitter break-up with its long-lasting consequences for Austrian politics. In Austria the controversy surrounding the relationship between the two men lingers on, even though the policy differences that ended their friendship are largely forgotten. Kreisky, of course, is no longer here to defend his side of the dispute. But from an outsider's point of view, it is hard to ignore Kreisky's intemperate and often irrational behaviour. There are parallels with his attempts to destroy Simon Wiesenthal's reputation.

The first signs of strain emerged in 1974 when President Jonas, Austria's head of state, was seriously ill and known to be close to death. Androsch and Vienna's powerful Mayor, Leopold Gratz, met informally to discuss possible candidates to become the next head of state. The two men threw out feelers to the sixty-four-year-old Kreisky as to whether he might be prepared to run. Later, Kreisky always referred to this episode as a manoeuvre to oust him, and as part of a sinister plot engineered by Androsch to wrest the chancellorship. Following this, Kreisky claimed, he could never again trust his Finance Minister.

The real version is very different. Kreisky responded to the suggestion that he might consider the presidency with the argument that his candidacy might provoke a fresh wave of antisemitism in Austria. Public opinion would not be prepared to accept a Jewish head of state. Androsch and Gratz countered that his argument was hardly convincing, given that Kreisky's chancellorship had not triggered any increase in antisemitism. However, the three leaders decided that for a quite different reason, that the idea of a Kreisky presidency had to be dropped: at the time, Kreisky was such a popular Chancellor that he was irreplaceable in that post.

After Jonas's death, and without much further ado, the Social Democrats nominated Rudolf Kirchschläger as their candidate. He was elected and became a modest, highly respected President.

— * —

Once Kreisky had come to see Androsch as a rival, all trust between the two men was gone. And yet the relationship might not have deteriorated so dramatically had it not been that Jonas's death and the issue of his succession coincided with the early impact of the 1973 oil price increases, which provoked a slow-down of Austria's hitherto remarkable economic expansion. Kreisky, fearing for the full employment policy, was set on devaluation of the Austrian currency.

Androsch resisted. The Austrian economy had caught up with the German one; in some sectors even overtaken it. He had no doubt that maintenance of the hard currency policy, with the value of the schilling shadowing the DM, was the only sensible course for Austria. True, the export sector would probably have preferred a weaker currency, but when the powerful Benya put his weight behind Androsch and the hard currency policy, Kreisky became isolated and was forced to let Androsch have his way. Economic growth resumed.

But Kreisky continued to believe to the end that 'Austria's economy had reached a stage where the country could have afforded to define its own exchange rate policy'. He questioned whether his Finance Minister's 'vanity had played a role in persuading him to walk alongside the DMark'.[6]

Helmut Schmidt, Germany's Chancellor between 1974 and 1982, has always thought that Kreisky was wrong, both on the substance of monetary policy, and on his suspicion that Androsch had hidden motives in holding to Austria's currency alignment with the DM. Looking back on that debate, Schmidt remains convinced that Germany and Austria 'had common economic interests. It was therefore a natural evolution,' for the two currencies to maintain their unofficial link. Schmidt was firmly on Androsch's side, and interpreted Kreisky's inflexibility as a manifestation of the generation gap: 'Kreisky belonged to an earlier generation, whose approach to economic issues had been fixed in the pre-Hitler years'.[7]

For a man with Kreisky's temperament, his defeat over exchange rate policy was not easy to accept. Like so many political super-egos, Kreisky was deeply disturbed by a senior colleague's popularity, and could not be disabused of the idea that Androsch was working to oust him sooner rather than later. Nevertheless, in 1976 he named Androsch his Vice-Chancellor – a move that misled many foreign observers into assuming that Kreisky still thought of him as his natural successor. They were mistaken. Kreisky had different motives: if he advanced Androsch, he could hold at bay other ambitious rivals for the Vice-Presidency, and could stave off manoeuvres to identify his successor. Kreisky also assumed that he could deter Androsch from his growing drive to leave the Finance Ministry and secure the directorship of Austria's Central Bank. Kreisky had not yet begun efforts to discredit Androsch's integrity, but his feelings towards the younger man had already fundamentally changed.

The gulf widened as Androsch accumulated international recognition for the management of Austria's economy. In 1978 he was elected to the presidency of the OECD. In 1979, he was given a standing ovation by a packed audience of leading British bankers, industrialists and diplomats after he addressed them at the Royal Institute of International Affairs in London. Kreisky's reaction, when he heard of it, was typical of his growing jealousy: 'It was just a claque, organised by the Austrian Embassy for any visitor from Vienna'.[8] Mutual trust between Kreisky and Androsch eroded and was replaced by growing bitterness. There were no more ski holidays. Before long they stopped talking to each other, and communicated through third parties.

Policy differences became harder and harder to reconcile. Androsch had never quarrelled with the goal of full employment, but could not accept featherbedding and subsidies for inefficient, uneconomic state industries: Kreisky was perverting the concept of full employment into one of guaranteed job security. He warned that budget deficits would run out of control if Kreisky continued to resist his Finance Minister's proposals for radical cuts in expenditure on the welfare state. Austria's high standing in the IMF and OECD would suffer; foreign investment would decline.

There were other bones of contention over economic policy. Energy supply was one of them: Androsch was a firm supporter of nuclear energy for Austria. Rightly or wrongly, he became convinced that Kreisky, sensing popular objections, had changed his original views and had adopted an ambivalent attitude towards the controversial Zwentendorf nuclear plant, which was completed but has never been made operational. Kreisky's decision to stage a referendum on Zwentendorf in 1978, followed by the decision to abide by the negative outcome of the vote, gained Kreisky a great deal of praise from Europe's environmental lobbies. But it further convinced Androsch that Kreisky was far too easily swayed by short-term political gains, and that he had failed to understand the need for Austria to reduce its dependance on energy imports. Ironically, even though Austria deprived itself of domestically produced nuclear energy, it now imports sizeable quantities from neighbouring countries, especially Germany and Switzerland.

Androsch had no illusions that Kreisky and he were on a dangerous collision course: 'Exchange rate policy – different concepts; financing the welfare state – different concepts; energy policy – different concepts; nationalised industries – different concepts. Each one of these elements were enough to generate conflict. All four combined compounded to make it worse.'[9]

Policy disputes between prime ministers and finance ministers are endemic in Western democracies, but when they acquire the explosive character of this one it is, to say the least, odd that it took over seven years before the final rupture occurred in 1981.

Kreisky wanted to rid himself of his Finance Minister, but also knew that his removal would damage Austria's international standing. Several factors were at play which delayed the inevitable: the success of the hard currency policy; strong Social Democratic backing for Androsch as the lead architect of Austria's economic miracle; external concern to safeguard political, and hence economic stability in Austria. Austria was basking in the generous praise for the country's economic achievements that its friends abroad were lavishing on the country. Kreisky was naturally gratified by this: he recognised that the country's high economic standing secured added clout for his foreign policy endeavours.

Kreisky was wont to stress that he lacked expertise in economic management. Yet he seems to have convinced himself that he understood economics well enough to carry on without Androsch. Others knew better. Left to himself, the Chancellor would probably have preferred to have Androsch go long before 1981, but senior colleagues in the Social Democratic Party insisted that Androsch must stay.

Willy Brandt was among those who tried to heal the rift between the two men. Others, who admired Austria's economic and financial policies, and who argued that Kreisky should hold on to Androsch included Henry Kissinger, the British Labour Party's economic guru Harold Lever, and ex-Austrian banker Eric Roll. Androsch himself was tiring of his policy battles with the Chancellor. From 1977 onwards their disputes spun out of control. That was the year when Kreisky switched tactics and embarked on a drive to discredit Androsch personally by mounting a conflict-of-interest case against him. Kreisky alleged that Androsch, while in office, had maintained links to Consultatio, the family accountancy firm. Androsch denied any improper conduct. The confrontation over this developed into an extraordinarily bitter dispute which eventually involved the courts, divided Austria's elites, and ended Androsch's political prospects – though not his political influence.

In December 1980, the flimsy thread that still bound Kreisky and Androsch, snapped. Early in January 1981, Androsch left office for good. At Benya's insistence, Kreisky appointed Androsch first as Deputy, and soon afterwards as Managing Director, of the Creditanstalt, then Austria's largest and still publicly owned bank. He remained in charge of the bank until 1988. Kreisky himself remained Chancellor for another 29 months; but with Androsch out of the government, its economic competence faltered, and the economy suffered.

Kreisky was already seriously ill. The economic programme drawn up by the new Finance Minister, Herbert Salcher, was lacklustre. Both the budget deficit and unemployment rose. Kreisky's popularity diminished. In the general election of April 1983, the Social Democrats lost their absolute majority in parliament and were forced into a return to coalition government. Kreisky, however, was unwilling to preside over a coalition, and, abandoning the Chancellorship, he retired, profoundly unhappy over the turn of events, to his villa in Majorca.

It has to remain an open question to what extent the destruction of Androsch's political career contributed to Kreisky's own demise. But there is no doubt at all that the long-drawn-out confrontation between Kreisky and Androsch occupied an inordinate number of column inches in the Austrian media. It was one of the longest-running sagas of Austrian political life since 1945. Abroad, its complex nature defied detailed explanation. The Soviet Union and its Communist bloc allies showed little interest or concern. They knew Kreisky more intimately than Androsch, and were conditioned by doctrine and experience to assume that the man in charge of a government is more powerful than his subordinates.

Western governments only followed the convolutions of the Kreisky-Androsch saga at the periphery. They saw no serious danger for Austria's remarkable stability, and treated it more as a soap opera drama than as a quarrel with ramifications beyond Austria's domestic political life. Only Germany and Switzerland, with their particularly close links to the Austrian economy, took a close interest.

When the Androsch resignation finally came, *The Economist* described the feud with Kreisky as 'Austria's longest political thriller'.[10] The *Financial Times* had an apt account of the contradictions, inherent in Austria, that had led to the impasse between Androsch and Kreisky: 'The much admired Austrian system of political and social consensus is undergoing its severest test yet. The economic outlook is cloudy. But far more important, the exit of Dr Hannes Androsch, Minister of Finance, Vice-Chancellor and once the chosen successor of Dr Bruno Kreisky has encouraged widespread cynicism about how the country is run.

'Dr Androsch this month resigned and retired from politics, having become the target of a fusillade of unsubstantiated allegations. They go back to 1978, when it became public knowledge that the Finance Minister at the same time was part owner of a very successful accountancy firm. In a country where backstairs influence and tax evasion are commonplace, that may have been accepted as tolerable; though neither Dr Kreisky nor the main opposition party thought so…'[11]

In Bonn, there was considerable concern that Austria, under new economic management might be less inclined to work closely with Germany. Chancellor Schmidt, unwilling at the time to comment publicly, let it be known that Androsch's departure was a 'personal disappointment' to him. Schmidt had admired his pragmatism and competence. But he 'realised that the collaboration between Kreisky and Androsch had become impossible'.[12]

Kreisky no doubt convinced himself that he was on strong ethical grounds in driving Androsch out of government. But in terms of maintaining popular support for his Social Democrat government, it was an unwise move. 'The Chancellor had failed to appreciate how widely Androsch's views on the precarious stability of the ever-expanding welfare state were shared by a substantial group of party functionaries and by the very voters whom Kreisky hoped to draw into the Social Democratic Party,' concludes the historian Pierre Secher in his political biography of Kreisky. As a result 'the Social Democratic Party was no longer able to mobilise its traditional voter potential in the 1983 election and lost its absolute majority in Parliament for the first time since 1971'.[13] Kreisky was propelled into involuntary retirement.

Whether they agreed or disagreed with the contention that Androsch's links with Consultatio overstepped the mark of the politically acceptable, many commentators felt uneasy about the venom that Kreisky unleashed against him, even from retirement in Majorca. In two high-profile interviews, Kreisky heaped invective on him and thundered away that the confrontation with Androsch was the cause of his deteriorating health. Androsch fired back that he would not comment on a statement that spoke for itself.

'The remarks of the two leading Socialist politicians are a reflection of the personal hatred that has divided Kreisky and Androsch for many years. Kreisky is clearly worried that the Social Democratic Party might want Androsch's return to a key position – at some distant point. Kreisky wants to prevent a return under all circumstances of "the all-out capitalist", who would be "damaging" to the Socialist party'.[14] Most objectively-minded observers felt that Kreisky was damaging his own and his country's reputation by perpetuating his feud with Androsch. But this did not prevent a certain ambivalence from emerging, and there was widespread agreement that Austria's public life should be cleaned up. Until then all attempts to end privileges and double incomes in Austria had failed because of lack of political incentive within Austria's elites. The Androsch controversy triggered many calls for clear blue water to be put between private business and political office. The impact of such calls was limited and diffuse. Demands to end questionable practices in high places continues to this day. In particular, the far right Freedom Party has made the issue its own, and has undoubtedly gained votes with its campaign against privilege and corruption in public life.

There are many versions, and still more interpretations, of the Kreisky-Androsch conflict. Kreisky's death did not close the book on the controversy. It rumbles on more than two decades after Kreisky first embarked on the drive to discredit his Finance Minister. Androsch himself has prospered, his national standing largely restored. After seven years at the Creditanstalt he reinvented himself to become one of Austria's major industrialists and an influential figure in the international business community. Nationally his views again command considerable attention.

None of this stopped Androsch from continuing to battle his way through the courts to clear his name from Kreisky's allegations against him. Moving from one appeal court to the next, no final verdict had been obtained by the start of the new century. However, quite regardless of the legal outcome, there would always be voices in Austria claiming that Androsch betrayed his office and popular trust, and that he acted improperly with respect to his private interests while he was Finance Minister.

But his Austrian critics should not have been surprised that, seen from abroad, there were many observers of the Austrian scene who remained convinced that Androsch was the best Chancellor that Austria never had.

NOTES ON CHAPTER IX

1. Senior trade union source, interview with author, November 1978.
2. *International Herald Tribune*, 26 March 1980.
3. *The Economist*, 11 December 1998.
4. *Financial Times*, 15 April 1982.
5. *Arbeiterzeitung*, 19 March 1979.
6. Bruno Kreisky, *Im Strom der Politik*, Siedelr, Kremayr & Scheriau, 1988, p 173.
7. Interview with Helmut Schmidt, Hamburg, 5 October 1998.
8. Peter Weiser, 'Kreisky and Androsch', confidential memo.
9. Interview with Hannes Androsch, Vienna, 16 December 1998.
10. *The Economist*, 24 April 1981.
11. W.L. Lütkens in *Financial Times*, 1 Januray 1981.
12. *Frankfurter Allgemeine*, 14 December 1980.
13. H. Pierre Secher, *Bruno Kreisky, Chancellor of Austria: A Political Biography*, Dorrance, 1993, p 140.
14. Hanni Konitzer in *Frankfurter Allgemeine*, 24 August 1983.

— X —

Austria in the Dock

The Waldheim Saga

The Kreisky era had just about run its course. By the beginning of 1983, it had lost much of its high gloss. Kreisky, seventy-two years old, was seriously ill; increasingly his obstinacy clouded his judgement. The economy was suffering from deficit budgeting; the Chancellor's international stature was waning.

But none of this prevented Austria from retaining a place of privilege as a secure democracy safely delivered from the throes of the Cold War. Shortly before the 1983 general election, a *Financial Times* survey of Austria had no hesitation in asserting that no-one in Austria 'has any fears about the durability of social consensus, labour peace and political stability... The fact alone that after 13 years of Socialist rule Austria's political and social structure is more stable than ever, that regardless of the outcome of the elections Austria is bound to remain an island of sanity and prosperity, precariously poised on the dividing line between the democratic West and Communist East, is perhaps the greatest tribute both to the Kreisky era and to the underlying strength of the entire political system.'[1]

But the same *Financial Times* survey also warned prophetically that Austria's structure was a house of cards: Austrians knew how to hold it together, but if outsiders were allowed to apply pressure at the wrong points and the whole edifice might collapse. This very apt perception was to be tested sooner than anyone imagined.

Only three years later, in 1986, the Waldheim nightmare began. During the six years of his presidency, Austria's international reputation and moral credit-rating plummetted, and the compromises on which Austria's post-war identity was constructed became unsustainable. With rare exceptions, the international community treated Waldheim as a pariah; and Austria, the country that had defiantly elected and continued to support the man with a tainted past, was made to suffer from guilt by association. The world which had warmed to the Austria of Mozart, *The Sound of Music* and the Sachertorte, and had admired the achievements of the Kreisky era, all of a sudden perceived the small central European country in a much harsher light. Nazi stereotypes were revived. Austria came to be viewed less as a victim of Nazi Germany, and more as a nation in league with Hitler, a common enemy during the war. 'The Waldheim scandal exposed an unpleasant side of the country; its antisemitic undertones and a tendency to indulge in collective amnesia,' wrote the *Times* correspondent in Vienna. 'It resulted not in a more exacting examination of the past, but in its citizens closing ranks resentfully against the rest of the world. The Third Reich continues to sit like an undigested lump in the body politic.'[2]

Before Austria could recover its good name, Austrians would be forced to engage themselves in all those uncomfortable home truths that Kreisky had knowingly avoided: they had to discard self-deception, purge themselves of the lies on which so much of Austria's national consensus had been built, and acknowledge the true extent of their collaboration with the Nazis. The widely-acclaimed Kreisky era had delayed the day of reckoning. Austria had to absorb the lessons of the Waldheim era and finally accept that the long sleep was over, if it wanted to be in the mainstream of post-Communist Europe. It could not continue to suppress the realities of the Nazi era.

Even in the waning days of his rule, 'Kaiser' Bruno refused to consider that he had made mistakes, whether related to economic policy, Middle East affairs or to the country's skeletons. The nearest he could come to self-criticism during his last election campaign was to acknowledge in his private moments that he was running out of steam. He had wagered everything on securing one more absolute majority for his Social Democratic Party; otherwise he would retire, he had warned the country.

But as he campaigned tirelessly around the country, the realisation grew that he had over-reached himself. 'His sharply tuned political instinct had told him that the general election could bring about a brutal end to a political career that had spanned 30 years in political office and secured his place in post-war history as one of its leading, even if controversial statesmen,' I wrote in the *Guardian* after travelling with Kreisky during the concluding stages of the campaign.

He fought 'like a wounded elephant'. His election speeches were always fine-tuned to respond to changing audiences. Naturally his emphasis was on economic achievement. The gist of his theme was that Austria had become a green and pleasant land which had gained international standing and scarcely knew the winds of recession. I quoted from one of Kreisky's campaign speeches: 'With my hand on my heart, I ask you whether so many people in this country have ever had it so good?' As the crowd roared approval, he turned to me: 'Can you name me one other country in the world where a politician could make such an assertion today and still be acclaimed by his audience?'[3] I could have referred him to similar pronouncements by Harold MacMillan, but refrained from reminding him how rapidly popular politicians are apt to fall from grace in an age of fast-changing loyalties.

— * —

Kreisky's wager with the electorate misfired. The Social Democrats emerged four seats short of an absolute majority – though it remained the largest party. Inevitably, this meant a return to coalition government – and Kreisky's withdrawal from active political life.

The new Chancellor was Fred Sinowatz, a Social Democrat leader virtually unknown outside Austria's borders. Instead of turning to the old format of a grand coalition with the other major party, the People's Party, the Social Democrats opted for the formula that had attracted Kreisky at the outset of his reign: coalition with the small right-wing Freedom Party. Its leader then was Norbert Steger, an anodyne figure who attracted little attention abroad. The Social Democrat coalition with the Freedom Party in 1983 caused none of the outcry that Jörg Haider's Freedom Party triggered after its inclusion in government in January 2000.

Kreisky's retirement triggered widespread regret abroad. Typical was the reaction of Canadian Prime Minister Pierre Trudeau, who wrote to Kreisky saying how much he had admired his economic policies and the stamp that he had put on international affairs. He singled out Kreisky's 'support for the United Nations, which had fully justified the decision to designate Vienna as a European centre for the international body'. Trudeau also emphasised Kreisky's endeavours for a Middle East settlement, 'which have become a central factor in the Middle East peace process. Moreover your persistence and energy have advanced the North-South dialogue.'[4] 'All who are committed to world peace and better understanding between nations stand in Bruno Kreisky's debt,' said a prominent British Labour Party member of parliament, Giles Radice. 'Under Bruno Kreisky, socialist Austria has become a model for successful and progressive economic and social development.'[5]

In a fulsome tribute, the *New York Times* said that Bruno Kreisky had succeeded in raising Austria's profile beyond the conventional image of a small country content with chamber music and replete with men in Lederhosen. Alone among the countries once under Habsburg rule, Austria had become an independent democracy. Under Kreisky, Austria had undergone a rebirth as a country freed from Great Power rivalries, and as a haven for refugees from communist countries. Perhpas the newly unemployed Kreisky should be invited to advise on solutions to the conflict in Afghanistan?

The head of Austria's Cultural Institute in New York, Peter Marboe, was less sanguine about the impact that Kreisky had made on public opinion in the US. In his assessment of the Kreisky era he wrote that Austria's image in America had suffered from the perception that the Jewish Chancellor had connived in promoting antisemitism in Austria. Some American Jews demonised Kreisky. The country remained ill-understood; perceptions of Austria were not clearly differentiated from Germany's; its relationship to the West was unclear to Americans, and the shadow of its past loomed large in the American mind. According to Marboe, Austria had acquired a seriously distorted image in the US. Before and after, some Americans saw Austria simply in terms of Mozart, the Vienna Boys' Choir, Lipizzaner horses; others thought that Austria was behind the iron curtain; confusion between Austria and Australia remained suitable material for stale jokes; and 'in those areas of the US where there are large concentrations of Jews, Austria is so closely associated with the Nazi past that any attempt to discuss contemporary Austria becomes wholly futile'.[6]

In the UK, where the Jewish lobby is less prominent, views about Kreisky were far less influenced by his difficult relationship with world Jewry and with Israel. 'Bruno Kreisky has been a good neutral... His departure is a sad event,' *The Economist* pronounced. 'The Swiss and the Swedes are professional neutrals. But the unsung Austrians have performed at least as worthily. It was they who took in the refugees from Russian attack in Hungary in 1956, from the Russian attack on Czechoslovakia in 1968, from the Russian threat to Poland in 1981/82 and from endemic Russian antisemitism throughout these years. It was a brave stand from a country that is so exposed, and that said goodbye to the Russian armies only in 1955. As Chancellor since 1970, Mr Kreisky tried to act publicly and privately as an honest broker between those rare Palestinians and Israelis who are prepared to accept that the other side has a genuine case... Mr Kreisky's successor will have to manage a country where for the first time in years the consensus between capital and labour of which the Austrians are inordinately proud and careful... may be under threat.'[7]

The *Guardian* also had mixed praise for Kreisky with uncertainty about the future. 'Austria under Kreisky has been remarkably active and even controversial in foreign policy while remaining committed to the western democratic concept. Thus Austria's Jewish Chancellor was the first western leader to recognise the PLO, and has consistently shown exceptional tolerance towards Poland under military rule and Colonel Gadhafi's Libya. All this has been a remarkable display of domestic confidence and international independence by a small country sandwiched between NATO and the Warsaw pact. Bruno Kreisky can be said to have surpassed even Konrad Adenauer in the rehabilitation of his country.'

But there was a twist in the tail. The national consensus built up by Kreisky had relied on the compliance of a 'small band of fellow-septuagenarians... The greatest contribution open to him is to ensure a smooth handover to a new generation.'[8]

— * —

Was Sinowatz, Kreisky's political heir, the right person to handle the controversial legacy? When the new Austrian Chancellor formed his government in May 1983, he was tolerably well known in Austria itself, but was an unknown quantity for the outside world. Though younger than Kreisky, Sinowatz, aged fifty-four, could hardly be said to have represented generational change. He was shrewd, and in a lifetime of Austrian politics he had acquired the reputation of a moderator and conciliator. But nobody knew whether he had the personality and the judgement to be able to act decisively and address the problems left behind by Kreisky.

One of Sinowatz's first decisions was to fall in with his predecessor's preference for a 'small' coalition with the Freedom Party rather than to attempt a grand coalition with the People's Party. This turned out to be an unhappy decision when, less than two years into the government's life, the Freedom Party Defence Minister Friedhelm Frischenschläger shook the hand of a convicted war criminal on his repatriation from gaol in Italy. This action brought opprobrium on Austria from abroad, caused deep misgivings at home, and very nearly brought down the Sinowatz government.

Sinowatz was less patrician than Kreisky, and more inclined to adopt a collegial approach to decision-making. He won the respect of those who worked with him, but suffered from a lack of charisma, and unlike Kreisky did not know how to make himself loved by the electorate. His bravest and most principled act – though his compatriots did not necessarily all see it that way – was to resign after Kurt Waldheim won the presidential election in 1986. His most sensible, and probably most perceptive, move was to accept the need for generational change and promote Franz Vranitzky, so that he became his natural successor as Chancellor.

When Sinowatz formed the Social Democrat-Freedom Party coalition, the English-speaking world expressed little concern about this unnatural alliance between Social Democrats and a right-wing party. It was as if the change of leadership in the Freedom Party – the controversial Friedrich

Peter, focus of so much opprobrium in 1975, had withdrawn in favour of the colourless Steger – had brought respectability and liberation from Nazi connotations.

In Germany, where these matters were followed more closely, there was considerable surprise that Sinowatz, yielding to Kreisky's last-gasp machinations, had opted for the small coalition formula. There was no need to be a prophet to forecast a difficult time for the new government. It was an uncertain political experiment, greatly disliked by the left wing of the Social Democratic Party. Possibly the only factor in favour of the small coalition was that a grand coalition would have made greater inroads on Social Democratic freedom of action within the government. With its large number of parliamentary seats, the People's Party could have demanded more significant policy concessions than the much smaller Freedom Party could wrest from the Chancellor.

Sinowatz had been a competent Minister of Education under Kreisky. He had faithfully carried out 'Emperor' Kreisky's injunction to create a well-educated, highly motivated society. He had been made Vice-Chancellor after Hannes Androsch had been propelled into resignation. Sinowatz was short, portly, soft-spoken, and a freemason. He would never have been described as handsome. However, he was known for his Jewish sympathies, and had even been awarded a decoration by Vienna's Jewish community.

Within Austria every move of the new government was scrutinised minutely, and endlessly debated. There was continuous speculation that Kreisky was still pulling strings behind the scenes. But the outside world showed little interest. Sinowatz did not have Kreisky's foreign policy ambitions; he had no desire to strut the international stage, and the outside world did not encourage the unknown new quantity in Vienna to assert himself.

It was a time of intense East-West manoeuvering. In Western Europe there was the divisive debate about the deployment of medium-range nuclear missiles. In Germany, the Social Democratic government collapsed, and Helmut Kohl was embarking on his long stint as Germany's Chancellor. Leonid Brezhnev had died in 1982, and his successor, Yuri Andropov, was floating proposals to halt the arms race which caused more alarm than interest in Ronald Reagan's Washington. 1983, the year of Kreisky's retirement, was also the year of Reagan's 'Evil Empire' speech and his controversial 'Star Wars' proposal.

Margaret Thatcher dominated the British political scene. Social democracy in Europe had become unfashionable; the Socialist International was virtually moribund. In the larger picture, Austria was an insignificant minnow.

— * —

Unlike Kreisky, Sinowatz made no attempt to impose his views or build alliances with world leaders. For close to two years, Austria was out of the world's headlines.

Then, on a cold January day in 1985, there was a rendezvous at an airfield near Graz between former SS Major Walter Reder and Defence Minister Frischenschläger. The meeting was intended to take place in strict secrecy. Reder was a convicted war criminal who had been given a life sentence by the Italian courts for his role in the mass killing of Italian civilians in 1944. Italy had now agreed to commute his sentence, and he was being repatriated. Frischenschläger, the son of a Nazi Party member, was counted among the more liberal, less nationalistic, members of the Freedom Party. When Reder emerged from his plane, the two men briefly shook hands.

If that handshake had done no more than harm Frischenschläger's reputation it would soon have been forgotten. But it turned out to have far greater repercussions. The handshake convulsed international opinion, as hard evidence that Austria remained unreconstructed in its attitude towards the Nazis. With the wisdom of hindsight, it is obvious that the Frischenschläger-Reder handshake was the prelude to, and the trigger for, Austria's fall from grace during the Waldheim era. It also precipitated Haider's rise to the leadership of the Freedom Party, and with it the gnawing concern that neo-Naziism was alive and well in Austria.

From the outset, Haider was described by the Western media as a rabble-rouser who belonged to the extremist right-wing faction of the Freedom Party. With him in charge, it was hard to see how the Freedom Party could adjust its positions to operate within Austria's deeply rooted concensual system.

As luck would have it, the Frischenschläger-Reder handshake coincided with the first ever meeting of the World Jewish Congress (WJC) in Vienna. The gathering had been intended as a signal of recognition that Austria's relations with its Jewish community were improving. A number of foreign correspondents not normally in Vienna were covering the Congress, and saw at first hand the anger that greeted news of the Reder-Frischenschläger meeting. The President of the WJC, Edgar Bronfman, expressed acute shock. The writer Elie Wiesel challenged Sinowatz to admit that an ethical error of considerable proportions had been made. The Mayor of New York, Ed Koch, angrily blamed the absent Kreisky for perpetuating and encouraging a political climate in Austria which had led to Reder's rehabilitation. One speaker after another castigated the Austrian cabinet.

Sinowatz rushed in to apologise, and admitted that a distressing mistake had been made. Frischenschläger also made a public apology, although he told his intimates that he felt he had done no wrong. Many years later, reflecting on the handshake incident, he still refused to concede that he had been at fault. He continued to see Reger not as a convicted war criminal but as a returning prisoner of war. He recalled that the airfield meeting had come about because the Social Democrat Foreign Minister, Leopold Gratz, had asked him as Minister of Defence to make the arrangements for receiving Reder on his return from imprisonment in Italy. Frischenschläger admits that it may have been a misjudgement to meet Reder in person. However, he never felt any guilt for his gesture. 'It was a humanitarian action. Moreover, I felt that I was closing a chapter of our history. I never thought that I had committed a moral error.'[9]

Frischenschläger also insisted that Austria's political and religious leaders, including Kreisky and even Cardinal König, had long lobbied the Italian government for Reder's release. The former Chancellor had told Frischenschläger that Reder was a sick man, and that he had feared if Reder died in prison he would become a martyr to Austria's neo-Nazis.

The vociferous critics who were appalled by the handshake had rather different concerns. For the first time since Kreisky's resignation, Austria was again big in the news abroad. Under the heading 'Turning a blind eye to the traumas of the past', the *Times* correspondent in Vienna wrote that 'the furore in Austria over the action of Dr Friedhelm Frischenschläger, the Defence Minister, in greeting the returning war criminal, Walter Reder, has not only damaged the coalition government's credibility but has also emphasised Austrians' ambivalent attitude towards the past... Unlike the West Germans whose national conscience bears all the scars of guilt inflicted by the crimes of an Austrian, Adolf Hitler, Austrians themselves rarely manifest regret or even responsibility for the role they played in the "thousand year" Reich.'[10]

Most of the critical comment abroad recognised that Austrian society should not be treated as a monolith – that there were good as well as bad people with an exemplary record as well as those who had embraced Nazisim with enthusiasm. But what disturbed public opinion abroad was that both those who were critical of the handshake and those who endorsed it or saw no harm in it were nevertheless united in opting for national amnesia instead of a candid examination of the past.

In an editorial comment – only the second on Austria since the State Treaty – *The Times* underlined that 'Austria has an ambivalent relationship with the Nazi past. Officially it has always been regarded as "the first country to fall victim to Nazi aggression", and of course it is true that many Austrians resisted heroically the Anschluss and the ensuing Nazi rule. But many welcomed it and fought willingly as Germans in the Wehrmacht during World War Two... By and large the world accepts that the Austria of today represent the former rather than the latter and the willingness of the World Jewish Congress to meet in Vienna is evidence of that. But the presence of someone like Herr Frischenschläger in the government inevitably casts doubt on that assumption, and is bound to put a strain on relations between Austria and those who like to be her friends.'[11]

There was a prevailing view abroad that Austria had not dealt adequately with its past. This impression was further reinforced by an account of the fate of paintings once owned by Austrian Jews published in the highly respected US magazine *Art News*. The magazine article had unearthed explosive information that Jewish-owned works of art sequestered by the Nazis, instead of being returned to their owners, had been kept by the Austrian authorities, hidden away in Mauerbach, a monastery near Vienna.[12] These disclosures, together with the Reder-Frischenschläger incident led some commentators to ask whether Austria's 'socialist-liberal' government was being transformed into a 'neo-national socialist' government. In Strasbourg, the Council of Europe even made a formal protest to the Austrian government and called for Frischenschläger's resignation.

The *New York Times* pointed to Austria's 'half-buried Nazi past', and its special correspondent in Vienna wrote, 'for decades, Austria has lived with a half-truth that has enabled it to skirt the part it played in the crimes of the Nazis'. The controversy surrounding the seemingly isolated handshake episode had 'rippled outwards into the country's political establishment, revealing widespread and compromising links to the Nazi past'.[13] The controversy was compounded by the fact that Haider, in 1985 the Freedom Party's leader in Carinthia, had said that his colleague Frischenschläger's apology had been unnecessary because Reder was not a war criminal but 'a soldier who had done his duty for the Fatherland'.

When I interviewed Sinowatz a month after the handshake, he strongly rejected allegations that the incident was characteristic of widespread pro-Nazi sentiments in Austria. 'He is obviously profoundly concerned by the widespread adverse comments in some Western countries where the Ministerial welcome for an old Nazi has severely dented Austria's image as a post-war miracle of economic and political probity,' I wrote. 'In no way can a misjudgement by a junior Minister be interpreted as a signal of official rehabilitation for Nazis in Austria, Sinowatz argued… He acknowledges of course that the country has a hard core of rightwing extremists… They have a nuisance value; but they do not possess the power of moral influence over the country's life.'

Sinowatz secured a vote of confidence for his government, and felt no compelling reason to part company with the Freedom Party, and force a break-up of the coalition. He would have been obliged to call an election under circumstances that would undoubtedly have polarised Austrian politics to a dangerous degree. But even without a bruising election campaign, the handshake's repercussions affected Austria's comfortable existence. Austria, I wrote, 'had looked forward to 1985 to celebrate 40 years of unblemished democracy. It had also hoped to bask in international approval when it marks, May 15, the 30th anniversary of its State Treaty. Instead the country is now looking unhappily inward, asking itself whether its nasty past is catching up with its pleasant present.'[14]

— * —

The thirtieth anniversary of the State Treaty in 1985 was indeed a low-intensity event compared to the festivities of five years earlier. But the Foreign Ministers of the four wartime allies turned up again, with Andrei Gromyko the only one of the original signatories. This time, however, he no longer came as Krushchev's representative but as the representative of the newly installed, and still little understood, Soviet leader, Mikhail Gorbachev.

The West was curious, expectant. Would Gromyko in Vienna lift the veil on the new regime? Gromyko, very likely out of sympathy with Gorbachev and soon to be replaced by Edouard Shevardnadze, gave little away. But at least Sinowatz had the satisfaction of observing that Vienna was once again being used as a high-level international meeting ground, and that the country's visitors were paying only minimal attention to his crisis-prone coalition.

Matters were rather different a few weeks later when it was discovered that, in an attempt to up-grade the Burgenland's sweet wines, lethal anti-freeze had been added. The amounts involved were not very substantial, but Austria's good name in the wine trade was destroyed, and its uncontaminated wines became as unsaleable as the dangerous ones. The US banned imported Austrian wine for a time, and Austria postponed plans for a major wine promotion campaign in the US. In Japan the panic led to a sharp drop not only in sales of Austrian wines, but also led to a boycott of Australian ones! Australia's Ambassador in Tokyo even felt compelled to issue certificates promising that 'Japanese consumers of Australian wines can be sure that they are tasting Australian sunshine'. Pronunciation problems and media errors had caused confusion among Japanese wine buyers, the Embassy explained.

Taken on its own, the wine scandal would have hurt Austria's commercial interests, but in all probability would soon have been dismissed as a foolish transgression by a minor wine growing country. But being Austria, and with the Frischenschläger handshake still raw in the memory, the wine tampering became a parable for deviousness. It was portrayed as characteristic of Austrian efforts to hide its weaknesses and to present itself to the world as more honourable than its blemished past justified.

— * —

Yet all this was only the prelude to what came next: Kurt Waldheim's decision to run in the 1986 Austrian presidential election. It started quietly enough as a party political quandary in Austria.

Though Waldheim had failed in his presidential bid in 1971, he had never abandoned the ambition to become Austria's head of state. Since the end of his second term as UN Secretary-General, he had been scheming a re-entry into presidential politics.

In 1985, a year ahead of the next presidential election, Waldheim asked Sinowatz whether the Social Democrats could be persuaded to back his candidacy jointly with the People's Party. Kreisky, who had encouraged Waldheim to nurture an elder statesman's role, hinted from his retirement home in Majorca that the proposition for a joint candidacy deserved consideration. But Chancellor Sinowatz was non-committal, and before it was taken any further the People's Party formally announced that Waldheim was to be its candidate. The Social Democrats responded by naming their own candidate, Kurt Steyrer, a worthy politician who had never succeeded in impinging, even remotely, on the awareness of the outside world. It was assumed on all sides that by naming the candidates so far ahead of the election date boredom would be the most worrying factor in what was expected to be a low-key campaign.

Little attention was paid to an Austrian Radio (ORF) profile of Waldheim in June 1985 in which it was asserted that during the war he had served in a unit – the Heeresgruppe Mitte – which also included some SS groups. Questioned about this in the *Kurier*, Waldheim said he 'had not seen a single SS person during the whole war'.[15] That was patently untrue. Yet it was all of a pattern with the line he had taken earlier, in 1981, when the *New York Times* was preparing a major profile to coincide with his attempt to secure a third term as UN Secretary-General. 'Fortunately I didn't last long in the army,' he had told his interviewer, Jane Rosen. 'I was badly wounded in the ankle, I couldn't walk and they gave me a medical discharge'. Any suggestion that he supported the Nazis was 'nonsense; I was against the Nazis'. Israel's Ambassador, Yehuda Blum, asked to comment, supported Waldheim's denials: 'We don't believe Waldheim ever supported the Nazis and we never said he did. We have many differences with him [over Middle East policy] but that isn't one of them.'[16] Three years later, the *New York Times* and Israel were to tell a rather different tale – and so were opinion-formers around the world.

During the winter of 1985, Waldheim's campaign for the presidency was surging ahead of his Social Democratic rival. He was trying to rally support by staking claims to world stature. Everywhere there were posters exhorting voters to rally to 'Kurt Waldheim, the Austrian the world trusts'. The Social Democrat leadership was badly rattled. It calculated that Waldheim was well on the way to victory, and had to find new ways of thwarting his advance.

Around the turn of the year, rumours intensified that Waldheim's army record was rather less pure than he had represented it throughout his political career, and that there were some nasty Nazi skeletons in his past. The German magazine *Stern* reported that he had been a member of the Nazi Student League; some former army officers alleged that Waldheim had links to the notorious General Walter Löhr, who had been responsible for the deportation and death of tens of thousands of Jews in Yugoslavia. An article in the Austrian weekly, *Profil*, alleged that Waldheim had been under Löhr's command in Yugoslavia and had been on his staff during a series of massacres. Hearing these rumours, the WJC began to dig into Waldheim's past, primarily by exploring sources available in the US, but also by sending one of its senior aides, Eli Rosenbaum, to Vienna to investigate.

The storm broke in March. The WJC had unearthed documents confirming Waldheim's former membership of both the Nazi Youth League and also of a 'brown shirt' (SA) riding club. Within a day of each other *Profil* and the *New York Times* published articles exposing Waldheim as a liar and worse. 'Files show Waldheim was a war criminal,'[17] the paper blazoned across its front page. 'Ex-UN chief accused by the Jews', *The Times* headlined, while adding Waldheim's resolute denial that the allegations against him were true: 'I was never in a unit which had anything to do with the SS'.[18] 'Missing years in former UN Chief's Military Past,' the *Guardian* headed a massive feature detailing the massacres and deportations in Yugoslavia for which Waldheim's army unit had been responsible. 'Although Dr Waldheim has maintained his innocence, the documents [published by the World Jewish Congress] have aroused dismay and bewilderment at the UN. Secretariat officials and diplomats are asking why the accusations were not made known long ago.'[19]

That was just the beginning. For the remainder of Waldheim's election campaign, the WJC kept up an almost daily fusillade against him, and secured a wide hearing for its findings both in America's political community and in the media world village. For a while the WJC held back from accusing Waldheim of war crimes, but it released documents showing the Yugoslav authorities had sought Waldheim for murder, and that he had been on a list of suspected war criminals.

The WJC labelled Waldheim 'a Nazi, a liar who has deceived the world for forty years'. A cartoon in the *Chicago Tribune*, captioned 'Nazi victim... lost his memory', depicted four figures: a man who had lost his home, a woman who had lost her husband, a second man who had lost his property, and finally Waldheim, who had 'lost his memory', and was reading a memorandum entitled 'my role'.[20] 'Dr Waldheim, for his own sake, and for that of his country, should withdraw his candidacy,' the *Guardian* advised.[21] He refused to listen to such entreaties.

The WJC's activism triggered an investigation by the US Department of Justice's Office of Special Investigations (OSI) to determine whether Waldheim should be put on the US Watch-list, a move that would ban him from entering the US. The Los Angeles-based Wiesenthal Center launched a postcard campaign in support of such a ban. In the US Congress there were hearings to gather evidence about Waldheim, and the Senate passed a resolution endorsing the Watch-list investigation. The OSI recommendation to impose the visa ban was leaked to the US media on the eve of the first round of Austria's presidential election in May 1986. Waldheim exploited the threat of a visa ban to hammer home his refusal to be intimidated by outside interference.

Reactions in Austria were belligerent. The country was plastered with posters screaming, 'We Austrians will vote for the person of our choice', later backed with the slogan 'And now all the more so' (meaning support for Waldheim).

The first round of the election did not give Waldheim an absolute majority. But in the second, and final, round of the election Waldheim won with 53.87 per cent of the vote.

— * —

Immediately after Waldheim's election as head of state, Sinowatz resigned. He had been widely blamed for the leaks about Waldheim's past which triggered the WJC campaign. Now that Waldheim was President, Sinowatz felt his own position had become untenable. But at least he was able to engineer it that his candidate for the chancellorship, Vranitzky, won Social Democratic approval to succeed him.

There was no let-up in the WJC campaign against Waldheim after the election, and little discernible softening by the US administration in its attitude towards him. Reluctant Western capitals only sent perfunctory telegrams of congratulations to the new head of state; the US Ambassador in Vienna, Ronald Lauder, failed to attend Waldheim's inauguration, citing 'family reasons'. Israel not only boycotted the ceremony, but arranged for extracts of the French film about the Holocaust, *Shoah*, to be shown in the Israeli parliament, the Knesset, on the day of the inauguration.

Moscow had sprung to Waldheim's defence during the election campaign, and had claimed that he was being victimised by opponents of the UN, although the Soviet Union never endorsed him to the extent of inviting him to Moscow.

As President, Waldheim was treated as an international pariah, shunned virtually everywhere except in the Arab world and by the Vatican. He exchanged visits with King Hussain of Jordan, and was lavishly praised by Colonel Gadhafi, who proclaimed that he had struck a blow against Zionism. At one point, when Turkey signalled its intention to invite Waldheim to visit, the US threatened Ankara with an end to aid. Ankara readily understood, and abandonned the plan. International meetings in Vienna were reduced to a minimum as Western leaders became reluctant to make the obligatory protocol calls on Austria's head of state. Pope John Paul II's decision to receive Waldheim in June 1987 was heavily criticised in the US, where this gesture, like the 1994 decision to give him a papal knighthood, was interpreted as renewed evidence of the Vatican's ambiguous attitude towards the Jews and the Holocaust. When Czech President Vaclav Havel attended the Salzburg Festival in his official capacity he was accused of throwing principles to the wind.

Refusing to heed the Austrian government's entreaties, the US put Waldheim on its Watch-list in 1987 and banned him from entering the US. Secretary of State George Schultz, urged by some of his own advisors to delay the visa ban on foreign policy grounds, had refused to make any exceptions. 'It's long overdue,' he said. To keep Waldheim off the Watch-list 'would be a travesty'.[22]

The WJC was in possession of the damning OSI file on Waldheim as soon as it was completed in 1987, even though its publication was not authorised until 1994. The WJC used the data it contained to level its accusations of war crimes.

In an attempt to clear Waldheim's name, the Austrian government appointed an independent international Historians' Commission. Their terms of reference were limited to Waldheim's personal history, and they were not concerned with the wider issues of Austrian behaviour under the Nazis. Their report, published in 1988, was inconclusive. Though the Commission stopped short of war crimes charges against Waldheim, it agreed that he had certainly been 'exceptionally well-informed', and had known far more about the atrocities committed in the Balkans than he had brought himself to admit. He 'had been involved in the process of knowledge and action', and had 'tried to let his military past pass into oblivion, and as soon as that was no longer possible, to make it less harmful'. He was 'undoubtedly far more than a junior level desk officer', and his work in collating intelligence information made him 'excellently informed about what was transpiring in the war... Even if Waldheim was absent during certain periods from Salonika, he must undoubtedly have noticed that a fourth of this city's population [its Jews]... had suddenly disappeared.'[23] Clearly Waldheim's amnesia went beyond conventional bounds of credibility. 'In bringing to light the incredible capacity for repression and forgetfulness of a man who, in the manner of Dr Faustus, imagined that he could permit himself two lives entirely independent of each other, the historians leave Austria morally and psychologically in ruins,' the French newspaper *le Monde* commented.

Even though they abstained from designating Waldheim a war criminal, the findings of the Historians Commission did not persuade the US authorities to remove his name from the US Watch-list, or to lift the visa ban. Even three years after his retirement as head of state, Waldheim was refused a visa to join Javier Pérez de Cuéllar, the other living former UN Secretary-General, for the festivities held to mark the organisation's fiftieth anniversary in 1995. The Watch-list distinguishes between the private person and his public office: Waldheim was banned from the US as a private individual and not as an Austrian office holder.

From the outset of the anti-Waldheim campaign, it was inevitable that the case against him would develop into a case against Austria. 'His lie is only a symbol of Austria's lie,' Bronfman asserted. 'The issue is not Kurt Waldheim. He is a mirror of Austria. His lies are of secondary importance. The real issue is that Austria has lied for decades about its own involvement in the atrocities Mr Waldheim was involved in – deportations, reprisal murders and others too painful to think about.'[24] The WJC had justified its intervention against Waldheim from the beginning as a mission to force Austria to confront its past.

Simon Wiesenthal, whose own long-running efforts to prod the Austrian conscience had made little headway, was convinced that such outside pressure would be wholly counter-productive. He bristled against the WJC's intrusion into Austrian politics, and bitterly resented the Los Angeles-based Wiesenthal Center's anti-Waldheim postcard campaign. Wiesenthal's own office in Vienna had only loose links with Los Angeles, and he had not been consulted on the postcard campaign. He predicted, correctly, that anti-Waldheim actions orchestrated from abroad would achieve the very reverse of what was intended.

The WJC would not be swayed: 'My organisation is proud of its role in helping to make Austria – indeed the entire world – again face up to that nadir of man's inhumanity to man, the Nazi era,' WJC President Edgar Bronfman wrote in the *New York Times*.[25] Both men were right: Wiesenthal's fears were realised. The 'liar' Waldheim was elected for a six-year term as Austria's President; the WJC did provoke antisemitism: the Freedom Party, shifting to a right-wing xenophobic platform after Haider replaced Norbert Steger, made important electoral gains.

But Bronfman's drive to make Austria adopt a more honest approach to its history also proved successful. Whatever one may think of the WJC's tactics or its strategy – and I certainly do not count myself among its admirers – there can be no doubt that the exposure of Waldheim's lies led directly to a crucial turning point in Austrian thinking. It propelled Vranitzky in 1991 to deliver his formal admission that many Austrians had backed Hitler's Third Reich and had been instrumental in its crimes.

— * —

When the Waldheim affair burst unexpectedly upon the world it became immediately clear that the man could not be divorced from his country. If he was in the dock, so also was Austria. Overnight, benign neglect of

Austrian affairs was transformed into the closest possible scrutiny of its record since 1945. Media interest rose dramatically. Until then, there had been no time when so much, and for such a long time, was written and broadcast abroad about Austrian politics, morals and the country's recent history.

Interest was particularly marked in the Anglo-Saxon world. Just as happened 14 years later, when Haider's Freedom Party entered government, Austria's image underwent radical change with the focus on its domestic politics, antisemitism and wartime role. Soon after Waldheim's past began to be exhumed the American and British media shifted from personal to collective criticism of a 'defiantly xenophobic' country. Waldheim's character was also Austria's character: expert in the art of forgetting, with a lack of moral fibre, opportunism, servility, a reluctance to undertake self-criticism. As UN Secretary-General, Kurt Waldheim had often been likened to an expert waiter – polite, affable, servile. This assessment was now being applied equally to Austria. Indeed the country acquired a new image, synonympus with Waldheim's. Even in the American hinterland there was widespread comment that the popular image of Austria deserved radical correction. The *Buffalo Times*, for example, said that 'the Austria revealed by the Waldheim controversy is not a place unburdened by history, moving happily through time to the graceful strains of the waltz. It is a land with a complex and unsettled legacy from World War II, a country ambivalent about a vast invaluable Jewish heritage. It is a remnant of a once powerful empire, unsure of its national identity and insecure when stripped of its carefully wrought facade.'[26] From the US capital, the *Washington Post* wrote that 'Austria's choice can only diminish its international reputation… Austria has many good friends in the United States. But President Waldheim will remain an unwelcome symbol of Austria's least attractive side: a refusal to look back at the recent past out of fear of the truths that may be found there.' These were among the kindlier perceptions.

More crudely, the picture of Austria shifted to project an image still frozen in a wartime frame: a country of unreconstructed Nazis and opportunists, more enthusiastic than the Germans about the ideas of their countryman, Hitler. Indeed the Germans tried to profit from this perception, and it became much in vogue in West Germany to point to Austria and draw comfort from the idea that Naziism had been an imported product.

Austrian diplomats fanned out to combat Austria's deteriorating image and growing international isolation. But most of this was futile as long as Waldheim remained in office. On one occasion, when the Austrian Ambassador in Washington was instructed yet again to protest against America's treatment of Austria, he happened to see a Waldheim caricature pinned up in the office of a senior State Department diplomat.

The drawing was similar to old FBI posters that had been posted up to hunt the robber barons of the wild west. Beneath the drawing, the caption read, 'Wanted: Kurt Waldheim'.

Governments and the media were not alone in revising their views of Austria. Prominent historians joined the fray with research to back the contention that Austria, and by no means only Waldheim, had engaged in historical revisionism. In America, Professor Robert Herzstein dug up a horrific picture of merciless Nazi behaviour in Yugoslavia during the time that Waldheim served with General Löhr's German Wehrmacht unit. Though he ultimately came to question whether there was enough evidence to accuse Waldheim of war crimes, his work illuminated the lies that Waldheim had spread. Austria itself does not emerge well from his research.

Another historian, Gordon Craig, wrote in the New York Review of Books that the 1943 Moscow Declaration had enabled Austrians to stand back and leave it to Germany alone to come to terms with the Nazi era. The disclosures surrounding Waldheim's past had put an end to Austrian escapism. The Waldheim affair was symbolic of Austrian collaboration with the Third Reich. Austrian reactions to the exposure of Kurt Waldheim's past had revealed xenophobia, antisemitism and defiance, and had demonstrated that Austrian society's biggest problem was its relationship with itself.

In the UK, Robert Knight argued that the Waldheim affair must not be interpreted merely as a one-off blemish on what could otherwise be considered a story of consistent Austrian post-war success. On the contrary, it was an integral part of Austria's recent history. Waldheim was only the most immediate manifestation of the self-deception in which Austria had luxuriated since 1945. After Waldheim it would no longer be possible for Austria to portray itself as a Nazi victim which had succumbed despite massive resistance to Hitler. 'Post-war Austrian governments argued that Germany was the fount of all evil and that the Austrians had been, as one British diplomat put it, "the proto-martyrs of Europe…" The real basis for Austria's post-war political settlement was a compromise between the Social Democrats and the People's Party which demanded a generous exercise of selective amnesia by both sides,' Knight wrote. This included turning a blind eye to most of Austria's Nazi Party members. 'Denazification which attempted to go beyond political or judicial procedures by undermining the economic and social bases of Naziism would have torn the new Austria apart.' Moreover, 'Austrian governments were consistently readier to compensate Nazis for losses incurred as a result of denazification than to provide compensation for their Jewish victims… This is a moral blot on Austria's record and is the price the country has paid for its undoubted economic and political success.'

Knight also argued that the role of the Austrian resistance had been greatly inflated, and that it never amounted to a 'movement'. He asked whether 'suppression of the truth and self-deception affect the viability of a political system?' Knight provided his own answer: 'On the whole, Austria's post-war history suggests that it does not'. Perhaps Kreisky had been right to argue that it would have been an unnecessary diversion to focus on the past when he wanted the country to concentrate on building solid foundations for the future. Gloomily, Knight remarked, 'If you run your shop efficiently and let sleeping Nazis lie, business may well prosper. It is a depressing conclusion.'[27]

Some of Austria's politicians were particularly riled by Knight's assertions. Peter Jankowitsch, Kreisky's former private secretary whose brief tenure in 1986 as Austrian Foreign Minister coincided with the international clamour against Waldheim, made an ill-conceived attempt to enlist prominent Austrian historians to take issue with and contradict Knight's assertions, and those of other Western academics whose findings served to reinforce Austria's deteriorating image abroad. His arguments were given short shrift by the academics. The Minister's letter is instructive, since it illustrates a mindset that wanted to preserve the comfortable half-truths on which Austria's post-war consensus rested, and was so fearful of redefining its identity on the basis of the challenge that the Waldheim crisis had thrown up. He appealed to Austria's historians to act so that isolated examples such as the Waldheim case and the Frischenschläger handshake would not be allowed to distort the image of Austria which its society had carefully nurtured since 1945. 'During the last few months there has been growing international controversy surrounding Austria and its manner of dealing with its recent history... Many old prejudices have been revived, not only because of the Waldheim controversy but also in the wake of the Frischenschläger-Reder incident.

'Initially the debate was confined to the media. But it has now spread to academia.' The Minister referred to Knight's writings, and warned that the British academic's analysis would lead to a radical re-evaluation of Austria's record since 1945. 'The consequences are obvious. The values that have hitherto been regarded as Austria's hall-mark might be turned upside down.' Austria might be forced to turn back on itself, to focus again on the Anschluss and on other matters that it had thought it had left behind. 'I believe it is time for Ausrtria's experts on contemporary history to rebut the dangerous theses put forward by Prof Knight.' The Minister wanted Austrian historians to counter with articles in foreign journals, and with lectures abroad. Above all, he wanted them to organise a symposium in Austria to take issue with the thesis that Austria's contemporary history was in urgent need of reappraisal. 'We must prevent the gross distortions of history.'[28]

Jankowitsch's intervention was firmly rejected. In his reply, one of the historians who had been approached argued that if Austria's image abroad was poor the country itself was largely to blame. If Knight's article served as a reminder of unpleasant facts, it was hard to see where the damage lay. 'I share the view that after the liberation from fascism – by allied forces and not by our own people – enormous effort was applied to ignore Nazi crimes and Austria's share of responsibility... If Austria's image has deteriorated, we ourselves are to blame... There is no need to panic over commentaries that remind us of facts that we have collectively sought to push into the subconscious.'[29]

Oliver Rathkolb, head of the Kreisky Archiv, was similarly firm in rejecting a confrontation with Knight. Open discussion of Austria's fault-lines would do far more to create a positive image for the country than any attempts to suppress debate. These academics were certainly not the only Austrian voices to argue that it was high time to abandon the national lie. Many Austrian intellectuals came to the conclusion that the Waldheim affair represented a challenge for the Austrian conscience. Could Austrians find the courage to put their democracy to the test, or did they prefer to live in the greater comfort of a consensus based on a mirage of mirrors and a lack of responsibility?

For the first time since the end of the war, there were deep divisions in Austrian society. The controversy over Waldheim had brought to the surface issues which the Austrians had long sought to forget. The Waldheim affair, and the claims over resurgence of antisemitism, were bound to make a profound impact. But there were imponderables: would the effect be cathartic, and help to bring all the issues about Austria's past out for full discussion? Or would it encourage xenophobia? Or would both strands figure in Austria's future?

Austria was united in hating the criticism from abroad, but deeply divided in its response. The most common grass-roots reaction was outrage over alleged foreign interference in Austria's internal affairs. Some of Austria's media, most notably *Profil*, joined in the international drive to expose Waldheim's lies, although the attacks on Austria's good name continued to cause widespread resentment, and helped to strengthen Waldheim's standing within Austria.

Even after the Historians Commission published its damning findings, Waldheim still had plenty of defenders in Austria. There was widespread anticipation abroad that public opinion in Austria would force him to resign. But the People's Party remained behind him, and Vranitzky, though he never hid his unhappiness with Waldheim, could not even rally sufficient support from his own party to take a firm stand. The President's supporters in Austria liked to argue that he was the victim of a Jewish conspiracy concocted in the US after he and Kreisky between them had antagonised the Jewish lobby over their approach to the Middle

East peace process. Both men had been heavily criticised by Israel and US Jewry for pursuing pro-Arab policies. At its most virulent, Austrian antisemitism was reflected in the assertion that 'you Jews got Christ; but you will not get Waldheim in the same manner'.[30] These were the sentiments of the Deputy Mayor of Linz, Carl Hodl, expressed in a letter to Edgar Bronfmann. An outraged Ronald Lauder, the US Ambassador in Austria, commented that in every other Western country the author would have been sacked within 15 minutes.

Such extremes of antisemitic sentiment were exceptions in Waldheim's Austria. At the other end of the spectrum there was the Austrian dramatist Thomas Bernard's controversial play *Heldenplatz*, performed in the national Burgtheater. In the play Austria was likened to a sewer, the Viennese depicted as more virulently antisemitic in Waldheim's Austria than they had been in 1938. Another example of anti-Waldheim sentiment in Austria was a political satire in which Waldheim was awarded a prize by 'Amnesia International'. Even more notable was a huge anti-Waldheim demonstration in Vienna in March 1988, held to coincide with the fitieth anniversary of the Anschluss. The demonstration appeared to confirm that the Waldheim affair was at last beginning to trigger a deep, traumatic self-examination among Austrians over the country's behaviour during the Second World War. 'The agonising reappraisal of its recent history has been forced on a reluctant people by the wide publicity given to President Waldheim's role in the German Wehrmacht which coincided with the commemoration of the Anschluss. The conjunction of the two events has undermined not only the traditional consensus between the two grand coalition partners, but has split the Austrian people right down the middle. For the first time in 40 years, the public and the body politic have found themselves passionately involved in a nationwide debate on an issue of major national and international importance.'[31]

Austria had suddenly come to the realisation that it could not live in the present, continuing to see itself as a 'blessed isle' floating happily and with good conscience in quiet waters away from the turbulence of the East-West relationship. But Austria and the world had to wait another three years before official Austria braced itself to accept that Kreisky and his predecessors had been wrong to try and draw a line under the past. The inevitable could not be staved off for ever: the history of the Nazi era would have to be tackled as a national duty, both to repair the damage to Austria's international standing and, above all, to strengthen the foundations of modern Austria. Inevitably there were dissenters; Haider, too, was on the rise.

NOTES ON CHAPTER X

1. *Financial Times*, 10 March 1983.
2. Anne McElvoy in *The Times*, 25 April 1992.
3. *Guardian*, 25 April 1983.
4. *Wiener Zeitung*, 6 May 1983.
5. *Guardian*, 27 April 1983, letter to the Editor.
6. *Profil*, 31 January 1983.
7. *The Economist*, 30 April 1983.
8. *Guardian*, 22 April 1983.
9. Interview with Frischenschläger.
10. *The Times*, 2 February 1985.
11. *The Times*, 30 January 1985.
12. See Chapter 13, 'The Go-slow Saga of Restitution'.
13. *New York Times*, 9 March 1985.
14. *Guardian*, 22 February 1985.
15. Hans Fischer, *Reflexionen*, p 388.
16. Jane Rosen in *New York Times* magazine, 13 September 1981.
17. *New York Times*, 4 March 1986.
18. *The Times*, 5 April 1986.
19. *Guardian*, 7 April 1986.
20. *Chicago Tribune*, 27 May 1986.
21. *Guardian*, 24 April 1986.
22. Henry Grunwald, *One Man's America*, Doubleday, 1997, p 589.
23. *The Waldheim Report*, international commission of historians designated to establish the military service of Lt/1st Lt Kurt Waldheim, submitted to Chancellor Vranitzky, 8 February 1988.
24. *New York Times*, 16 February 1988.
25. *New York Times*, 11 June 1986.
26. *Buffalo Times*, 30 November 1986.
27. *Times Literary Supplement*, 3 October 1986.
28. Letter from the Minister for Foreign Affairs to Dr Karl Stuhlpfarrer, 28 November 1986.
29. Letter from Prof. Dr Karl Stuhlpfarrer to Minister for Foreign Affairs, 12 December 1986.
30. *New York Times*, 10 November 1987.
31. *Financial Times*, 11 April 1988.

XI

From the Mozartkugel to Klimt and Schiele

Clichés inevitably attach themselves to public perceptions of a country's character. Mention of Austria to foreigners will bring to mind the chocolate Mozartkugel as well as Mozart; mention of Johann Strauss and conjure an image of the romantic blue Danube, its shores awash with elegant dancers waltzing into a rosy sunset. The kaleidoscope of Vienna as fertile ground for seedy black marketeers derives from *The Third Man*; the perception of the country as a pastoral alpine paradise owes a huge debt to *The Sound of Music*. The multitude of Egon Schiele reproductions has created the impression that Austrians are particularly attracted to eroticism; Gustav Klimt's legacy has been to associate Austria with the image of the Kiss and a love of sensuous beauty.

None of this adds up to a true picture; much of it reflects the distortions of commercial exploitation. Music, paintings and films have had as decisive an influence – perhaps an even greater one – in shaping the contemporary image of Austria as have Bruno Kreisky, Kurt Waldheim, Jörg Haider, tourism, or controversy surrounding the country's attitude to its Nazi past. Politics have their own momentum, and spin-doctoring has its limits; but in the arts there is scope for playing on peoples' imaginations and gullibility.

Mozart's genius has long established him among music lovers as one of the world's greatest treasures. But it was the play, and above all the successful film, of *Amadeus* that mixed fact and fiction to create often misleading, but highly persuasive impressions of both high and low life in Vienna. Purists were unhappy with the work; marketing experts were happy: chocolate pralines wrapped in silver foil bearing the portrait of a young man in powdered wig and labelled with the magic word 'Mozart' could be sold world-wide as a taste of Austria. Production of these chocolates has increased very satisfactorily; the Mozart cliché has conquered the community of chocolate lovers. It has helped to market Austria as much as have the world-class performances of Mozart's music in Salzburg and Vienna.

— * —

If *Amadeus* – though filmed in Prague and not in Vienna – has shaped the way foreigners imagine imperial Vienna, its impact on popular culture has nevertheless been less marked than that of *The Third Man* or *The Sound of Music*. These two films, both of them now classics, created indelible images of Austria. The first was set in Vienna in the immediate aftermath of the war, the other in Salzburg in 1938, before and during the Anschluss. Though totally different in substance and treatment, both were tales about good and evil, meanness and generosity; about morals and amorality. Neither film, however, made any serious attempt to address the underlying issue of Austrian complicity with the Nazis.

The Third Man, based on Graham Greene's novel, was made in 1949, and used fictional characters to highlight a world of sleeze and spying, profiteering and romance in war-worn occupied Vienna during the early few years after 1945. Since the chase through Vienna's sewers depicted in the film, this sinister underground network has entered the list of the city's claims to fame. The theme tune, played on a zither – an instrument rarely used outside Austria – provokes instant recognition and nostalgia. Visitors to Vienna still search out the big wheel, the Prater Riesenrad, that was used to such sinister effect in the film.

Directed by Britain's Carol Reed, the film earned an Oscar for its screenplay. Its monochrome treatment has made such a vivid impression that 'tourist guides in Vienna recount, wearily, how American and British tourists are quite surprised when they see that Vienna is not just black and white'.[1] It was co-produced by Alexander Korda and one of Hollywood's big film moguls, David O. Selznick. While the film was being made, there was much transcontinental bickering over the message it should communicate. Selznick wanted a film that would both portray Vienna in an idealised way 'as a city of culture, beauty, cheerfulness', and at the same time see Austria as 'a microcosm of the East-West conflict'.[2] This had little to do with any personal commitment to use the film as a Cold War propaganda instrument. It belonged to a marketing strategy which assumed that *The Third Man* would sell much better in America if it contrasted Vienna's glorious past with the indignities it had to suffer from the Soviet soldiery in its midst during the occupation. Selznick complained that Reed's version showed all too little of Vienna's current misery, and the way this contrasted with the magical brilliance and cheerfulness of its former incarnation as a world metropolis.[3] Selznick urged Reed to take his cue from a *Life* magazine feature entitled 'Vienna: it is a strategic city of want, waltzes, quiescent struggle'. The article stressed that post-war Vienna was trying to recapture the essence of the clichés that had always captured the popular imagination. 'For millions of Americans who have never visited Europe, Vienna always appeared more as an idea than as a reality. The idea is made up of Strauss waltzes, of Wiener Schnitzel and Habsburg princes surrounded by the elegance of the baroque. It is pointless to assert that such a Vienna has never really existed. What is so surprising is that now, in 1948, after three decades of economic crisis, revolution and dictatorship, the old idealised image of Vienna still persists.'[4]

Korda and Reed successfully resisted Selznick's desire to pander to these distorted perceptions among the cinema-going public. They wanted to show Vienna the way they saw it during this murky post-war period: as a city and a people who were damaged goods and therefore fertile material for Graham Greene's tale of corruption, corrosion and loneliness. They were not interested in evoking the old myths of baroque grandeur, or promoting new myths about the Viennese caught in a bitter East-West struggle. Yet their film ended up creating its own mythical cityscape of a Vienna composed of the ruins of war and hallmarked with zithers, sewers, cemeteries and petty criminals.

— * —

The Sound of Music was made 16 years later, in 1965. It was based on the Rodgers and Hammerstein musical, which in turn derived from the true story of the von Trapp family. The film was financed in Hollywood. There was never any intention to portray the precise events that had transformed the von Trapps from upper-class Austrians to a singing group in the US. The film was always intended as a fairy tale, with Salzburg and its surroundings providing an idyllic background for tear-jerking romance. Though the Anschluss was an integral part of the story-line, it only makes a cursory, crude and superficial appearance in the film. Its main purpose was to reinforce the image of a stable, prosperous country disagreeably disturbed and victimised by the intrusion of German Nazis: paradise lost. The Anschluss scenes are anodyne and do not reflect the true extent of the welcome accorded to the Nazis by the burgers of Salzburg. Yet permission to film even a watered-down version was only given after considerable pressure was applied. 'The city fathers were strictly opposed to the American request to put up Nazi flags on the Residenzplatz (one of the city's principal squares) "No, no, you cannot do this, because the people of Salzburg never belonged to the Nazi party," they said. Permission to put up the Nazi flags was only given after after the Americans warned that they would use real-life newsreels from 1938 which show how the people of Salzburg greeted Hitler's arrival with cheers and great joy. The producers of *The Sound of Music* had to promise that there would be no attempt to portray the cheering crowds of 1938.'[5]

Salzburg had good reason for seeking a *Sound of Music* free of any reminders of economic crisis, of social division, or which portrayed the prevalence of Nazi sympathies in the Austria of the late 1930s. The doctored, idealised version of Salzburg served their ends so much better. The finished film boosted tourism more than any publicity campaign ever could have done. Many Americans still think that the film's theme tune, 'Edelweiss', is Austria's national anthem. Schloss Leopoldskron, the villa outside Salzburg where much of the film was shot, has become a place of secular pilgrimage. Scarcely a day goes by when foreign tourists do not come to look. Typically, during a recent train journey to Salzburg I overheard a quartet of well-heeled Americans discussing what they should do during a brief stop-over in Salzburg. They had guidebooks, but they were not interested in the city's baroque treasures; not even Mozart's birthplace aroused their curiosity. The only Austria they wanted to see was 'that Schloss' where *The Sound of Music* had been filmed!

Hollywood's myth-making has worked its wonders: American tourists in search of an idyll, the idea of Austria the 'blessed isle' perpetuated.

— * —

Fortunately Austria has also provided the world with an antithesis to the populist Mozartkugel, 'Edelweiss' and *Third Man* underworld image of Austria. A trinity of modern artists, Gustav Klimt, Egon Schiele and Oskar Kokoschka have ensured that modern Austria is also recognised as a breeding ground for universal art. Klimt and Schiele are far removed from the *The Third Man* and *The Sound of Music*, both in time – Klimt died in the Spring of 1918 and Schiele during the influenza epidemic at the end of World War I – and in the artistic importance of their achievement. Together with Kokoschka, who lived much longer and only died in 1980, they have become the best-known Austrian painters of modern times.

Kokoschka and Schiele were true modernists, and masters of expressionism; Klimt developed a more traditional style, and his large range of paintings and decorative design, much of it done for the Wiener Werkstätte, formed an integral part of the Sezession movement at the turn of the century. All three worked in Vienna before and during the First World War. Klimt was the oldest, having been born in 1862; Schiele was the youngest, and, as he was only twenty-nine when he died, also the shortest-lived of the trio. While Kokoschka lived long enough to be recognised internationally in his own lifetime, Schiele's and even Klimt's talents went largely unnoticed abroad until decades after their death. Even Kokoschka's following before World War II was largely confined to the German-speaking world. He was eminent enough in Germany to merit the 'honour' of having his work banned by the Nazis as *entartete Kunst*. But he had to wait until the 1950s to secure fame outside the German-speaking world and to command serious sums for his paintings internationally.

The work of Klimt and Schiele had to wait even longer. It only became international currency two decades after the end of the Second World War. The two artists had established their reputation in Austria during their lifetime: Klimt was the pre-eminent artist of the 'Sezession', and Schiele might have achieved similar status had he lived longer. But for a long time their fame did not spread widely. In their lifetime and beyond – until well after 1945 – neither artist had made a serious impression on the international art market. What a contrast with their standing now, when Klimt and Schiele's grip on popular culture, as well as on serious collectors on both sides of the Atlantic and beyond, is on a par with the French impressionists. Since 1988, when the copyright on reproductions of the works of Klimt and Schiele ended, there has been an explosion of reproductions which have been used on an endless procession of commercial products. They now belong to the handful of artists whose work commands instant recognition. Through over-use as illustrations on chocolate boxes, scarves, porcelain, book illustrations, greetings cards, calendars and much else, the reproductions of their art have become clichés on a world scale.

Kokoschka had first-hand experience of sponsorship by important patrons of the arts. But Klimt and Schiele, had they still been alive, would also have recognised that their international fame owes a great deal to the persistence of Austrian emigré art dealers in London and New York. In the UK, Harry Fischer at the Marlborough Gallery became Kokoschka's champion. His son Wolfgang Fischer became a Schiele enthusiast, and also specialised in Klimt. In New York, another emigré, Otto Kallir, founder of the Galerie St Etienne, doggedly promoted Schiele's art, even though for many years he only found buyers among other emigrés, such as the film director Billy Wilder and the financier Hans Popper.

Harry Fischer, a bookseller and publisher in his former Viennese incarnation, had managed to reach England in 1939. After internment on the Isle of Wight as an 'enemy alien', he volunteered for the British army and found himself in the Pioneer Corps together with a great number of other refugees, such as Arthur Koestler and other prominent names. Invalided out, he found a job as archivist at the *Financial Times*, and soon moved on to the St George's Gallery in London. Harry had no capital, but with another friend, Kurt Levai – whom he had met on kitchen duty in the Pioneer Corps, and who had changed his name to Frank Lloyd – they opened their own gallery in London, the Marlborough Fine Arts. At the beginning they dealt mainly in antiques, rare books, French Impressionists and post-Impressionist art. Lloyd's family had been antique dealers in Vienna, and his brother, who had emigrated to Sweden, was able to help him launch the gallery with a small amount of start-up capital.

Fischer already had a thorough knowledge of the avant garde works and artists of his generation. He understood the appeal of the Impressionists. But he was even closer to the Expressionists – who initially had far less appeal for the British, and had formed a close friendship with Kokoschka. In 1951, he mounted the first important exhibition of the artist's work in the UK. During that critical period, he also helped the him win several important portrait commissions, including Agatha Christie, Konrad Adenauer and the Duke of Hamilton. London's Tate Gallery finally opened its doors to Kokoschka in 1962, with a big retrospective which included political paintings from the pre-war period such as his 'Alice in Wonderland', his ironic portrayal of the Anschluss.

Kokoschka always had an ambivalent attitude towards his native country – and it showed in his work. His paintings were often harsh; they never tried to idealise the country or its people. He had passed some of the best times of his artist's life at the turn of the century when Vienna's intellectual and artistic ferment was at its zenith. He knew all the leading figures of the period, including the influential architect Adolf Loos and Alma Mahler, Gustav Mahler's widow, with whom he had had a tortuous affair. But he felt that Vienna was too attached to traditions that had lost their meaning. The Vienna of Kokoschka's early achievements was of little help to him in promoting his work beyond Austria's borders.

It was only after the First World War, when he left Vienna for Berlin and later Dresden, that he gained recognition across the German-speaking world; that was, of course, before Hitler's rise to power. The Anschluss and the Austrian embrace of Naziism added to Kokoschka's estrangement from the country. After the war, the reluctance of official Austria to encourage his return from exile only served to confirm his cynical assessment of the Austrian character.

In 1955, Austria finally grasped that one of its native sons had become a major figure in the international art world. Kokoschka was given his first important retrospective exhibition in Vienna, and was commissioned to do a painting of the rebuilt Vienna State Opera House. Now that Austria had the State Treaty, and had regained full sovereignty, the promotion of Kokoschka's work was also a tactic to demonstrate Austria's desire to heal the rift with emigrés, and to help re-establish the country's intellectual credentials. In 1957 Wilhelm Furtwängler invited OK – as Kokoschka was known to his intimates – to design Mozart's *Magic Flute* for the Salzburg Festival, and in 1958 Vienna's Künstlerhaus staged a massive Kokoschka exhibition. To mark Kokoschka's seventy-fifth birthday in 1961 the City of Vienna made him an *Ehrenbürger* (honorary citizen).

Kokoschka had become a British citizen soon after the war, and was even awarded the OBE. He waited until November 1947, when he already had a British passport, to make his first post-war visit to Vienna. But in 1953, he left London to settle in Switzerland. That same year he also helped to found the Sommerakademie für Bildende Kunst (summer academy for the arts) in Salzburg, and taught there for many years. Students from several countries attend these painting courses, and have been taught to understand that to look intently is an essential ingredient of the art of painting. If these budding artists have followed the advice of Kokoschka – and other Austrian artists such as Georg Eisler, who have also taught at the summer academy – they will have formed a truer picture of Austria and its character than the foreigners who know Salzburg only from *The Sound of Music*.

Unlike Klimt and Schiele's work, reproductions of Kokoschka's art have not so far been exploited commercially outside the art world; it has not yet become a cliché. Perhaps it never will, as it lacks both the sweetness of Klimt's work and the dramatic eroticism of Schiele's.

— * —

After their period of fame during the Sezession, Klimt and Schiele were almost forgotten outside Austria, and suffered from partial neglect even in their own country. Klimt's work was always the more accessible, and far less controversial than that of the Expressionists. It was decorative, happy and appealing. Having lived so much longer, he left behind a much larger *oeuvre* than Schiele. Austria did not have to be prodded into buying Klimt's work by pressure from outside; it was finally launched upon a willing world with a major exhibition, 'Vienna Around 1900', staged in Vienna in 1964. It proved a big success, attracting considerable international interest and stimulating a vogue in Art Nouveau which has spread around the world and has had an incalculable influence on design.

In London, the Marlborough Gallery scored considerable success with an exhibition of Klimt graphics in 1966. His renown rose further with the 1985 'Dream and Reality' exhibition in Vienna. It far exceeded the 1964 exhibition in interest and attendance, and edited versions of the exhibition were taken around the world, to cities including London, Tokyo and Paris. The value of Klimt's work rose by leaps and bounds, much faster than Schiele's, though eventually both artists have come to command sky-high prices.

Austrians have not been alone in exploiting Klimt's commercial potential, although even now there is only a single Klimt painting in a

17. Richard Nixon used Bruno Kreisky as a sounding board during his presidency and liked to stop off in Austria on his way to high-level meetings elsewhere. Kreisky was invariably flattered.

18. Bruno Kreisky frequently consulted and holidayed with his protégé, the Finance Minister Hannes Androsch. They were good friends until they became bitter enemies.

19. During the presidential elections of 1986, Kurt Waldheim knew he was on a winning streak when he called on Austrians to vote for him rather than cave in to the outside world's attempts to discredit him as an alleged war criminal. 'A Man of Experience, a Man for Austria', and 'Now even more so' the ubiquitous placards proclaimed.

20. Over decades Nazi-hunter Simon Wiesenthal was the thorn in Austria's conscience and reviled by Bruno Kreisky along with many other Austrians. But in his grand old age his image turned. He became a national treasure and an icon.

21. *(above)* Frank Vranitzky, Chancellor from 1986 to 1997, was the first post-war leader in Austria to confront the nation with its true history. It took until 1991, more than half a century after the events, before official Austria accepted responsibility for its participation in the Holocaust.

22. *(below)* Cardinal Franz König earned international distinction for his open-minded outlook and efforts to build bridges across religious and political divides both as head of Austria's Roman Catholic Church and in his retirement. During the Cold War his initiatives created openings for dialogue with the Communist bloc.

public collection in the UK: the portrait of Hermine Gallia in London's National Gallery. Reproductions of his work, however, have become almost over-familiar. A romanticised image of Vienna, of its Art Nouveau, and of Klimt's paintings have become fused in cosmopolitan popular culture.

— * —

Schiele had by far the hardest climb to international renown. Though it is generally known that he was Austrian, he has never been mistaken for the easy-going stereototype of his country. Though largely misunderstood, he is often seen as an essentially tragic, flawed product of Austrian society. His genius is linked to a perception of Vienna that fostered eroticism, even pornography. Even in his own country, his work had a much harder time securing acceptance and support. In 1922, four years after his death, Schiele's mother was unable to persuade the Austrian State Gallery to buy one of his paintings. The only way to have his work put on display was for her to donate a painting. But one of his fervent admirers, Otto Nirenstein, the art dealer who later changed his name to Otto Kallir, who was so convinced of Schiele's lasting significance that he chose an exhibition of Schiele's works for the opening of his New Gallery in Vienna in 1923. A handful of Austrian collectors and museum directors recognised their importance, and bought drawings as well as paintings. Yet in 1937 Schiele was still so utterly unknown that the Nazis forgot to class him among the group of banned 'degenerate' artists.

After the Anschluss, Schiele's work was not treated as harshly as that of other Expressionists. A dozen of his drawings from Vienna's Albertina collection were included in a 1943 exhibition under the patronage of Baldur von Schirach, Hitler's Gauleiter in Vienna during the war. That same year, commemorative articles were authorised in the 'Ostmark' media to mark the twenty-fifth anniversary of Schiele's death.

Between 1945 and 1955, Schiele's work was included in several exhibitions in Austria. The most important among them was an exhibition in Linz in 1949 which included over 200 Schiele works, and which was later seen in Salzburg and in three German cities. Rudolf Leopold, a young Austrian opthamologist who eventually amassed the largest collection of Schieles, was beginning to scour all available sources of his drawings and paintings.

Elsewhere in Europe, Schiele was virtually unknown. In the US, however, he had gained an ardent advocate. Nirenstein had managed to bring a considerable Schiele portfolio when he emigrated to New York after the Anschluss. In his new St Etienne Gallery he persisted with promoting Schiele's works. In 1954, he secured his first breakthrough when the Minneapolis Institute of Arts bought one of Schiele's last paintings, the portrait of the painter Albert Paris von Gütersloh. Three years later, the Museum of Modern Art in New York acquired its first Schiele from Kallir, who was by then established as perhaps the world's leading dealer of the artist's work. From that point onwards, Schiele's standing in the US steadily improved. In the mid-1950s, museum directors in Holland and Switzerland began to show an interest, but the work was still so little known that it commanded laughably low prices. Erich Lederer, an Austrian emigré in Switzerland who possessed a large number of Schiele drawings, was giving them away as New Year or Christmas presents! In London, the market for Schiele remained virtually non-existent during the 1950s. Arthur Stemmer, an Austrian emigré in London who possessed three of Schiele's most important paintings, was unable to find a buyer in the UK, and had to sell them to Rudolf Leopold in Vienna for a mere £500.

Harry Fischer and the Marlborough Gallery passed up every opportunity to acquire Schieles until 1964, when his son Wolfgang pressed the Marlborough to hold an exhibition of the artist's work. Wolfgang had been to see the paintings in Vienna and was enthusiastic; excepting Kokoschka, his father Harry had initially been reluctant to handle the Expressionist school. It was understandable: in the 1950s and 1960s the overhang from World War II still affected the art market. There was a lack of enthusiasm for German works, and no distinction was made between them and those of Austrian artists – after all, what could have been more characteristically German than Expressionism?

Under the influence of Kokoschka, Harry Fischer was particularly reluctant to deal in Schiele. Kokoschka, probably out of jealousy, always dismissed Schiele as 'that little crook, that pornographer'. However, the 1964 exhibition in London, followed by another in 1969, aroused great interest, and considerable controversy. Artists, including Alberto Giacometti and Friedrich Hundertwasser, were fascinated. Critics pondered the narrow line between art and pornography. In any event, Schiele had finally had a prominent outing in the UK.

Even so, Wolfgang Fischer is convinced that 'Austria excepted, America after World War II made by far the greatest contribution to Schiele's reputation'.[6] An exhibition at the Guggenheim Museum in New York in 1965 set in motion a bandwagon that led to purchases by several major US museums, and inflated the value of his work to boom levels. By 1970, Schiele's reputation was firmly established in the US, the UK and Germany. 'Kokoschka's lifelong feud with Schiele was history, although the old master himself had never conceded.' Official Austria grasped that it was in the country's interest to identify itself with the work, to remind the art world and those beyond that Schiele was an Austrian artist. Stimulated by the perceived eroticism of his work, interest in Schiele was no longer limited to the narrow confines of the art world, and began to arouse the attention of the more popular media. The Schiele boom was on its way. Wolfgang Fischer describes how 'journalists homed in on one important, if not necessarily crucial aspect of Schiele's life: the eroticism of his work with its supposed "Lolita fixation" and the preference for pubescent female models which had on one occasion led to his arrest and two weeks' incarceration'.

Exhibition followed exhibition throughout Western Europe and North America. In 1990, Schiele was given one of the UK's highest accolades for artists: a major exhibition at the Royal Academy of 'Schiele and his contemporaries', a collection of the works in Leopold's possession. There had been considerable difficulty in finding sponsors: many were reluctant to put their names behind an artist whose work was associated with pornography. The doubters misjudged: the exhibition was certainly controversial, but it was also popular, and received marked critical acclaim. Every major newspaper gave the exhibition long reviews. Again and again the question was asked: was it eroticism, pornography or art; or all three?

The *Times* critic argued that interest in Schiele was clearly linked to the Jugendstil movement and the 'Viennese sunset in the years before the first world war'; it reflected the 'new willingness to see decadence as divine', concluded that 'Such is their [the paintings'] artistic integrity that even the stuffiest Academy regular is unlikely to be more than mildly ruffled'.[7] Another eminent London art critic emphasised the erotic nature of Schiele's work, but insisted that 'we should not lightly surrender our capacity to be shocked by art. Once we lose that, we also lose the ability to be moved.'[8] An editorial in the same paper argued that Schiele's work provided 'a healthy antidote to the marshmallow joys of Monet'.[9]

The *Guardian* concluded that 'Schiele is a significant artist, he is unique... He brings art nearer to pornography than any other modern draughtsman.' But the reviewer, Tim Hilton, was more interested in puzzling out the motives that had led Leopold to become such an obsessive Schiele collector. He thought that Leopold's interest began 'in the peculiar atmosphere of Vienna just after the war. This was not the city that pretended to be an operetta, nor the city that once had known intellectual life. It was the Vienna of *The Third Man*, the Vienna divided into military zones, a smoky twilit world, full of refugees, spies, contrabandiers, people who knew how to keep their dealings quiet.' This led Hilton to a prescient comment: 'Little is known about the network of contacts that allowed Leopold to locate and purchase his paintings. If we were aware of their provenances, no doubt our knowledge of Vienna's cultural patterns would be much enlarged. Were any of them, for instance, pictures that had been confiscated from the Jews?'[10]

This question was to be repeated, far more loudly and with far-reaching repercussions for Austria's handling of restitution claims, seven years later when the Leopold collection was on display at New York's Museum of Modern Art. When the exhibition ended, two paintings, 'Walli' and

'Tote Stadt III' were seized by the New York authorities following claims by two emigré families that the paintings had been illegally acquired.

The spotlight was not only on Leopold, but on the Austrian state, and the Americans sought answers not only to the provenance of the two Schieles but on the fate of countless works of art once in the ownership of Austrian Jews and expropriated by the Nazis. Schiele had been made the unwitting agent of a new bandwagon: external pressure for Austria to return stolen property and to discharge its debt to the Austrian victims of Nazi persecution.

NOTES ON CHAPTER XI

1 *Guardian*, 28 August 1993.
2 Jacqueline Vansant, 'Die Entnazifizierung Österreichs in Amerikanischen Filmen' in *The Sound of Austria*, Laxenburger Internationale Studien, 1995, p 172.
3 Ibid., p 173.
4 *Life*, 18 October 1948, p 173.
5 Vansant, 'Die Entnazifizierung Österreichs in Amerikanischen Filmen', op. cit., p 179
6 From Wolfgang Fischer's monograph on Schiele.
7 *The Times*, 23 November 1990.
8 *Independent*, 27 November 1990.
9 *Independent*, 19 November 1990.
10 *Guardian*, 28 November 1990.

XII

Exit Waldheim, Enter Haider

Have the Lessons of the Past Been Absorbed?

In 1990, Austria was bubbling with optimism. The shackles of the Cold War had been lifted; the economy was in good shape; foreign investment was flowing in; entry into the EU was in the offing; the outlook was good for expanding trade and economic links with Eastern Europe; Austria no longer formed a precarious bridge between two heavily armed enemy camps. It had full freedom to acknowledge its affinity with the West and to re-establish its historic role as a political, cultural and diplomatic crossroad between different European worlds.

In 1986, the country had acquired a new Chancellor, Franz Vranitzky. He was the first head of government to belong to the post-war generation. He also became the first to insist that Austria must retain its neutral status and still secure full membership of the EU. Even more significantly, Vranitzky was the first to be persuaded that the Austrian state and its parliamentary institutions had no alternative but to acknowledge and accept responsibility for the crimes of Austrian people during the Nazi era.

Kurt Waldheim, resisting heavy pressure to resign, and intent on serving out his term of office until 1992, was still at his desk in the Hofburg. But his role as head of state had become marginalised, his disgraced presidency almost invisible. It would be up to his successor to recapture the moral high ground for the office.

In sum, as the last decade of the twentieth century began the wind seemed set fair towards a bright, largely untroubled future for Austria. A British journalist in Vienna observed that 'Austria is like a contented child gently rocking in a hammock. The movements are rythmical enough to send any child to sleep. If the child were to wake up, it would find in Austria a world full of reassurance.'[1] And yet all was not as it seemed. Tempting though it might have been, there was no justification for complacency. Just as it looked as though the long post-war apprenticeship for normality was nearing completion, a shadow, growing inexorably longer, darkened the political horizon, exerting a damaging influence on policy formulation and engendering deep unease abroad. The phenomenon had a name: Jörg Haider. The outside world saw his Freedom Party as a reincarnation of the fascist tendency that brought Mussolini and Hitler to power. His critics in Austria preferred to portray him as an unscrupulous opportunist, a demagogue without principle or ideology.

Even if it is an exaggeration to cast him as a neo-Nazi, the presence on the Austrian scene of this 'yuppie fascist' – as the European Parliament dubbed him when he became leader of the Freedom Party in 1986 – has reawakened fears that, as in 1938, there is a sizeable number of Austrians ready to follow a far right populist whose rhetoric carries fascist overtones and whose growing power not only polarises opinion inside Austria but also threatens the political order in Europe. If Austria thought it had achieved peace with itself and with the world at large, it was mistaken. If the international community hoped that Austria had finally come to terms with its past, and no longer sought to paint itself as a victim of contemporary history, it was to be disappointed.

At first, Haider was the phantom at the feast. But since the October 1999 general election and the Freedom Party's subsequent entry into a coalition government with the People's Party, Haider has acquired not just virtual power, but has become the real *eminence grise* behind the throne. His abrupt decision in February 2000 to give up the formal leadership of his party left his influence undiminished.

International preoccupation with Haider and his brand of politics has surfaced regularly since 1986, when he ousted Norbert Steger as leader of the Freedom Party. The outside world watched with growing concern how Haider transformed the party from the spent force it had been when he took it over, to the popular acclaim it achieved, making it Austria's second-largest party at the beginning of the new millennium. In the space of only 14 years Haider increased the party's share of the vote from 5 per cent to just over 27 per cent in the 1999 federal election. Subsequent public opinion polls showed that the Freedom Party's standing surged ahead in the weeks that followed the election, reflecting further disillusion over the inability of the two traditional governing parties – the Social Democrats and the People's Party – to renew their coalition agreement. It must also be interpreted as a knee-jerk reaction to the international furore over the decision of the People's Party to throw in its lot with Haider's party. The campaign by EU countries, Israel and the US to punish Austria by isolating it politically initially reinforced support for Haider even from Austrians who dislike and mistrust him. Once again, many Austrians felt victimised. But the suspension of bilateral relations with Austria by the EU countries also prompted a far-reaching political debate in Austria, which carried the seeds of a more realistic accceptance of the country's dark past.

Even though Haider decided against joining the federal coalition government formed in February 1999, in which the Freedom Party secured a series of key ministries, he confidently predicted that he will emerge as Chancellor in the not-too-distant future. Unperturbed by the international outcry and the imposition of sanctions, Haider jeered at his critics that 'there is panic in the chicken coop even before the fox has got in'.

— * —

Haider's neo-fascist image owes its origins to his publicly-voiced admiration for Hitler's employment policies, to his attendance at an SS veterans' meeting – at which he described the participants as men of decent character – to his upbringing by parents who were enthusiastic Nazi Party members wedded to the ideal of the greater German nation, and to the knowledge that his wealth derives from the acquisition of Jewish property in 1939 at bargain prices.

At the Los Angeles Wiesenthal Center's Museum of Tolerance, a life-size photograph of Haider was, for a while, placed alongside pictures of Idi Amin and Saddam Hussein. The trio was part of a display of modern tyrants. But even without such hyperbole, Haider has always given cause for concern with his anti-establishment populism, his encouragement of xenophobia and carefully-coded hints of antisemitism, his exploitation of narrow nationalist instincts, and his distortions of Austria's record during the Nazi era and attempts to bracket Austrian victims of the Holocaust with Austrian members of Hitler's Wehrmacht who had been taken prisoners by the Soviet Union.

Haider's growing army of supporters in Austria are less concerned with the wider implications of Haider's rhetoric. His popularity owes a great deal to political antennae that led him to attack the *Proporz* system – the system under which the two old-established parties entrenched themselves in Austria's power structure. Haider struck a deep vein of resentment. For more than five decades the two big parties had divided not only key posts, but also jobs much further down the ladder in both the public and private sector, between their own supporters. This created an elite network, and engendered a climate of cronyism which prevented outsiders from gaining jobs on merit alone. Though the Social

Democratic and People's Party leadership asserted that *Proporz* was already on the wane, removal of the system became an important issue which Haider exploited with considerable success.

As early in Haider's ascent to power as 1990, careful observers of the Austrian scene identified the characteristics that singled him out from rivals on the complacent Austrian political scene. 'The attraction of the FPÖ [Freedom Party] is its populism... Haider has attempted to revamp the image of the party in two ways. First he has appealed to the small man who feels aggrieved by the gargantuan bureaucracy perpetuated in Vienna... He has identified Vienna as the den of privilege and corruption where jobs for the boys are handed down in return for political loyalty. Mr Haider wants an end to that... More worrying is the way the FPÖ unashamedly uses the influx of East Europeans for political ends. Austrian xenophobia is never far from the surface.'[2]

This analysis was just as apt ten years later, when Haider emerged to an international chorus of denunciation as the triumphant king-maker in Austrian politics, whose party could no longer be kept out of government. The international media recalled his notorious remarks in 1990 to veteran members of Hitler's Waffen SS, the force responsible for the extermination of countless Jews. As well as telling the veterans that they were decent people of good character, and praising them for sticking to their convictions despite the greatest opposition, he 'appreciated' the efforts of the Waffen SS in 'a struggle for freedom and democracy'. When this had originally become public knowledge, soon after the 1990 meeting, he defended himself with the argument that 'the Waffen SS was part of the Wehrmacht, and hence deserves all the honour and respect of the army in public life'. Reminded that the Nuremberg trials had branded the Waffen SS a criminal organisation, Haider replied that this 'does not interest me in the least'.

After the 1999 general election, when Haider embarked on a charm offensive to gain international trust, he changed tack, apologised to Holocaust survivors and Austrian Jews for his 'ambiguous statements', distanced himself from the Nazis, and described himself as 'a passionate Austrian democrat'.[3] When the Freedom Party entered government in February 2000, Haider went further, putting his signature to a joint declaration with the People's Party committing it and the Austrian nation to a 'self-critical scrutiny of the National Socialist past' and to acceptance of 'her responsibilities arising out of the tragic history of the twentieth century and the horrendous crimes of the National Socialist regime'.[4] Yet, on the same day, the German weekly *Die Zeit* quoted from an interview with Haider in which he asserted that 'all this business of apologising for the Nazi past will only lead to emotions flaring up. People will ask "what is the meaning of all this after so many decades?" Sooner or later one has to make a break with one's past.'[5]

But then Haider – sometimes dubbed 'Teflon Man' – is past master at disowning or modifying awkward facts and statements when they no longer suits his purpose. There are so many striking examples of constantly changing position that it becomes impossible not to conclude that he deliberately sets out to obfuscate and confuse.

After the uproar caused by his endorsement in 1991 of Hitler's 'orderly employment' policies, Haider subsequently claimed that he had been misinterpreted, but had nevertheless decided to 'take back the remark with regret'. On another occasion, having identified himself as an advocate of the greater pan-German nation – shades of the 1938 Anschluss – and described Austria in 1988 as an 'ideological miscarriage' and as a country that would eventually return 'to the German Fatherland', Haider turned *volte face* after he saw that Austria's post-1945 national identity had become set in cement. He converted into the fervent Austrian nationalist he is today.

Haider's positions with respect to the EU have undergone repeated change. Initially a supporter of Austrian membership – because he saw it as a way of moving closer to Germany – he opposed membership during the 1994 referendum campaign to join the EC. But after Austrians voted with a two-thirds majority for joining the EC, he swiftly switched to endorse membership, but turned his guns against enlargement and against participation in the Euro-zone. After the 1999 election, he first threatened to use the Austrian veto against enlargement but again reversed that position, claiming that as part of the Freedom Party's coalition agreement with the People's Party, he was now prepared to accept the Euro, and to co-operate with the EU 'in a trusting manner'.

In 1994, the Freedom Party, alone among Austria's parliamentary groups, voted against the establishment of a compensation fund for Austrian Holocaust survivors. By 1999, Haider conceded that he might have 'hurt the feelings of the victims of Naziism', and that his past statements were 'not in line with the personal values of tolerance and humanity which are the basis of my political work'.

Haider's first reaction to French President Chirac's forthright warnings after the 1999 federal election against allowing the Freedom Party to participate in government was to condemn him as a 'leader who has done everything wrong in recent years'. Reprimanded by Austria's President Klestil, Haider delivered a tongue-in-cheek apology: 'If anybody feels insulted, then I withdraw these remarks with regret. But I also expect people to respect the result of the Austrian election.' Haider's charisma is such that his supporters appear to have few problems with his chameleon-like utterances. Whatever Haider thinks is appropriate is apparently good enough for his acolytes.

It has become a cliché to describe Haider's 'youthful good looks' as another reason for his appeal to voters, although not everyone subscribes to that view. Nicholas Fraser, the producer of a British documentary film on Europe's far right parties, shown in the Spring of 1999, came away from a Haider interview with this impression: 'He wore extravagantly large Puritan Maid white or dark blue collars over sportive leisure suits in lurid brown or electric blue, giving him the appearance of a character from an alpine porn movie. When I interviewed him, it was his empty fixed expression that I noticed and the wardrobe that stuck in my memory. It didn't seem likely that fascism would return to Europe wearing brown trousers and a toothbrush moustache. Instead we would find ourselves with something like Jörg Haider in open-collared leisure wear.'[6]

Haider's electoral advance has to be seen in the context of the far right movement in Europe, and on his record so far he is certainly the most seductive and successful leader within that movement. Fear that Haider's success in Austria could have a domino effect elsewhere – in Germany, France, Belgium or Portugal – in part explains the vehemence of European and American reactions to the Freedom Party's entry into government.

— * —

Haider was only thirty-six years old when he became party leader. 'Handsome and dapper and with an indisputable concern for the little man, Haider seduces most audiences with his innocent style and his appeals for justice and an end to corruption,'[7] the *Guardian*'s correspondent wrote during the 1986 election campaign. Vranitzky, as leader of the Social Democratic Party, had called the election after Haider had captured the Freedom Party leadership from Norbert Steger, who was at the time Vice-Chancellor in the Austrian cabinet. In the wake of what Vranitzky described as an 'unacceptable ideological shift' in the Freedom Party he refused to renew the 'small coalition' between the Social Democrats and the Freedom Party over which his predecessor, Fred Sinowatz, had presided. In a contemporary account of the Haider phenomenon, the Central European expert Misha Glenny wrote that 'Behind Haider's playful image lies not only a shadowy past but a present that is hard to pin down... For three years he has been building up nationalist sentiments in his adopted powerbase of Carinthia, eroding the support of both parties. The Carinthian branch of the Freedom Party has traditionally been a melting pot of rightwing ideology since the party's foundation in 1956, and Haider has had no difficulty in wooing its constituent elements and increasing its strength.'

'Dig back a little further and one finds Haider a student involved in organisations with an avowed commitment to greater Germany... Another issue dogs him: the source of his wealth. It stems entirely from an estate inherited from his great uncle, William Webhofer. He bought the estate in 1939 from its Jewish owner after the start of Hitler's 'aryanisation' programme. Haider insists that the transaction was quite legal but cannot explain how the price was but a tenth of the property's actual value. The 80-year old Mathilda Roifer, who now lives in Israel, says the estate still belongs to her. Haider dismisses the idea as absurd.'[8]

As US Ambassador to Austria in the mid-1980s, Henry Grunwald kept a close watch on the new Freedom Party leader, the shrewd postmodern Haider. 'He told me that he was not really a German nationalist, but used that rhetoric to satisfy "the old folks". It was hardly a reassuring explanation. After several more meetings with him I felt that calling him a neo-Nazi was too simple. I saw him as a populist, radical opportunist who gladly appealed to lingering pro-Nazi sentiment, but would also appeal to anything else that might lead him to power.'[9]

My own reaction to Haider's emergence into the political limelight in 1986 reflected fear that Austria would remain a twilight state, never wholly able to shed its extreme right-wing factions. At the time, I reported from Vienna that Haider 'had avoided any taint of anti-semitism and extreme nationalism'. This had not altered my belief that 'the Austrian election results are likely to be seen by the outside world as a further black mark against Austria and, like the election of Dr Kurt Waldheim [earlier in 1986] as President, as another fateful step backwards to Nazism... Austria's history, geography and culture give it a pivotal role in central Europe. But Dr Vranitzky recognises that it can only fulfil its role if it can reestablish its international credentials... The Haider phenomenon, emerging so soon after Dr Waldheim's election, will be widely interpreted outside Austria as a further fall from grace.'[10]

In the 1986 election, the first fought under Haider's leadership, the Freedom Party succeeded in doubling its vote and confirming his powerful influence on the electorate. The Social Democrats and the People's Party leadership sensed that the Haider phenomenon spelled danger not only for the popular appeal of their own party platforms but also for the future standing of the Austrian nation. They reached a tacit understanding to co-operate in countering his influence and to set aside any idea of inviting the Freedom Party to join a coalition government. The grand coalition was maintained, even though the two mainstream parties found it increasingly difficult to work together, and public confidence in their ability to provide effective government was steadily diminishing.

Five years on, in 1991, the Freedom Party secured 23 per cent of the vote in Vienna's important municipal elections. Haider had succeeded in breaking the hitherto impenetrable defences of social democracy in Vienna: much of his support had come from blue-collar workers.

Haider was now imposing his xenophobic rhetoric on the national scene to such an extent that curbing immigration had become a major political issue. Just as the country was nearing the end of six years of ostracism under Waldheim's presidency, and was negotiating EU membership, Austria's old spectres were taking new forms. Austria was 'in the throes of a xenophobia that Jörg Haider skilfully exploits for his own aims. Frustrated voters are clearly prepared to overlook Haider's habitual nods to his party's limited clientele of aging Nazis. The FPÖ [Freedom Party] is making steady gains helped by young professionals drawn by reformist pledges... Its success owes much to Mr Haider's effective highlighting of cronyism and corruption within the two [mainstream] parties... Haider's appeal must be distinguished from France's Jean-Marie Le Pen. Haider is more subtle, and potentially more pernicious... Until Austrian politicians find the courage to confront directly Haider's contemporary intolerance, answering legitimate elements of his reform programme where needed, he will continue his ascent towards the federal Chancellery.'[11]

Early in 1993, Haider promoted a national petition to outlaw immigration altogether. That was defeated. But far from concluding that the government had been vindicated in maintaining a generous asylum policy, Vranitzky and his coalition partners decided to trump Haider by imposing highly restrictive curbs on immigration. Even this was not enough to silence Haider on this issue. He has never allowed the issue to go away. He used it to make his case against EU enlargement, arguing that new members on Austria's borders would open the floodgates to immigration and deprive Austrians of their jobs.

By 1997 Austria had become a respected member of the EU, and was about to hold the presidency. 'The spotlight falling on Austria next year will reveal a mature and prosperous society,' the *Financial Times* proclaimed in its 1997 survey of Austria. But Haider's presence was casting a pall over the country's political future. 'His party never misses an opportunity to test the increasing political faultlines within Austria's coalition government. If Mr Haider were to achieve his ambition of becoming Chancellor after the 1999 elections then Austria might once again find itself being snubbed on the international stage as it was during Mr Waldheim's days.'[12]

As a tactic to neutralise the Haider effect, the coalition government continued to make concessions towards the policies he championed – immigration was further cut back to near zero levels, and the challenge of EU enlargement was approached with a degree of coolness that Austria's fellow members deplored. They had assumed that Austria would act as a docking platform for new EU members in Eastern and Central Europe. But fearful of playing into Haider's hands, EU members refrained from pressurising the coalition to act more constructively in the run-up to the 1999 Austrian elections. The possibility of a Freedom Party presence at meetings of the EU was seen as a nightmare prospect. But Haider was not to be deflected. He has always deftly seized his opportunities. For years he had enjoyed the support – which he lost after the 1999 federal election – of Austria's largest circulation paper, the *Neue Kronenzeitung*; his assault against the coalition barricades increased in intensity, and gradually the mainstream parties' defences began to crumble. Haider's share of the popular vote grew dramatically both at national level and in key elections at regional, Länder level, most notably in Carinthia, Vienna and Upper Austria.

Haider had rapidly become unstoppable. He secured 42 per cent of the vote in regional elections in Carinthia in March 1999. Carinthia had always been a special case. Haider had made it his home. It is also a region which has always had a strong core of voters on the far right, resentful of its Slovenian minority and concerned to keep out further migration from neighbouring Slovenia. Even so the swing to Haider in Carinthia caused widespread anxiety abroad. He had gained an important springboard for the next national election campaign. Jewish communities in Austria and abroad went on alert, interpreting his victory in Carinthia as a victory for racism.

In September 1999, Haider went on to secure control of the government of Upper Austria with 27.5 per cent of the vote.

Soon afterwards came the federal election, which gave the Freedom Party 27.2 per cent of the vote. It proved to be a decisive breakthrough for the party's advance to national power. With the Freedom Party marginally ahead of the Peoples' Party, it brought about a radical realignment of the political landscape. The political will of the two mainstream parties to resist Haider crumbled. Suddenly it no longer seemed impossible that the grand coalition should be replaced by a new formation.

While the Social Democrats held fast against forming a government with the Freedom Party, the People's Party saw it as their chance – very likely their last chance for years to come – to regain the Federal chancellery. Their leader, Wolfgang Schüssel, who had insisted on the eve of the election that he would rather take his party into opposition than go into a coalition with the Freedom Party, changed his mind – and jumped. Weakly, Schüssel ceded key ministries, including Finance, Justice and Defence to the Freedom Party. Haider decided against joining the federal cabinet and ceded the party leadership to one of his trusted lieutenants, Vice-Chancellor Susanne Riess-Passer. But even though he remained instead as Chief Minister of Carinthia, nobody was left in any doubt that his lieutenants in the federal coalition would take their cues from him. Far too many Austrian voters failed to understand – or simply did not want to know – that the outside world had long seen Haider as a sinister figure whose populist message endangered political stability and undermined democracy.

Austria's liberal establishment has watched Haider's progress with a mixture of surprise and foreboding, but remained complacent and consistently underestimated his ability to capture the high ground of Austrian politics. In the business community there was a growing view that Haider's advance had become inevitable. Given the bankruptcy of ideas among mainstream politicians, perhaps, the argument went, he should be given a chance either to prove his democratic credentials – or to implode.

For Austria's Social Democrats, Haider's success in persuading the People's Party to form a coalition with him was a nightmare come true. Fears of such an outcome had already crucially affected Vranitzky's handling of the Waldheim crisis in the late 1980s. There was much outside speculation then that Vranitzky might have been able to force through Waldheim's resignation had he not been deterred by Haider's growing political influence.

Vranitzky had publicly threatened, if Waldheim stayed, to leave office himself, deliberately telling me and other foreign media of his exasperation with Waldheim. But before long Vranitzky withdrew his threat to resign, which would have broken up the coalition – and so Waldheim remained. The *Financial Times* described how 'the Socialists, acutely aware of the international isolation of Austria as a result of the Waldheim affair, wanted the President to step down in the interests of the country. However their conservative partners have fully supported Mr Waldheim's stubborn refusal to relinquish his office... At one stage in February this year [1988] it looked as if the coalition would fall with Mr Vranitzky threatening to resign because the Waldheim affair was taking up more and more of his time.

'The Chancellor eventually changed his mind... Though the exact reasons are not clear, it seems that he feared resignation could lead to the formation of a coalition between the People's Party and Jorg Haider's Freedom Party.[13]

— * —

1 January 1995 was a red letter day in Austria's post-war history. It was then that Austria took possession of its seat in the EU. The acquisition of membership is surely one of the three most important markers of Austria's post-war history – together only with the proclamation of the Second Republic in 1945 and the completion of the State Treaty in 1955. These events were the principal stepping stones along Austria's slow march to normalisation and European integration. The road to Brussels was tortuous.

While the Cold War lasted, membership of the EC always seemed more of a mirage than a realisable goal. Successive Soviet leaders had been unwavering in their 'niet' to Austrian desires for closer links with Brussels. Austria's political classes had become innured to the idea that the country's neutrality constituted an enduring barrier to full EC membership; furthermore, if it came to a choice between the two, neutrality was assumed to be a safer haven than Brussels. The economic successes of the 1960s and 1970s had persuaded many Austrians that neutrality was not just a safeguard of security, but also the key to prosperity. Such optimism masked Austria's need for more external investment and for a better framework for its foreign trade.

New vistas for Austria opened up when Mikhail Gorbachev arrived on the world stage. He brought blasts of fresh air to the Kremlin which fundamentally changed the Cold War climate in which Austria's neutrality had matured. In charge in the Kremlin, Gorbachev introduced himself to the world with the new language of *glasnost* and *perestroika*. He called for co-operation to build a new 'European home', and at a snail's pace inched away from the old Soviet view of the EC as a NATO dependancy and part of the West's anti-Communist arsenal. Gorbachev understood the imperative of expanding Soviet trade with the West, and that the EC could become an important trading partner for the Communist bloc.

Enter Vranitzky, also new to the top job in his country. As Chancellor, the former banker and Finance Minister needed little persuasion to seek new approaches to membership negotiations with Brussels. He read the signals from Moscow correctly, and sensed that the Soviet Union might now become more pliable on Austrian EC membership. The time was approaching to break the great neutrality taboo. In January 1987, the Chancellor made it known that Austria would be willing to go along with new thinking in Brussels, and was attracted by a 'global concept' of membership, including full participation in the single market, and in economic and monetary union. Even before Manfred Scheich, the Austrian diplomat most closely associated with the EU negotiations, could plead in Vienna for a more open and constructive attitude to Brussels, Vranitzky made it plain to him that he was already among the converted. As Scheich told a Brussels audience several years later, the Chancellor greeted him with the remark: 'Don't you think it is time that we joined the EC, albeit with some kind of reservation about our neutrality?'[14]

Soon afterwards a working group was set up in Vienna to begin the lengthy process of preparing a formal application to Brussels. It had the full support of Alois Mock, the People's Party leader and Foreign Minister in the coalition government. But there was no applause in Brussels, where there was little eagerness to expand the EC club. The existing members pleaded uncertainty about Gorbachev's attitude to Austrian membership. They would have preferred for Austria to remain in line with the other EFTA neutrals and content itself with the 1984 Luxembourg Declaration on closer trade and other co-operation between the EC and EFTA. The EFTA states themselves were also disturbed by the change of attitude in Vienna, and demanded solidarity. Their reaction, Manfred Scheich recalls, 'wavered between scepticism and annoyance with Austria's lack of solidarity, while Moscow, to put it mildly, remained suspicious'.

The breakthrough in Moscow came in the autumn of 1988, when Mock met his counterpart, Soviet Foreign Minister Edouard Shevardnadze and was agreeably surprised to find him far more flexible than previous Soviet officials. According to Scheich, who was present at the Moscow talks, the Soviet Foreign Minister wanted to know how Austria would reconcile its commitment to neutrality with EC membership, but no longer asserted that these were two irreconcilables. Towards the end of the meeting between the two Foreign Ministers, Shevardnadze hinted further at changed attitudes in Moscow. Mock felt encouraged to assume that Austria was at last free to press Brussels for membership. 'He suggested that the situation might be radically transformed in the mid-nineties – that old Soviet attitudes might be discarded – if the shift towards East-West detente was maintained, if the process of dynamic disarmament continued, and if cooperation between East and West became the accepted reality in place of confrontation and suspicion.'

Soon afterwards, Gorbachev's spokesman, Genardi Gerassimov, endorsed the 'Sinatra doctrine' enabling Communist bloc countries to 'do it their way', a remark which was interpreted as a further hint of shackles being removed in Eastern and Central Europe, leaving it open to Austria to interpret its neutrality status far more flexibly than in the past.

By the end of 1988, Austria was fully decided and ready to launch its EC membership application. But Jacques Delors, President of the EC Commission, tried to throw one more spanner in the works by proposing the establishment of a 'European economic space' that would give the EFTA countries access to the single market but exclude them from decision-making. This suited Switzerland and was enough for Sweden, but Austria wanted more.

On 17 July 1987, the Austrian membership application was tabled. This was, as Austrian diplomats like to point out, a particular act of political courage because it took place several weeks before the fall of the Berlin Wall fatally undermined the Soviet Union's authority in European affairs, and thus before Vienna could feel absolutely safe in making its approach to Brussels. Denmark and Sweden, two countries which had far less to lose in terms of their relations with the Soviet Union, waited many months longer before they applied for EU membership.

The response in Brussels to the Austrian application was, to say the least, muted. The Commission decided to set in motion the usual process for evaluating a membership application, but warned that negotiations with Austria could not begin until the European single market entered into force at the end of 1992. A further delay was introduced when Austria was kept at bay until ratification of the Maastricht Treaty.

Reluctance to enlarge the EC at a time when Brussels was preoccupied with economic and monetary union and closer political integration was self-evident. It was like a kitchen, originally designed for a family of six, which had been doubled to 12, the spokesman for two Dutch Commission members explained. It was already overcrowded, and its defective refrigerator would have to be repaired merely to accommodate the needs of the existing membership. There was no space, for the present, for more entrants.

Austria was impatient with the constant delays to full-scale negotiations. One of Mock's aides, Ambassador Wolfgang Wollte, compared the often 'arrogant and negative attitude of the Twelve EC members with the Elvis Presley song 'The lady loves me, but she doesn't know it yet'.[15]

With the 12 so reluctant to accept the logic of bringing Austria into the club, its diplomats used the cultural card to soften the EU's attitude, bringing the Vienna Philharmonic and other cultural attractions to Brussels. They hoped to persuade Brussels that the small alpine republic could enrich the EC's cultural life. Doubts about the Austrian ability to meet its obligations as a member, if it also held to its neutrality, surfaced regularly – as they continue to do to this day. Britain's Foreign Secretary, Sir Geoffrey Howe, responded to the Austrian application by questioning 'the serious issues for the future of the Community if one country's neutrality qualified its acceptance of future developments'. Germany's Foreign Minister, Hans Dietrich Genscher, was more positive, and argued that it was not for the EC countries to worry about Austrian neutrality if the Austrians themselves were willing to take on all the responsibilities of membership.

Belgium appeared to be the most concerned by possible Soviet objections. The Commission should not be empowered to probe the Austrian application until clarity could be established about the Soviet attitude. Vienna was infuriated by a suggestion from Belgian Foreign Minister Mark Eyskens that the EC should negotiate with Moscow to free Austria from its obligations as a neutral state. It reflected Belgian ignorance about the fact that neutrality had been adopted by the Austrian parliament only after, and not as part of, the State Treaty. 'Senior Austrian diplomats had to interrupt their summer holiday to brief the Belgian Foreign Ministry on the subtle differences between the State Treaty and Austria's neutrality law. However, Eyskens later became a true friend and supporter on the way to Austrias's EU membership.'[16]

Austria was kept in the Commission's waiting-room for almost four years without being able to negotiate the substance of the membership terms. Its impatience was plain for all to see. Austria belonged to the heartland of Europe, an *aide memoire* handed to the Commission in February 1990 insisted. The country's neutrality would be 'Austria's contribution to the peace and security in Europe'. Its links with the countries of Central Europe would enhance the EU's weight.

EU countries were hard to convince that Austrian neutrality would be an asset to the grouping. When the entry negotiations finally got underway in 1993, EU countries were already deeply embroiled in Yugoslavia's disintegration, and wanted to know the limits of a neutral Austria's willingness to join in military measures to end the fighting or to police a possible settlement. Austrian negotiators were closely questioned about the practical application of neutrality, and had to provide assurances of solidarity with the EU's goal of achieving a common foreign and security policy. At the same time there were growing doubts whether neutrality still had much meaning in the post-Communist world, and whether Austria was right to continue to cling to neutrality, even if its prime purpose had been, and still was, to bolster Austria's sense of national identity.

The debate about European security has of course moved way beyond the situation that prevailed during Austria's membership negotiations. With Hungary, Poland and the Czech Republic now admitted to full NATO membership, Austria has to decide whether it wants to be seen as a non-combatant island surrounded – bordered not only on the west but also now on the east – by a military alliance involving itself ever more deeply in post-Communist European security affairs. The debate became acute after the NATO intervention against Yugoslavia over ethnic cleansing in Kosovo.

However, even though Austria was within its rights to deny its airspace to NATO war planes, the action caused other EU countries to question Austria's commitment to the pursuit of common foreign and security policies within the EU and the new commitment to establish its own defence identity. Austria's political leaders have yet to give an unequivocal answer to that challenge. During the entry negotiations, its diplomats constantly stressed Austria's connections with Eastern and Central Europe as a crucial asset in weighing up its membership qualifications. With Hungary, Poland, and other ex-Communist bloc countries clamouring to join the EU, Austria could act as locomotive, bringing the nations of the old Austro-Hungarian monarchy back into a common institution. During the negotiations they were still counting without the steam of xenophobia conjured up by Haider, and the fear of cheap labour pouring into Austria across open frontiers.

After a final marathon round of negotiations, Austrian accession was finally secured on 1 March 1994. The European parliament approved the accord three months later. To complete the process, the referendum vote in Austria on 12 June 1994 delivered a two-thirds majority in favour of membership. The triumph was all the greater since Haider had run an 'Austria first' campaign against entry. He quickly absorbed the lessons of this defeat, and switched from opposition to EU membership to concentrate on opposition to enlargement, an issue where he has found consistent support.

When the day came in January 1995 for Austria to take its place as a full member, it signalled 'a certain coming of age after a long and lonely post-war adolescence as a small neutral buffer between the cold war blocs,' the *Guardian*'s correspondent in Vienna wrote. 'Is this the end of an era, a farewell to the Vienna of the sticky chocolate cake and sugary

Strauss? Hello to an uncertain world of breached taboos, populism and Euro-federalism?

'For the big EU powers, Austria's accession is a mixed blessing. Affluent Austria will be a net contributor to the Community's coffers... and already the country's leaders talk positively of monetary union. Germany is delighted to see Austria in the EU since it means she is no longer alone in bordering the less stable half of the Continent... yet these common interests and the eastward shift in the Union's centre of gravity have provoked fears in Paris.'[17] Indeed President Francois Mitterrand had complained that German unification and Austrian entry meant that there were now three German states in the EU.

The perception of Austria as a German state was an image that its political leaders had fought to discard since 1945. Vranitzky told the French President in no uncertain terms that 'We are the first and only Austrian state. There will be no spectre of a teutonic state in the EU.'

— * —

Vranitzky was equally determined that Austria's small size should not prevent it from occupying a place in the EU's premier league. The other members were watching closely as Austria's coalition government used the long-established social partnership with industry and trade unions to drive forward the privatisation process, and curb the welfare state to bring the budget under control – and work towards meeting the criteria for economic and monetary union and the launch of the Euro. 'EU membership has put new strains on a society already struggling to cope with the liberalising forces of the past decade',[18] the annual *Financial Times* survey found at the end of 1995. But a year later it was already obvious that 'Austria is proving a model member of the European Union in many respects... Today it is among the half dozen richest members of OECD countries. It still has one of the lowest unemployment rates in Europe, enviable price stability and a well-trained labour force'[19] – familiar observations to those recalling Austria's progress in the 1960s, but no less welcome for that. Moreover, Austria's performance within the EU continued to improve.

Vranitzky stepped down in January 1997, and there was a smooth transfer to his chosen successor Viktor Klima. The country had succeeded 'in renewing its strong historical ties with its Central European neighbours and consolidating its position as one of the world's richest and most stable countries. Austria's economy, after a two-year hiccup, was starting to motor again, and there were flattering statistics to demonstrate the country's economic and social maturity. Its record of the highest long-term productivity growth of any OECD country was being maintained. Its unemployment rate was still less than half the European average and its inflation rates remained one of the world's lowest. Its citizens were recognised as being among the best educated in the world and its record of peaceful labour relations could only be bettered by Switzerland.'[20]

One Austrian citizen credited with making a considerable contribution to Austria's standing within the EU is Franz Fischler, the Commissioner responsible for administering the Common Agricultural Policy. He quickly mastered the intricacies of the farm policy, and became a familiar face on TV screens throughout the EU. At first, 'he was not seen as a big political hitter'. But as the Commission s came under heavy fire for incompetence and corruption, Fischler remained untainted. 'Ask any European diplomat to name the most effective of the 20 commissioners, and Fischler invariably comes in the top five or six.'[21]

During the second half of 1998, Austria took over the presidency of the EU. With Austria centre stage, there was deliberate symbolism in the fact that 'the Chancellor and his ministers sketched their ambitions in the white and gold chamber where Metternich chaired the Congress of Vienna that recast the map of Europe in 1815'.[22]

As the Austrian presidency drew to its close, the *Financial Times*, once more publishing its annual survey of the country, said that 'Viktor Klima could be forgiven for feeling a touch of pride... Today Austria is once again a regular port of call for Europe's politicians.' Even though not on a par with Metternich, Chancellor Klima had acquitted himself well during Austria's first six months' spell in charge of the EU economy. 'The Austrian economy is once again growing faster than the EU average... Fears that Austria will be one of the main casualties of any fallout from Russia's financial turmoil have been overstated. As often is the case with Austria, there is a yawning gap between image and reality... While some of Austria's banks are more exposed than they should be to Russia's economic turmoil, most Austrian companies have escaped unhurt.'[23] Enlargement poses headaches for Austria, but these should be seen as a huge opportunity. Again there is a big difference between the image of gloom and doom conjured up by Haider and the reality, that 'Austria has already derived considerable benefit from the opening up to the East. An estimated 100,000 jobs have been created... If enlargement is successful, then Vienna could become the hub of the most dynamic region of Europe.'

— * —

For Austria to regain a pre-eminent place in Europe, it was never going to be enough for it to be confirmed as a stable, democratic and a prosperous member of the EU. It required one more element: the gap had to be closed between the myth and the reality of Austria's relationship with Nazi Germany, and the Austrian people had to be confronted with the historical truth. After long years of prevarication, Vranitzky and his successor, Klima, finally gave the lead, so that the Austrian nation, after decades of evasion, could be brought to confront the shadows of its

Second World War past. At last, Austrians were emerging from their amnesia, and the international community applauded. Before Vranitzky, a blind eye had been turned to the skeletons of the Nazi era. The Waldheim presidency made it impossible to sustain this posture: unless Austria wanted to remain an international outcast, it had to accept its responsibilities for Nazi crimes.

Yet even though Vranitzky understood the strength of this argument, he was slow to act, and it was not until 1991, when Waldheim's controversial term of office was nearing its end, that he finally had the political courage to appear before parliament and acknowledge Austria's guilt and apologise in the name of the whole nation for the crimes of Austrian Nazis. Vranitzky should have read the writing on the wall when he became Chancellor in 1987. Had he urged Austria to confront historical truth when he presented his first government programme to parliament, Austria would have had a credible defence against its critics, the Waldheim effect might have been neutralised, and Austria might have avoided its pariah status during the Waldheim era. But he missed the opportunity then, and tackled it only half-heartedly during the commemoration of the fiftieth anniversary of the Anschluss in 1988.

On that occasion Vranitzky acknowledged that individual Austrians had been guilty, but attached no blame to the nation itself, and limited himself to urging Austrians to reflect and reassess Austria's role in 1938. 'For Austria today it is not so much a question of what happened 50 years ago... but rather our present attitude towards it. It would be a mistake to think that these things are too far in the past to be relevant today.' In place of 'pragmatic amnesia', Vranitzky wanted to 'draw on the historical canvas, highlighting three areas which Austrians should study in some detail: the period of Austria's own clerico-fascist state, 1934–8; the transformation of independent Austria into the German Reich's "Ostmark"; and Austria, defined by the Allies as Hitler's first victim, under four-power occupation'.[24]

Abroad, this was certainly taken as a step in the right direction; but it still fell far short of an unqualified frontal attack on the selective interpretation of history. Vranitzky had ignored advice to use the Anschluss anniversary to direct the Austrian nation on to much firmer ground. Soon after he became Chancellor, he had set up a small council of 'wise men'. One of them, Hugo Portisch, had outlined a whole series of positive measures to combat the image of Austria as a 'Nazi country'. He had urged the government to go before parliament to confirm both Austria's acceptance of moral responsibility and outline a generous approach to restitution and to reconciliation with Austria's widely dispersed Jews.

The ideas that Portisch put forward in his confidential memorandum prevailed, but only after a delay of four years. Vranitzky seems to have agreed with the Portisch prescription from the outset, but dithered.

Portisch had addressed himself to Austria's image abroad, whose ugly contours had been exacerbated by Waldheim but had been present earlier. Experience had shown, he argued, that the outside world saw Austria as a country 'that had thown itself into Hitler's arms, had participated in his crimes, but had decided to lie about all this and instead to portray itself as a victim. The burden of the allegations against Austria was to unveil it as a Nazi country.'[25] Obviously the Moscow Declaration and the readiness of the wartime Allies, even during the post-1945 occupation era, to treat Austria as Hitler's victim had been one reason why Austria had been able to hide itself from the truth for so long. But if Waldheim's Austria was being demonised by the international community, much of the blame must be attributed to Austria's long record of self-delusion: with Austria's failure to recognise its responsibility towards its Jewish victims, who had died in the concentration camps or at best been driven out of the country. Not only moral considerations, but self-interest, demanded a radical change of attitude. Austria's handling of the restitution issue had been bureaucratic and inhumane. Many of the refugees themselves, as well as their children, had come to occupy positions of influence abroad. They had become embittered and angry, and portrayed Austria in a far worse light than was justified by the country's real behaviour, Portisch stressed.

The impression of a 'country that felt no responsibility for the fate of Jews had been further worsened by its Middle East policies: the premature recognition of the PLO by Chancellor Kreisky, invitations to Yasser Arafat and Col Gadhafi; constant criticism of Israel. Neither the US nor Israel were prepared to accept that a country that bore co-responsibility for the Holocaust could assume this degree of freedom in the Middle East.'[26] A third factor that had contributed to Austria's poor image was scarcely its fault: the UN had come to be perceived in the US and in Israel as an instrument of pro-Arab policies. For ten years, the UN had had Waldheim as its Secretary-General. The connection had rebounded on Austria to generate yet more negative feelings towards the country.

How could the world be convinced that Austria deserved to be judged more positively, and could be trusted? How could the damage of the Waldheim presidency be contained? Portisch was adamant: Austria could never prove its good faith, could never convince world opinion by relying on legalistic arguments or a recital of denazification processes undertaken after 1945. Like Germany, Austria must deal with its contentious history as a political and humane problem. Portisch advised Vranitzky that the Austrian government should, at the earliest possible opportunity, make a formal declaration acknowledging and assuming responsibility for all the deeds of its citizens during the Nazi era. The government should also recognise the material and moral obligations that would flow from such a declaration. Austria should take a leaf out of Germany's readiness to come to terms with the Nazi era. Germany's post-war leaders had recognised the country's responsibility for Nazi crimes much sooner, and had handled restitution issues with generosity. This had been a key factor in reducing anti-German feeling abroad.

Among the facts that the Austrian government had to acknowledge were the deportation and murder of 65,000 Austrian Jews, the forced emigration of another 100,000, and the involvement of many Austrians in the persecution of the Jews. Austria must recognise its guilt and share of responsibility, although the Great Powers, who did nothing to help Austria after the Anschluss, were not blameless. Among the practical measures that Austria should take, Vranitzky was advised, were acceleration of reparations and generosity in response to claims. Austrian emigrés should be made to feel that Austria remained their country, and was at their service, especially for the elderly and those in need.

Speed was of the essence, Portisch argued in 1987. Three years later, the Austrian government had still not acted on his advice; Waldheim's Austria was still ostracised by large parts of the world, and Austria still led a schizophrenic existence – admired for its economic achievements but reviled for perpetuating its victim image. Portisch went public and issued a challenge: he wrote an article in Austria's leading Jewish journal, *Das Jüdische Echo*, and broadcast a commentary on Austrian television, in both insisting that Austria must finally be brought to face the facts. Portisch's stature was such that his intervention created a big stir in Vienna.

Finally, in July 1991, Vranitzky felt that public opinion was ready to accept harsh home truths. In an address to parliament, broadcast live on TV, he acknowledged for the first time in the full glare of publicity, that many Austrians had backed Hitler's Third Reich, and had been instrumental in its crimes. The declaration was an historic modification of the long-held state doctrine that Austria was Hitler's first victim. Vranitzky highlighted Austrian culpability in the Holocaust.

Without honestly evaluating its own history, he argued, the Vienna government could not expect to be accepted as a morally credible partner in present-day issues. And in a public gesture that would have been unimaginable even a decade before, he went on to apologise for atrocities committed by Austrians. Closely echoing Portisch's 1987 draft, Vranitzky acknoweldged the good as well as the evil of Austria's recent history: 'As we lay claim to the good, so we must apologise to the survivors and the descendants of the dead for the evil people among us'. He continued, 'Many Austrians embraced the Anschluss, supported the Nazi regime and upheld many levels of the hierarchy. Many Austrians took part in the repressive measures and persecution of the Third Reich, some in prominent positions. Even today we cannot brush aside a moral responsibility for the deeds of our citizens.' He added the promise that the Austrian government would do everything in its power to help those not included in previous reparation measures. He claimed that Austrian politicians had in the past frequently spoken on similar lines. But his declaration had a special significance, as it was being delivered in parliament to set 'a standard for the political culture of our country and as a contribtution to the new political culture in Europe'.[27]

Vranitzky's declaration did not produce an instant change in international opinion about Austria. The US and Israel were particularly hard to convince that a sea-change had occurred, or that the Austrian establishment was cured of its political amnesia. But gradually, as the government continued with its drive to make Austrians gain a better understanding of their past, and placed greater emphasis on restitution measures, the outside world began to accept that Austria was prepared to abandon the self-deception which it had enjoyed since 1945.

Vranitzky made another important confidence-building gesture during an official visit to Israel in 1993. In a speech at the Hebrew University in Jerusalem, the Chancellor restated the gist of his 1991 declaration, singling out the moral responsibility that Austria must bear for the Holocaust, and the forgiveness that it sought from survivors. But he also went out of his way to stress the important contributions to Austria's culture and character which the nation owed to its Jews. Austria's 'moral responsibility weighs double because we are aware of how much of ourselves, our own life, our culture has been destroyed by the firestorm of the Nazi barbarians. Much of what Austria is proud of today, from Sigmund Freud to Gustav Mahler, from Arnold Schoenberg to Ludwig Wittgenstein, from Karl Kraus to Theodor Herzl, from Stefan Zweig to Victor Adler, is part of our Austrian heritage. In sharing collective responsibility we appraise this heritage, we claim to be part of our history.'[28]

Vranitzky insisted that the Austria he represented deserved to be seen as 'a new, a modern and self-confident country, an independent democratic state that has been established as the antithesis to Naziism'. Austria had undertaken enormous financial effort in caring for the victims of the Holocaust. But the way it had been done often 'seemed to come out late, timid and in piecemeal fashion, as if to hide a bad conscience'. Since his 1991 declaration many measures had been taken to change the situation, and further improvements would be made, Vranitzky promised. The speech was well received in Israel, but not without caveats. While his own good faith was not in question, that of many of his compatriots remained in doubt.

'He has done more than any other Austrian leader to set the record straight on Austria's relationship with the Jewish people. Unlike many of his countrymen, Vranitzky does not suffer from the collective amnesia regarding Austria's actions between 1938 and 1945 when an estimated 70,000 Austrian Jews perished. Austrians have been fond of claiming that they too were the victims of the Nazis, a nonsense that Vranitzky has forthrightly exposed.'[29] If Austria really wanted to atone for its sins, it should end what Israel perceived as a pro-Arab bias in its Middle East policies. It should also do more to counter Haider's xenophobia.

Israel will never be fully convinced of Austria's good faith. But even Austria's harshest critics abroad could not ignore the new emphasis on education to achieve greater knowledge and awareness of the Holocaust in Austria. Political and church leaders have made great efforts to set the historical record straight. School books have been rewritten; anti-semitism has been decried. Both Waldheim's successor, President Thomas Klestil, and also Vranitzky's successor, Viktor Klima, have given a determined lead. A national fund was established for the benefit of Jewish survivors. The law was amended so that Austrian refugees who had settled abroad but wanted to reclaim their Austrian nationality were able to have dual nationality. Restitution claims are handled expeditiously. Under the terms of a declaration drawn up by Klestil, Chancellor Schüssel's government is 'committed to a self-critical scrutiny of the National-Socialist past', and to acceptance of Austria's 'responsibility arising… from the Nazi regime'.

The controversy surrounding the new Holocaust memorial in Vienna has focused on its location and not on its desirability; the controversial Wehrmacht exhibition in 1998, which confronted Austrians with unpalatable truths, was defended by the government in no uncertain terms. No relevant anniversary has been allowed to pass without official commemoration. An annual day of remembrance, 5 May, has been set 'in memory of the Victims of Naziism and against Violence and Racism'. Honours have been heaped on Simon Wiesenthal. Ordinary people have trekked in their thousands to Mauthausen, the site of Austria's most notorious concentration camp, and have listened in silence as Cardinal Franz König, Klima and other leaders have demanded that Austrians persevere with the long and painful process of facing up to the truth and correcting mistakes.

'Austria faces up to legacy of wartime collaboration,' the *Washington Post* headlined its verdict on Austria in 1998, 60 years after the Anschluss. 'A dramatic transformation is taking place in the way this nation of 8 million people looks at one of the most sordid chapters in its long history… In contrast to former President Kurt Waldheim, who for many years covered up his involvement in wartime atrocities, Austria's leaders now speak with striking candour about the fact that many compatriots were linked to Nazi crimes and that the rampant anti-semitism that culminated in the Holocaust found fertile soil here.'[30] Klima emphasised that all this was not just a matter of facing up to the past but of countering Haider's message. Austria's changing assessment of its historic culpability has gone beyond words. The country's two dominant parties, acting through their coalition government, recognised that they could not change history but that they could, and must, correct its mistakes.

The big unknown is how the Freedom Party will use its power, now that it is in government, to influence the course set by Austria's mainstream parties to confront Austrians with their controversial past and to win public support for generous compensation to the victims of the Holocaust. All the signs are that Haider believes that more than enough has already been done. He prefers to take a leaf out of the Kreisky era and plead for a line to be drawn under the past.

NOTES ON CHAPTER XII

1 *Financial Times Survey of Austria*, 25 June 1990.
2 Ibid.
3 Speech by Haider in Vienna's Hofburg, 13 November 1999.
4 Federal government statement 3 February 2000.
5 *Die Zeit*, 3 February 2000.
6 *Observer*, Nicolas Fraser, 14 March 1999.
7 *Guardian*, Misha Glenny, 20/11/86.
8 Ibid.
9 Henry Grunwald, *One Man's America*, Anchor Books, p 603.
10 *Guardian*, Hella Pick, 23 November 1986.
11 *Independent*, Michael Wise, 14 November 1991.
12 *Financial Times Survey of Austria*, 1 December 1997.
13 *Financial Times Survey of Austria*, 11 April 1988.
14 Lecture by Dr Herbert Batliner at the Euroa Institute, 29 May 1998.
15 Ibid, p 120.
16 Otmar Lahodynsky, *Oesterreichs europaeische Zukunft: Die kurvenreiche Strasse nach Brussel*, Signum Europa Bibliothek, 1996, p 119.
17 *Guardian*, Ian Traynor, 3 January 1995.
18 *Financial Times*, 12 December 1995.
19 *Financial Times*, 15 November 1996.
20 *Financial Times*, 1 December 1997.
21 *Financial Times*, 11 December 1998.
22 *The Times*, 2 July 1998.
23 *Financial Times*, 11 December 1998.
24 Vranitzky quoted in *New Statesman*, Misha Glenny, 26 March 1988.
25 Hugo Portisch, memorandum, 8 April 1987.
26 Ibid.
27 Speech by Franz Vranitzky's, 8 July 1991.
28 Speech by Franz Vranitzky, Hebrew University, 9 June 1993.
29 *Jerusalem Post*, 10 June 1993.
30 *Washington Post* and *International Herald Tribune*, 6 April 1998.

XIII

The Restitution Go-slow

In most respects, Austria's post-war history can be neatly divided between two eras: first the ten years of occupation, and then, after 1955, Austria's progress as a fully sovereign nation-state. But there is one important exception: the murky story of Austria's response to demands for restitution, and to claims for compensation, from survivors of Nazi persecution straddles both eras, and only took a decisive turn for the better after 1991, when Austria was finally persuaded to accept responsibility for its persecution of Jews and other minorities. Until then, Austria prevaricated and resisted external pressure for restitution – even to the point of defying provisions of the 1955 State Treaty. Austria's behaviour undoubtedly prejudiced its search for international respect, and alienated influential power brokers among Jewish groups abroad.

Between 1945 and 1991, official doctrine held that Austria as a victim state had no legal or moral obligation to compensate individual victims or restore their property. Even though this was not applied as a blanket policy, and some piecemeal compensation measures were adopted in response to pressure from Washington and Jewish lobbies abroad, Austria always contended that it was to Bonn that claims against the Nazis should be addressed. It was a spurious argument, and there is an apocryphal story to illustrate German Chancellor Konrad Adenauer's exasperation over the constant attempt to shift all responsibility for restitution on Germany:

he is said to have warned an Austrian diplomat that if he heard it once more he would send Hitler's ashes as a present to Bruno Kreisky.

The drive to make Germany pay for restitution claims was rejected by successive German governments. They refused to make themselves liable for Nazi crimes committed by Austrians within Austria. However, in sharp contrast to Vienna's negative attitude to restitution issues, the Bonn republic needed little prompting to respond to claims related to Nazi crimes in Germany itself. Beginning with Adenauer, the Germans understood that generosity towards Nazi victims was an essential component of Germany's rehabilitation in the international community. It was an example that Austria was reluctant to follow until 1991. Then, at last, restitution policy was radically revised. A combination of factors – the furore surrounding Kurt Waldheim's presidency, a desire to disavow anti-semitism, the end of the Cold War, and generational change – brought about a new awareness of Austria's flawed past. Step by step during the last decade of the twentieth century the Austrian government sought to demonstrate to the international community that it had turned over a new leaf in meeting its responsibilities towards Hitler's victims in Austria. But the groundswell of resentment built up during the long years of non-co-operation has continued to affect the way Austria is judged by the international community. Questions are still being posed whether Austria has really mended its ways, whether doubts about its good faith with respect to restitution can really be set aside, whether Jörg Haider's success signifies restitution fatigue.

If the outside world has been slow to wake up to the new realism in Austria's policy on restitution it is the consequence of long years of denial, which have served to undermine trust in Austria's willingness to recognise and meet its commitments to Nazi victims. There was a brief period in the early aftermath of the war when the Western Allies fully supported the Austrian government in its reluctance to grasp the nettle of restitution: their priority then was to prevent the Soviet Union from achieving its goal of securing for itself not only Austrian but also foreign-owned economic assets in the Soviet zone. They feared that concessions on restitution claims by Holocaust survivors could set a precedent and strengthen the Soviet case for reparations. But the US and UK could not long sustain this tacit accord to ignore inaction on restitution claims against Austria. By 1946, swayed partly by pressure from Jewish lobbies, the two allies changed tack and embarked on the long and thankless task of impressing on Austria that it could not be allowed to escape liability for the depradations of the Nazis.

Austria, however, was unyielding, and for decades refused to grasp the nettle. From the outset, restitution has been a deeply contentious issue in Austria's domestic politics, and a succession of post-war chancellors, beginning with Karl Renner and his successor, Leopold Figl, feared that their efforts to rebuild a national consensus would be undermined by a decision to accept liability for the victims' claims. Amid the destruction and chaos of the early post-war period, food and housing was short. People already resented the demands on scarce resources made by the tens of thousands of displaced persons, among them many Jews, scattered mostly in camps around the country. Antisemitism was much in evidence.

Renner did not want to antagonise domestic public opinion further by restoring to the survivors of the Holocaust or their heirs Jewish property and businesses seized by the Nazis in Austria. Out of fear that they would be accused of aggravating the acute housing shortage in war-damaged Vienna, Renner and his colleagues were not even prepared to encourage any of the emigrés to return to live in Austria – a mistake which deprived post-war Austria of valuable intellectual capital and instead only served to strengthen the anti-Austria lobby abroad. In fairness it must be said that among the Jews who had owned their own homes there was quite a number who succeeded in having 'aryanised' property restored to them, as did the relatively few Jewish landowners; a number of financial claims were also met. But all this was on a small scale quite disproportionate to what had been taken from Austria's Jews during the Nazi period.

Piecemeal, a handful of legislative measures were adopted during the early post-war years to establish a fund large enough to correspond to unclaimed, 'ownerless' assets, once the property of murdered Holocaust victims, and to set up administrative machinery for the return of property to the claimants who were still alive. But these measures were quite inadequate, and the fund existed only on paper, and was not endowed with any money. Many claimants were made to sell their property for meagre sums. Haider's properties in Carinthia are just one example of such exploitation. Political will was in short supply, and the legislation was never fully implemented. Soon the Americans were complaining bitterly that Austria must act more expeditiously. They insisted that restitution become an important agenda item of the State Treaty negotiations.

Overt manifestations of antisemitism, partly triggered by the pressure for restitution, became a major cause for concern to the Western Allies. Austrians vented their resentment over food shortages by demonstrating against Jewish inmates of the displaced persons (DP) camps, blaming them for lack of milk and other basic foodstuffs. When this was reported in the West as evidence of virulent antisemitism, Austrian leaders were embarrassed. Vienna's Mayor, Theodor Körner, protested against what he considered to be invented tales about antisemitism allegedly rampant in Austria. 'Letters and news stories reaching us indicate that certain circles abroad believe that Austria has retained its antisemitism even after the defeat of national socialism and its liberation from Germany. Such inventions have surfaced even in North America, and command widespread credibility.'[1]

Martin Herz, a senior political aide on the US High Commissioner's staff, concluded that the Austrian authorities, by protesting their innocence, recognised they had a credibility problem on their hands. 'The repeated denials of antisemitism published in Vienna's newspapers only serve to confirm that Austria's politicians, and to a certain degree even the general public, are aware of the damage caused by the impression abroad that antisemitism is alive and well in their country. Notwithstanding Vienna's Mayor Körner's outspoken denials, there can be no doubt that antisemitism continues to exist in Austria.'[2]

The cabinet discussions that led to the notorious recommendation to drag out implementation of restitution matters show quite unequivocally that antisemitism remained prevalent in post-war Austria. Almost all its post-war leaders could justly claim that they had never been Nazis. Several had experienced prolonged spells in concentration camps. But none of this prevented them from harbouring antisemitic feelings – a trait that many of them had in plentiful supply. In November 1948, the Austrian cabinet was weighing up its response to a US request for speedy action to activate the special fund, raised from the assets of Jews who had perished under the Nazis, so as to provide financial help for Jewish emigrés who were returning to Austria. Ministers argued that Austria had other, more important, priorities to rebuild schools, hospitals and the railway system. 'I cannot see why, at this juncture, any specific race should be given special privileges,'[3] Minister for Agriculture Joseph Kraus asserted.

A second Minister, Peter Krauland, responsible for economic planning, reminded the cabinet that they could not ignore the wider dimensions of the issue. Austria must take into account the pressure for action exercised from America by its Jewish population. 'There is no question but that needy Jews should be given assistance. We also have to weigh up the influence and the views of America's Jews.' This was quickly countered by the Minister for Food Supplies, Ernst Kolb. It was imperative to insist before the international community that Austria could not be held responsible for the plight of Jews. 'Austria was not responsible for the injustices suffered by the Jews. Austria and the greater German Reich were not one and the same state. They were separate entities.' Continuing the discussion, Minister of the Interior, Oskar Helmer, said that Austrians could not be entirely absolved from responsibility for the confiscation of Jewish assets. But that did not necessarily mean that the Jews should now be singled out for help. There were other equally deserving cases: 'I detect Jewish expansion all around, notably among doctors and in the trading sector in Vienna'. Drawing a parallel between the confiscation of Jewish assets after the Anschluss and the treatment of Austrian Nazis after the war, Helmer argued that 'the Nazis lost everything in 1945 and some of their academics have been forced to become labourers. We are no longer living in 1945. The English are now engaged in fighting the Jews in Palestine; the Americans have not implemented their promises [to the Jews]. The cruelties committed by the Jews during the fighting in Palestine are widely known.' The sum of these considerations led Helmer in 1948 to the conclusion that Austria should not rush to implement restitution measures. With that, the Minister pronounced his infamous phrase, which is quoted against Austria to this day: 'I am in favour of dragging this matter out'. The Americans, in Helmer's view, should be told that Austria had to take many issues into consideration before acting on the establishment of a fund for ownerless assets. 'There are people who understand this. Even the Jews themselves will understand [the complexity] of the issue, since they are themselves well aware of the antagonism that they arouse among many people. We should simply tell him [the US envoy] that we will consider the matter.'

The Chancellor had the last word. Endorsing the cabinet decision to put the restitution issue into abeyance, he emphasised that there would only be negative consequences if the government were to seek parliamentary approval for a special fund to aid the Jewish survivors. It would single Jews out for favourable treatment in unfortunate contrast to the 'difficulties' in which Nazis found themselves. Registered Nazi Party members had only recently been amnestied, and had their vote restored. The governing coalition could not afford to antagonise a voting bloc of 500,000 people. The Americans should be told that Austria had to sort out its budgetary problems before it could address the restitution issue. 'We shall explain: give us time to finalise our budget, and then we will see how we can help [the survivors]. Then we can also explore whether the Americans can provide aid'[4] to help pay the cost of compensation to the victims of the Holocaust.

As if it was not enough to dream up lame excuses for inaction on restitution, Figl that very same day indulged in a a public display of sympathy for Jewish concerns which would have been condemned as blatant hypocrisy had his audience known of the cabinet decision. The day happened to be the tenth anniversary of 'Kristallnacht'. Figl was attending a remembrance meeting organised by Vienna's Jewish community. In a breast-beating speech he declared that all of Austria bowed its head in sadness and in shame over the memory of what had taken place in Austria ten years earlier. He hastened to add that 'all these crimes had been planned and organised outside Austria's borders'.[5] The horror of the Nazi era could not be undone, Figl declared. Drawing a thick veil over the 'go-slow' decision taken by the cabinet earlier in the day, the Chancellor misled his predominantly Jewish audience with a promise to draw the lessons from what had happened and put 'reconstruction and restitution' high on the agenda. The Austrian government, he promised, would create the right kind of framework for a common future.

Even though the Austrian cabinet decision to stonewall on restitution was kept secret, neither the Jews nor the Americans were satisfied with

Austria's handling of victims' claims. There was constant prodding from the Americans, including warnings that the US Congress might become awkward over aid to Austria. American views were expressed in strong language in a letter from the US High Commissioner, Lt General Geoffrey Keyes to Figl in June 1949. It included a series of complaints about Austrian failure either to enact restitution legislation or to implement measures already adopted by parliament. Keyes was particularly incensed over the refusal to hand back flats where Jewish ownership had been clearly established, yet Nazis were allowed to remain in occupation. 'It is hard to understand why your administration has not taken the necessary measures to restore the flats to their rightful owners. It is surely unnecessary for me to spell out in greater detail the injustice of the situation.'[6]

US complaints were to no avail. Discrimination in favour of former Nazi Party members continued. Austria was naturally aware of foreign criticism, but at home the policy was not seriously challenged. During one cabinet meeting in 1950, the Minister for Education, Felix Hurdes, voiced a rare criticism when he observed that the principle of restitution was respected in favour of Nazi claims but not when Jewish claims were involved. 'The victims of Nazi oppression are always told that the impoverished state lacks the means to pay. But where Nazis are concerned, the impoverished state always finds the money. This is a double standard.'[7]

The Americans were reluctant to engage in a public dispute over the restitution issue. But the tone of their confidential missives became noticeably sharper. The US State Department noted in December 1952 that 'the Austrian government has made no progress in the matter of restitution or indemnification, and has in fact endeavoured to pass legislation that would compensate former Nazis ahead of victims of Nazi persecution'. This was becoming the stock theme of complaint and remonstrance from abroad. The Austrian cabinet repeatedly weighed up the risk of losing US financial support against the political and economic cost of setting up the ownerless assets fund. During a cabinet meeting in 1952 one of the Ministers observed that even if Austria met the State Department's wishes, 'it would not be treated one iota better'. Vice-Chancellor Adolf Schärf – before he became President – followed this up with the observation that American generosity was anyhow on a downward curve. At the same meeting, Schärf also questioned whether a sizeable number of Austrian Jews had really lost their lives. He was 'certain that the number of Austrian Jews who died [in the Holocaust] was relatively small. Most of them had escaped across the border.'[8] The implication of this was that if this was better understood the world would have a very different picture of Austria. No doubt it is all a matter of interpretation: the facts are that out of pre-war population of 190,000 Jews at least 65,000 lost their lives in concentration camps.

23. *(above)* In 1994 Austria acceded to the European Union, a milestone almost as important as the 1955 State Treaty. Austrians waved banners saying 'Europe is our future' as the two-thirds majority voted to join the EU.

24. *(below)* The increasing popularity of the far-right Freedom Party and its leader Jörg Haider *(below, seated, at a 1998 party rally)* was in part a popular reaction to the cosy arrangements and patronage which had dominated the Austrian political establishment since the 1950s.

25. *(above)* Jörg Haider, during the 1999 elections, declaimed that his far-right Freedom Party was the answer to all Austria's problems – including the issue of guilt about its Nazi past.

26. *(below)* Haider used every opportunity – including his own birthday celebrations – to create an image as a genial man of the people.

27. The emergence of Haider produced an outcry amongst many Austrians who, with their demonstrations, were keen to show that they shared the worries of the outside world.

28. *(above)* It was Wolfgang Schüssel's overwhelming ambition to become Austria's Chancellor which persuaded him into his controversial alliance with Jörg Haider's Freedom Party.
29. *(below)* President Thomas Klestil made no secret of his distaste in swearing in the Freedom Party as part of Chancellor Schüssel's administration, formed in early 2000.

While the politicians were willing to risk US displeasure over restitution, intellectuals in Vienna were prepared to alienate former colleagues who had emigrated after the Anschluss. The chequered story of the effort during the first few years after the war to re-establich the PEN writers' club in Austria, and reintegrate it with the international PEN movement is a typical example of procrastination, shows that there was a greater concern to reinstate Nazi sympathisers than to facilitate the return of Jewish emigrés, and a willingness to risk a poor image abroad rather than take decisions that appeared politically risky at home.

During the first few years after the war, the debate among the intellectuals focussed on the reluctance of writers in Austria to exclude Nazis from the post-war PEN club. This was countered by the determination of Austrian emigré writers, mostly in the UK, to secure not just the exclusion of former Nazi Party members, but also of anyone who had written for Nazi publications. Matters were further complicated by rumours on the one side of communist infiltration of Vienna's restored PEN club, and on the other of CIA penetration into Austria's intellectual life. There was good foundation to both. This led to endless disputes between right and left-wing PEN members, with some of the emigré writers drawn into the debate. Two delegates from Vienna were invited to the International PEN Congress, held in Zurich in 1947, to put their case for rejoining the mainstream of the movement. But Robert Neumann, who had emigrated to the UK and had founded the Austrian PEN club-in-exile, warned that Austria would not be allowed to re-enter the international community of intellectuals until it had cleansed itself of all Nazi connections. 'In Zurich you will have to overcome the reservations and doubts of all the countries who came to know the Austrians as participants and beneficiaries of the Nazi occupation [of Austria]... The view is widespread that Austria is far from denazifying its intellectual life.'[9] Eventually, in 1955, the Vienna PEN club was deemed sufficiently rehabilitated to host the annual International Congress. But the disputes over the politics of the Austrian club's membership were far from over; resignations and defections continued.

The fight over Bertold Brecht's move to gain Austrian citizenship was a typical example of the tensions that prevailed. Brecht, a German, had settled in the GDR after wartime exile in New York. The GDR treated him as their literary genius, as one who deserved to be put on display in person throughout the world. But travel on a GDR passport was cumbersome, and so the country's Communist Party, together with the Austrian Communist Party, decided that Brecht should secure Austrian citizenship. The Soviet occupation authorities endorsed Brecht's bid. But Friedrich Torberg, editor of the CIA-financed Austrian magazine *Forum* launched a protest campaign. The result was that Brecht secured his Austrian passport, but that his work was banned from Austrian stages – and he was in fact not performed there until the 1980s.

— * —

While these literary wars were seen as a test of Austria's intellectual honesty, the failure of international efforts to secure a satisfactory settlement of the restitution issue blighted Austrian efforts to draw a line under the Nazi era and to secure a clean bill of health for the post-war republic. The small Jewish community in Austria, always afraid of fanning antisemitism, was deliberately circumspect in pressing Austrian governments to adopt a more constructive policy on the victims' claims. But it had representatives on the Jewish Claims Committee (JCC) for Austria, which was formed by 22 Jewish organisations abroad. This was a forum where Austria's Jews could express themselves more plainly. The committee used its extensive influence in the US, UK and elsewhere to lobby governments to exert greater pressure on Austria to negotiate more expeditiously. Even so, it took eight years, from 1953 to 1961, before Austria finally agreed to pay $6 million dollars into a reparations fund. On a per capita basis this was substantially less that the sums that West Germany had already committed to reparation payments for Nazi victims. Much verbal blood was spilled in the process of securing the Austrian sum; Austria's good name suffered lasting damage. Throughout the negotiations, Austria denied legal liability, and said that it agreed to pay reparations only out of a sense of moral responsibility, repeating the same mantra: it 'had done no harm to anyone. For the actions against Jewish minorities, Germany alone must carry the liability – as it had annexed Austria.'[10]

Dr Nahum Goldmann, President of the World Jewish Congress (WJC), led the negotiations on behalf of the JCC. Its demands focussed principally on the establishment of a fund for needy Jews, arguing that the ownerless assets should be used for this purpose. The committee proposed an initial sum of 300 million Austrian schillings (approximately $11.5 million) – a sum that was immediately rejected by Vienna as excessive.

After much prompting from the US and British governments, the Austrian authorities finally agreed to open negotiations with the JCC in June 1953. But the meeting achieved little beyond Austrian promises of good intent. That autumn, both Goldmann and the US administration again forcefully urged Austria to act promptly and bring the negotiations to a satisfactory conclusion.

Austria's Chancellor Julius Raab initially ignored Goldmann's interventions, and eventually replied that Austria's freedom of action would remain circumscribed until the State Treaty was secured and Austria regained full sovereignty. In 1953 it was still far from clear when the Treaty would be finalised, but in any event Raab held that negotiations with the JCC could only resume six months after conclusion of the State Treaty. He also set out a long series of conditions, which only served to confirm that Austria was intent on stonewalling, even after it regained full sovereignty.

During a press conference in London in December 1953, Goldmann had no doubts that Austria was far more concerned to look after the interests of former Nazis than the Jewish victims. In a letter to Raab, he recalled that more than 65,000 Austrian Jews had perished under the Nazis, that whole families were decimated and had left behind significant assets which were of considerable utility to the Austrian economy: 'Surely no state would wish to take advantage from the murder of its citizens'.[11] The outcry abroad became ever more strident. At the end of 1953, the political director of the WJC portrayed Austria as the cradle of antisemitism, and insisted that the country had contributed significantly to the rise of the Nazis to power. Austria owed its existence to the generosity of the Western Allies. The least it could do now was to accept the 'minimal demand for $12 million restitution'[12] to help impoverished Jewish survivors.

By 1954 the State Treaty negotiations were entering their final phase. Jewish emigrés appealed to the Foreign Ministers of the US, UK, Soviet Union and France to prevail on Austria to act on restitution. Bruno Walter and Alma Mahler-Werfel were among the prominent Austrian emigrés who handed over a memorandum to the US Secretary of State, John Foster Dulles, in which they said that a majority of Austrians had actively supported the Nazi regime and had participated in its illegal activities. 'We can confirm from our own experience in that the Nazi movement in Austria was far from deriving exclusively from Germany. A majority of Austrians were active supporters of the Nazi regime, and participated in the atrocities.'[13]

Israel's Prime Minister Moshe Sharett expressed disappointment with Austrian inaction, and US Senator, Alexander Wylie, warned Austria that its international prestige was a stake. Goldmann told the American public that never before in negotiations with foreign governments had he experienced such disappointment and frustration as with Austria. The President of the American Federation of Jews, Gustav Jellinek, was even more scathing. He claimed that Austria had provided help for former Nazis but had done nothing for its Jews. 'The Austrian government likes to portray itself as the poor little man of Europe. But is it really so poor? With Marshall Plan aid Austria has achieved extraordinary economic recovery.'[14]

In November 1954, Raab went on an official visit to America. The JCC mobilised several governments to bring renewed pressure on Austria; while he was in New York, billboards were plastered with a call to Jews to boycott all events connected with the Austrian visit. The *New York Times* added its voice to the demands for justice for Austria's Jews, and highlighted the long-standing argument that Austria was far less inclined to aid Jews than to rehabilitate the country's former Nazis. Soon afterwards, the two leading US trade union leaders George Meany and Walter Reuther, not noted for their co-operation with one another, made a joint call on their Austrian counterparts to act: 'Free labour can do no less than work diligently to secure financial justice for the victims of naziism'.

The 1955 State Treaty included an obligation on Austria to return sequestered property to its former owners, and where that was no longer possible to pay compensation. It stipulated that this provision should be implemented within 18 months.[15] Austria turned a blind eye, and made no attempt to meet the time limit. In the absence of any attempt by the other signatories to enforce it, this section of the Treaty was allowed to become a virtual dead letter.

Desultory negotiations on restitution did resume after the State Treaty. But the exhortations to Austria to act with speed and decency continued to fall on near deaf ears. Adoption of a further handful of minor measures to help Austrian Jews only reinforced international demands for comprehensive legislation. The Austrian government, however, was far more mindful of domestic pressure, which was against generosity to the Jews. It listened sympathetically to insistent complaints from Austria's far right – the Freedom Party – that the Jews were over-reaching themselves and that their financial demands had no justification. I have already described in an earlier chapter how Dulles urged Raab in 1958 to end the debate over restitution by establishing a $5 million aid fund. Raab not only rejected this proposal but made matters worse by referring Goldmann and the WJC once again to Bonn.

By July 1960, Goldman's patience was close to exhaustion. He issued a long statement highlighting Austrian delaying tactics and the country's failure to make good on its promises. His confidence in Austria's good faith was almost gone, he said. He was convinced that the nations of the West would sympathise with the bitterness and sense of disappointment felt by Jewish survivors. 'In the name of the 22 members of the Jewish Claims Committee, I am in duty bound to make public that our confidence in the goodwill of Austria to settle the complex restitution issues has been shattered. We are convinced that public opinion in the West has full understanding for the bitterness that is felt by Austria's victims of persecution.'[16] As happened so often in the sorry saga of Austria's reluctance to come to terms with history, on this occasion too the country's leaders shrugged off Goldmann's strictures, showing far too little appreciation of what was at stake.

One Austrian should have known better. However, for a long time Bruno Kreisky kept his distance from the restitution issue. During the period from 1953, while Kreisky held public office, first as State Secretary for Foreign Affairs, and after 1959 as Foreign Minister, he felt that as a Jew he should avoid active involvement in this contentious issue. Finally, in 1961, he decided to change tack and participate in the negotiations. He wanted to signal that the Austrian government had at last become more aware of the damage which its posture was inflicting on its international standing. After a sharply critical article in the *New York Times*, Kreisky had sent Raab a memorandum in which he stressed that Austria must follow the German example and act on restitution if it was to avoid further international opprobrium. He warned that 'our reluctance to fulfill our obligations will lead to growing attacks, and damage our external standing and vital interests. Austria will become the whipping boy of public opinion, while Germany's standing continues to rise… [Until now] I have deliberately kept my distance from the restitution issue, fearing that any concession from me would be criticised [in Austria] as opportunism. But now, in my capacity as Foreign Minister, I consider it an obligation to emphasise my concerns.'[17] Kreisky added that he would urge Germany to relieve Austria of at least part of the financial burden of meeting its restitution obligations. At long last, in March 1961, a significant step was taken: the government successfully sought the endorsement of the Austrian parliament of the $6 million fund to compensate the victims of political persecution for loss of their assets. But this sum, though it went a considerable way towards satisfying the Jewish claims that were on the table at that time, could only be paid out against successful individual claims. Since Austria still refused to accept legal responsibility, the country was not prepared to make an across-the-board payment to every survivor or to the children of dead victims.

It was not until the fiftieth anniversary of the Anschluss in 1988 that survivors were offered a small one-off payment of 2500–5000 schillings. It was described as a 'payment of honour'. Perhaps Austria's conscience was at last stirring? Austria had so far only repaid a fraction of the sums represented by the arianisation of Jewish property, the smashing of synagogues, the loss of income. Or had Austria learned that it could not continue to blame the WJC for its bad image in the international community? Amends would have to be made; Jewish claims would have to be taken seriously.

One observer of the scene in 1988 wrote that meanness and 'muddled arrangements, endlessly revised, now result in just under 4000 Austrians receiving special pensions. Children taken to concentration camps, however, get nothing because they cannot prove contributions to the pension system. Former SS men have had few difficulties over pensions. Austria did not agree to pay any compensation at all for Jewish property until 1962 – and then only $91 million – despite the fact that the State Treaty had laid down that this was to take place within 18 months of its ratification. When it did, bureaucratic delay ensured it was not paid in full.'[18]

———— * ————

Helmer's phrase, 'I am in favour of dragging it out', has become a classic of Austria's political lexicon. The country's critics use it regularly as a bad character reference for Austria. It sums up in a few anodyne words a policy of stonewalling over restitution that prevailed in Austria for almost 50 years after the end of the war. The cabinet papers recording the discussion between Helmer and his cabinet colleagues during the early post-war years only came to light in 1988. Even though the disclosures only confirmed a posture that had been obvious to all engaged in the protracted negotiations for a settlement, the post-war mind-set of Austria's leadership, now confirmed in black and white, had not lost its power to shock. The cabinet minutes, going back to 1948, illustrated much worse than obfuscation and duplicity; they also provided evidence of deep-seated antisemitism, and confirmed that leading politicians in Austria were quite prepared to discriminate in favour of former Nazis while resisting help for Jewish survivors.

The British historian Robert Knight stumbled on the cabinet papers while researching in the Austrian National Archive in 1983. He was working on post-war relations between Austria and the UK. His discovery was seen as an embarrassment. Officialdom did its best to hamper publication. Knight was refused further access to the archive. The prominent Austrian historian Oliver Rathkolb, engaged in similar research on Austria's relations with the US, was also prevented from consulting the cabinet papers. It took almost five years before Knight's account of the cabinet minutes of the discussions between 1945–52 on compensation for Austria's Jews was published; even then, the German edition was handled not by an Austrian publisher but by a German.

The book touched raw nerves in Austria. Peter Jankowitsch, Foreign Minister when Knight's book was published, declared that it was a 'grotesque distortion' of Austria's post-war history. 'Just as Austria was beginning to feel that international indignation over Kurt Waldheim's wartime past had died down, a fresh set of revelations had some citizens wincing,' *Time* wrote. Its account was headlined 'Looking at a blemished past – new evidence of antisemitism after World War II'. It described Knight's book as a 'sober and academic account that reveals that some of the leaders of the post-war republic were indifferent, even hostile to compensation, and that at times they voiced their opposition in terms that smacked of anti-semitism.' It told its world-wide readership how 'members of the government were torn between allied demands for compensation for concentration camp survivors and the certain knowledge that many of their countrymen would not accept just restitution for Jews'.[19] The magazine singled out a remark by Figl in 1947: 'Jews want to become rich quickly'. Intended as further evidence of Austrian antisemitism, the article also pointed to another extract from Knight's book, in which Schärf's words from the 1952 cabinet minutes were reproduced: 'the number of [Austrian] Jews who had perished [in the Holocaust] was only small'. The *Time* article, typical of many others in the Western media, served to put Austria, still smarting from the concerted Western anti-Waldheim campaign, even more on the defensive. But Knight's disclosures also added to the pressure to reassess Austria's behaviour during the Nazi era and to improve on its response to the victims of the Holocaust.

The change of policy took a long time to gestate. New thinking on restitution had been precipitated first and foremost by the Waldheim crisis, but also by Knight's disclosures of an Austrian leadership voicing antisemitic sentiments and seemingly impervious to the claims of Holocaust victims. In 1990, when Chancellor Vranitzky was already weighing up when and how to discard the victim doctrine and acknow-ledge responsibility for Austria's share in Nazi atrocities, the government decided to pay pensions to all Jews who had in 1938 been children between the ages of six and fourteen, and therefore too young to make social security contributions. Money was also set aside for the maintenance of old peoples' homes for Jewish survivors in Austria, Israel and the US.

Both of these measures were among suggestions put forward several years earlier by Hugo Portisch as part of his confidential advice to Vranitzky on the ways and means of repairing Austria's poor world image. Portisch had also advocated the establishment of a special fund to pay compensation to survivors who had not yet benefitted from earlier measures. This proposal was implemented – but not until 1995, three years after Vranitzky had relaunched Austria as a nation that must come to a truthful understanding of the Nazi era. 1991 had marked the definitive break with the discredited post-war restitution policy. That was the year when Vranitzky delivered his landmark speech, abandoning the simplistic victim version of history and acknowledging the Austrian state's moral responsibility for the participation of Austrians in the Nazi persecution of Jews. He went on to declare that 'much remains to be done and the government will do everything in its power to help those and meet the moral and material claims of those who were only partially covered, or not covered at all by previous measures'.[20]

The era of turning a blind eye to restitution claims was over; matters had been dragged out long enough. The signal had been given for a reversal of policy which would show the world that Austria was capable of fairness to the victims of the Holocaust.

— * —

1995 marked the fiftieth anniversary of the end of the war, and of the country's rebirth as the Second Republic. By way of atonement for the

Nazi era the Austrian parliament endorsed the creation of a 500 million schilling ($50 million) Nationalfonds für Opfer des Nationalsozialismus (National Fund for the Victims of National Socialism), under which a payment of 70,000 schillings (about $6000) has been made to all surviving Austrian Jews. The fund was also intended to pay towards more historical research into the Nazi era in Austria, and for Holocaust memorials.

Of course full restitution to the victims of the Holocaust can never be made. Life cannot be restored. Survivors cannot be compensated for their loss of roots and the upheavals of emigration. The significance of the measures that Austria has taken since 1991 has less to do with the size of the sums involved than with the formal endorsement, for the first time, of the principle that Austria had to assume responsibility for the suffering inflicted on Jews and other minorities in Austria during the Nazi era. 'Austria has a special responsibility to recognise the suffering inflicted on people by the Nazis, and to provide help,' Vranitzky emphasised in his parliamentary declaration. The new fund was intended 'as a visible sign that the Austrian people was aware of the darker side of its history'. Letters were sent on behalf of the Chancellor to all Austrian emigrés who had responded to invitations to register with the fund. It urged them to reclaim their Austrian nationality, which they would now be able to hold alongside their new nationality. And it underlined the radical change of official thinking in Austria: 'The adoption of this act [the fund] is to show you, as a victim of national socialism, that in recent years a new more open-minded attitude has come to exist in Austria regarding its own history. It may also indicate to you that Austria is no longer suppressing its recent past and has not forgotten you or any other victims of national socialism, who were able to save their lives only by leaving their home country, but rather that you are part of the Austria of today and are welcome in this country.'[21]

With the existence of the new fund, the political will to make amends became tangible; that much even Austria's sternest critics were prepared to conceede. But it was still not enough to satisfy the rising tide of international opinion demanding settlement of all outstanding claims against governments and companies that had exploited Nazi victims and had benefitted from the Holocaust.

In 1998, the Austrian government, alert to the new pressures, decided to set up an International Commission of Experts to undertake a root-and-branch investigation both into expropriation in Austria during the Nazi period, and to analyse the adequacy of the restitution measures implemented since 1945. Knight, who remains a controversial figure in some Austrian quarters, was not initially invited to join the commission. But after Raoul Hilberg, one of the historians chosen from outside Austria decided to withdraw, the selection panel – which included Simon Wiesenthal – turned to Knight. He readily accepted, and very likely saw this as a vindication of his efforts to tell the true story of Austria's approach to the restitution issue.

Establishment of the commission is symptomatic of the sea-change that has taken place in official thinking in facing up to the more unpalatable facts of history, and in recognising the imperative of giving concrete expression to the affirmation of Austrian responsibility for evils committed during the Nazi era. A further significant step was taken when Austrian banks agreed in 1999 that a sum of $40 million should be made available in settlement of claims against them by Holocaust victims whose accounts had been sequestered during the Nazi era.

— * —

There is much unfinished business for Austria to tackle; the situation is like an onion, with more being revealed with each layer that is unpeeled: Nazi gold deposited in secret bank coffers, unpaid insurance policies, failure to compensate slave labourers, art works that had not been restored to their rightful owners. A further task for the International Commission of Experts is to ensure that the last layers of expropriation, looting, destruction and theft will be exposed, and amends made.

An important issue, which Austria may be able to close even before the commission concludes its investigations, concerns the multitude of works of art seized by the Nazis from Austria's Jews. Hundreds of the most important objects and paintings 'found their way' into Austrian museums. What happened was tantamount to plunder, even blackmail, and is graphically illustrated by the fate of the important Rothschild collection. Ownership was nominally restored to Bettina Looram Rothschild soon after the war. But in fact Austria's post-war governments treated these important Jewish collections as war booty. Under the terms of a law on the prohibition of art exports adopted in 1923 to protect national treasures, the National Monuments authority decided that the bulk of the Rothschild collection, and several other Jewish-owned collections were designated 'national treasures', and could not be taken out of the country or put on sale abroad. The 'price' for securing permission to export some of the lesser works in these collections was to 'donate' the important ones to Austria's national museums. The policy had its critics in Austria as well as abroad, but for years no amount of pressure could persuade the Austrian authorities to free the sequestered works and hand them back to their owners.

Now all this has changed. Since 1998, Austria has at last recognised the inadmissibility of its actions. The then Minister for Culture, Elizabeth Gehrer, acting with singular determination and fighting any colleagues still intent on delay, insisted that Austria must act rapidly and in good faith to clear up the art scandals in all their ramifications. To the surprise of the international art world, Gehrer was as good as her word, and the Rothschild collection was handed over complete in Spring 1999, and the family was free to take them out of the country and offer them for sale.

Austria remains reluctant to free other works of art, and not every claimant has so far met with the co-operation that was extended to the Rothschild family. Nevertheless, Austria has won praise from an unexpected quarter: from Ronald Lauder, the former US Ambassador to Austria and closely associated with the WJC, who has praised Austria as 'one of the few countries that have tackled this problem (of the sequestered artworks) correctly and comprehensively'.[22]

It was not always so. The history of the missing works of art works is similar to every other aspect of restitution, involving obfuscation, circumvention, a reluctance to respect the commitments of the State Treaty, piecemeal legislation inadequately implemented. Where it differentiates itself from the long battle for financial compensation is the extent of attention that the missing art has consistently attracted outside Austria, and not only from Jewish organisations. Since 1984, the art world has been in the vanguard of international pressure on Austria to give up its stolen treasures.

The trigger for this campaign was an investigative article in the US magazine *Art News* entitled 'Testament of shame'. It exposed the fact that not only had the Austrian government unotrusively stored thousands of works of art in a monastery at Mauerbach, outside Vienna, but that several hundred more had been scattered in museums, government ministries and Austrian embassies abroad. While former owners, seeking the return of missing art, had had many of their claims denied, museum visitors, diplomats in Austrian embassies and officials in their ministries had been able to enjoy them. The disclosures created an international outcry. Initially, this focused much more on the hidden treasure in Mauerbach than on objects housed elsewhere. Their turn was to come much later – in 1998, when two Schiele paintings, on exhibition in New York as part of the Leopold collection in Vienna, were sequestered pending the outcome of an investigation into their rightful ownership. By then Austria was eager to co-operate.

This had not been the case in 1984, when the art world responded to the *Art News* disclosures with a long and hard backward look: the magazine described how Hitler had stored much looted art in the salt mines of the Ausseerland; how the Allies during the occupation returned art works to the Austrian authorities on condition that they do everything in their power to return them to their former owners; how the Americans began to question Austrian behaviour in this matter, as in other aspects of restitution; how under the State Treaty Austria should have dealt expeditiously, but did not, with claimants, making only derisory attempts to seek out former owners; how it took until 1969 – and one of

Simon Wiesenthal's campaigns to alert international concern – for the Austrian government to agree to publicise a list of unclaimed art works in its care; how it had remained impossibly hard to prove ownership, and how by 1980 less than 100 had been returned.

Legislation on ownerless art adopted in 1969 had allowed the Austrian government to take possession of any unclaimed works. This was a task the bureaucrats appeared to undertake with rather more enthusiasm than than they displayed in their response to the claimants. 'The Austrian government never behaved as though it had been wrong in the past; never took the view that there was a wrong to be put right,' the *Daily Telegraph* argued. 'The situation did not improve in the seventies. Indeed if anything it got worse. Jews who claimed property under the 1969 law were subject to all manner of devices to deprive them of what was theirs – legal obstruction, deception, blatant lies. In one case, for example, the Austrians actually argued that because a painting had been in the 'control' of the Germans in 1945, when the war ended, it had legally passed into the possession of the Austrian state, and therefore did not belong to the claimant from whom it had admittedly been stolen.'[23]

After the appearance of the *Art News* article, Austria extended the period open for claims on works of art, and published a new list of 8153 objects in its possession. Only 367 applications were made during the claims period, which ended in September 1986, and of these only 21 – comprising 151 objects – were accepted. 'Fifty years after Kristallnacht it was harder than ever for Jews to prove their case; memories were fading, survivors were frail. Yet the Austrian courts insisted on standards of proof that were, quite frankly, unreasonable.'[24] But by now the art world's attention was firmly fixed on Mauerbach. The government recognised it would have to act in the matter as much as with other aspects of restitution. After securing the agreement of Austria's Jewish community, it was decided to transfer legal rights to unclaimed artworks to them, and to auction the contents of Mauerbach for the benefit of Austrian Holocaust victims. The necessary legislation was adopted in 1994. The sale 'will make something good out of something tragic,' said Christie's, the London auctioneers who agreed to organise the sale without commission.

The Mauerbach sale, when it took place in September 1996, provoked widespread comment abroad, which once again raked over Austria's poor record on restitution. 'The sale is the result of a complex web of events, at the centre of which lies a decades-long Austrian state secret and the efforts of those who fought to bring it to light,' the magazine *Art and Auction* wrote in its October 1996 issue. It continued: 'In all the current uplifting talk of the long overdue righting of an injustice, the stubborn, cynical and deceitful behaviour of the Austrian government in concealing the artworks for four decades in the Mauerbach monastery, and resistance to all efforts to restore them to their rightful owners, has been, if not forgotten, largely subsumed in feel-good, smoke-and-incense rhetoric of "reconciliation" and "new beginnings"... the Austrian government now turns around and says with macabre smoothness: "We are sorry".'

The *Daily Telegraph* magazine article ended its account of the Mauerbach saga with the conclusion that 'The Mauerbach objects have been victims twice, once of the Nazis, and again since then, like orphans of war from pillar to post, symbols not only of the immense wrongdoing that began on Krystallnacht but also of the way memory has been manipulated by history in the aftermath of war'. It is an epitaph that applies not just to works, or to all other aspects of material restitution, but to the indefensible way that remembrance of the human beings, the victims of Nazi persecution, was handled for so long.

Under Chancellor Viktor Klima, Austria set about, with increased energy, to tackle the unpalatable past. There is even an element of competition with Germany and Switzerland in efforts to show that Austria wants now to prove itself a model for others to follow in all aspects of material and moral reparation.

As the effort to right at least some of the wrongs of the past has gathered momentum, Austrians are being warned against heeding Haider's message, and instead listen to those of their political leaders, as well as to their friends and critics abroad, who urge them to resist the temptation to put all painful memories behind them. Having briefly opened the history books, they must not be tempted to close them again.

Cardinal Franz König summed up the dangers when he spoke at Mauthausen in May 1998 on the fifty-third anniversary of the liberation of this concentration camp. He pointed to the repeated efforts to cover up the horrific deeds of the Holocaust, and to avoid confrontation with the truth. Nothing could be more damaging. 'Those who choose to forget history are condemned to live through the same again. Those who do not want to know precisely what took place will never be able to learn the lessons of history... We have a duty to understand the past – and as far as possible, to accept wrong-doing and make amends.'[25]

NOTES ON CHAPTER 13

1 *Wiener Zeitung*, 9 February 1947.
2 Memo, 4 March 1947, quoted in Robert Knight, 'Ich bin dafür die Sache in die Länge zu ziehen', minutes of the 132nd cabinet meeting, 9 November 1948, p 165.
3 Ibid., pp 195–8.
4 Robert Knight (ed.), *Wortprotokolle der Österreichischen Bundesregierung von 1945-52 über die Entschädigung der Juden*, Atheneum, 1988, pp 196–7.
5 *Wiener Zeitung*, 10 November 1948, extracted from 'Ich bin dafür die Sache in die Länge zu ziehen', op. cit., p 198–9.

6. Letter from General Keyes to Chancellor Figl, 21 June 1949, reproduced in 'Ich bin dafür die Sache in die Länge zu ziehen', p 217.
7. 'Protokoll der 212 Ministerratsitzung vom 18/07/1950', reproduced in 'Ich bin dafür die Sache in die Länge zu ziehen', p 225–6.
8. 'Protokoll der 275 Ministerratsitzung vom 8/01/1952', reproduced in 'Ich bin dafür die Sache in die Lange zu ziehen', p 239.
9. Klaus Amann, *PEN – Politik, Emigration, Nationalsozialismus: Ein Österreichischer Schriftstellerklub*, Bohlau, 1984, p 89.
10. Dietmar Walch, *Die Jüdischen Bemühungen um die materielle Wiedergutmachung durch die Republik Österreich*, Geyer Edition (History Institute of the University of Salzburg), 1971, p 23.
11. Ibid., p 26, quoted from Gustav Jellinek, 'Die Geschichte der Österreichischen Wiedergutmachung', in Walch, *Die Jüdischen Bemühungen um die materielle Wiedergutmachung durch die Republik Österreich*, op. cit., p 404.
12. Ibid., p 30–1.
13. Ibid., p 33, quoted from *Forum, Österreichische Monatsblätter für kulturelle Freiheit*. Vienna, February 1954, p 2.
14. Jellinek, *Die Geschichte der Österreichischen Wiedergutmachung*, op. cit., p 405.
15. Austrian State Treaty, Article 26.
16. Declaration by the President of the Committee for Jewish Claims on Austria, 1960.
17. Letter from Bruno Kreisky to Julius Raab, 12 January 1961.
18. *Independent*, Edward Steen, 23 February 1988.
19. *Time*, 11 July 1988.
20. Declaration by Chancellor Vranitzky in the Austrian parliament, 8 August 1991.
21. Letter dated 6 July 1995, signed by Gerda Themel-Sterk on behalf of the federal Chancellor.
22. *Die Presse*, report from Washington. 2 December 1998.
23. *Telegraph* magazine, September 1996.
24. Ibid.
25. Kardinal König, Mauthausen 10 May 1998.

XIV

Small but Far from Insignificant

A Personal Assessment of Austria

This has been a voyage foremost of rediscovery, but also of discovery, of coming to a closer understanding of my roots and learning aspects of Austria's past and present which I had previously ignored. As one of those forcibly uprooted from Hitler's 'Ostmark' in 1939 and dispatched in a 'Kindertransport' to London, and who has since made her life outside Austria, it was inevitable that I grew to have an ambivalent relationship to my country of origin. Would I ever be able to see Austria as my 'Heimat'? For a long time the question did not even pose itself, even though I frequently came to Austria, both professionally as a journalist and on holiday. Alienation was too profound. Now something has changed. Researching and writing this book has brought me closer to Austria. It has been a kind of homecoming.

I had not anticipated this when it was first broached that I should look at post-war Austria from an outside perspective. The initial focus was narrow: to assess the significance of the Kreisky era in terms of the Austrian Republic's efforts to define its identity and win a place of influence in the international community. But it was soon self-evident that a much broader perspective was essential to an understanding of how Austria is perceived, and the place it has been able to carve out for itself. How did it come about that Austria consistently attracted so much outside attention – and caused such deep controversy – quite disproportionate to its small size? Why is it, as Hugo von Hoffmansthal observed, that 'Austria is a small stage where the big events are rehearsed'?

Kreisky's long period in office certainly provides some of the answers. But there were so many other factors: the country's imperial Habsburg past; the failure of the First Republic, between the wars, to establish a firm foundation for the shrunken Austrian nation; economic crisis and the near civil war circumstances surrounding the Anschluss. After the Second World War came the effort to suppress the ugly aspects of Austrian behaviour during the Nazi era. Add to this the fact that Austria found itself placed on the fault-line between East and West during the Cold War, with the Great Powers jostling over the country during ten years of occupation, climaxing in the 1955 State Treaty, and the long-lasting emphasis on consensus politics as a platform on which to refashion national identity. With Kreisky came the drive both to give neutrality a new meaning – by developing the concept of an activist foreign policy – and to cement economic recovery so that it developed into a story of outstanding success and eventual membership of the EU.

Austria's cultural icons, especially its music-making and its art, have added another dimension to its impact on the world. So have its attractions for tourism. But there are other reasons, dark ones, that account for Austria's prominence: in the 1980s there was the international furore over Kurt Waldheim's successful bid for the Austrian presidency. Then there was Jörg Haider's steady rise towards political power, culminating in January 2000 in his Freedom Party's emergence as a member of Austria's coalition government. The Freedom Party in government came as a thunderbolt, transforming perceptions of Austria, and undermining – at least temporarily – much of the good-will Austria had built up over decades. It provoked such concern abroad, especially among Austria's partners in the EU, that it triggered sanctions to isolate the country and to shun high-level contact with its politicians and senior diplomats.

In this book I have explored a complex, often contradictory, set of phenomena to assess the image which the outside world has built up of Austria's tortuous search for regeneration, identity and international respect. This is, naturally, an ongoing process. At its most elementary, Austria still has the problem of establish that it is not Australia, and that neither the idyll of *The Sound of Music* nor the romantic cloak-and-dagger underworld of *The Third Man* – and certainly not Haider's fulminations – are a true reflection of Austria yesterday, still less of today. And even for observers with a sound knowledge of Austria, the jury is still out as to whether antisemitism has diminished to the point of irrelevancy, or that the Austrian nation has really taken to heart the injunction to accept responsibility for the persecution of Jews and other minorities during the Hitler era – that the extremes of racism are banished for good.

— * —

There is no entirely objective way of assessing Austria's transformation from post-war Cinderella to one of the EU's more prosperous members. By the same token, difficult choices have to be made in the selection of foreign commentaries on the many facets of life and events in Austria. There are mountains of material that combine to create images of Austria abroad: prejudices and preconceptions, the national interests of other countries, moral attitudes and emotional responses inevitably colour judgement.

I hope my journalist's training and experience have helped me to avoid distortion, and to analyse situations and events dispassionately. Journalism has also opened important doors. As the *Guardian*'s longtime foreign affairs specialist, I had often reported on major events in Austria, and had come to know many of its leading personalities. My familiarity with the Austrian scene increased further after 1994 when I began work on Simon Wiesenthal's biography. But none of this quite prepared me for the in-depth examination of Austria to which this project inevitably led.

I remain convinced that one of the central themes running through Austria's post-war history has to be the 'big lie', the *National Lüge*, the self-deception that has prompted so many Austrians to assert that the country could not be held responsible for the Nazi persecution of Austrian Jews because Austria had itself been Hitler's first victim. This attitude, maintained as official doctrine until 1991, discredited Austria abroad, led to adverse comparisons with Germany's way of coming to terms with the past, and diminished the image of an otherwise successful democracy that had clawed its way back from the detritus of World War II.

But I have come also to understand much more clearly the extent to which the four wartime allies, with their 1943 Moscow Declaration, deserve to be judged as co-conspirators in promoting and perpetuating the big lie well beyond its political sell-by date. It is not difficult to see the motives – different in each case – which persuaded the US, Britain, the Soviet Union and France to subscribe to the declaration. It is less straightforward to grasp the logic behind the decision to incorporate the victimhood concept into the 1955 State Treaty, while at the same time yielding to Austria's last-minute demand to scrap the Moscow Declaration's injunction that Austria had to be held responsible for its part in World War II, alongside Germany. The State Treaty provided Austria with a certificate of innocence whose validity was not seriously challenged outside Jewish circles until the mid-1980s, when Waldheim's falsified wartime record hit the world's headlines. The mud that was slung at Austria then would not have been as deep or as enduring if the country had adopted a more balanced attitude towards the Nazi era, and had admitted much sooner the need for a more realistic interpretation of its history during the Hitler years.

Many of those interviewed for this book have sought to convince me both that I am exaggerating the significance of the 'big lie' and that I have not paid sufficient attention to the reasons that led Austria's political leaders to perpetuate it. Such views deserve respect. However, my research for this book has convinced me even more than before that the widespread Austrian belief in its victimhood as a quasi-absolution for all the crimes committed in and by Austrians is unjustified.

I accept that the situation is not clear-cut, and that there were always individuals and groups of people who challenged the official line and appealed to the national conscience to take a more balanced view of the Nazi era. The exhibition *Niemals Vergessen* ('Never Forget'), staged in Vienna in the autumn of 1946, and the public demonstrations two decades later in 1968 linked to the notorious Borodajkewycz case were probably the most public expressions of national concern to set the record straight. The Communist-sponsored exhibition included haunting drawings and accounts of the persecution of Austrian Jewry. The Borodajkewycz case exposed the continued presence of Nazi professors at the University of Vienna, and brought thousands of people out into the streets to protest against a teacher who was still preaching the virtues of Hitler and Greater Germany. Such anti-Nazi demonstrations, and other events, were honourable and good; but they only concerned a tiny minority in the country, and did nothing to soften the authorised doctrine that Austria must be seen as a victim state. Dissent was never substantial enough to alter my view that the long delay in amending the official version of history has done lasting damage to Austria's international credibility.

But at least I now understand better than before the circumstances and motivation that led the first generation of Austria's post-war leaders to cloak itself in the victim's mantle. Several of these leaders had been in concentration camps or Hitler's prisons, and justifiably saw themselves as victims – even though, unlike tens of thousands of Austrian Jews, they had not paid with their lives. They had known at first hand the profound divisions of the inter-war years that had destroyed the First Republic and opened the door to the Nazis. In the immediate post-war period, and under allied pressure, they adopted stringent denazification measures. However, once it became obvious that mounting preoccupation with the emerging Cold War had led the Western Allies to lose interest in denazification, Schärf, Figl and their colleagues felt free to concentrate on their first priority, the construction of a new national identity. They worked with mirrors. Austria, they held, was not under 'occupation', but only subject to 'Allied command', a subtle nuance, but one which highlighted their interpretation that Austria was liberated in 1945 and had regained its sovereignty. Austrian society, they concluded, must be inclusive; all political forces had to be drawn in, even the former Nazis. The concept of Austria as a victim state was seen as a unifying force;

decision-making by consensus became part of a national theology – and was instrumental in creating Austria's remarkable economic progress and political stability.

There was pecuniary gain from victimhood, since it was used – in collusion with the Western Allies – to disavow Austria's financial liability for the actions of the Nazi regime. If the country was forced to accept the Anschluss, the argument went, Austria could – and indeed did – claim that the state did not exist as a legal entity between 1938 and 1945. The post-war Second Republic could not therefore be held responsible for Nazi crimes committed during the nation's statelessness, or be made to pay reparations to the Soviet Union. All of this carries its own logic, and can even be rationalised in the context of the difficult circumstances of the decade that culminated with the signing of the State Treaty.

And yet, I am left with unanswered questions: was it reasonable, even during the uncertain, difficult early post-war years, to equate the suffering of limited number of Austrians imprisoned by the Nazis for their political beliefs with the systematic persecution and extermination of Austria's Jewish population? Indeed to what extent was antisemitism the root-cause of Austrian reluctance to accept responsibility for involvement in the 'final solution'? It is shocking enough to read the verbatim Austrian cabinet minutes of discussions on the thorny issue of restitution that were held between 1947 and 1952. It is equally shocking to learn of the concerted effort that was made to discredit the British historian Robert Knight after he accidentally discovered the papers many years later hidden away in state archives. The ministers quoted in these minutes had unimpeachable credentials as democrats. They could not have been accused of Nazi sympathies, but they were quite uninhibited in their antisemitic comments, and repeatedly confirmed that they were more interested in the rehabilitation and material well-being of ex-Nazis than in helping the Jewish victims of the Nazi era. Victimhood was fine, as long as the Jews were left out of the equation, and provided the issue of responsibility for the persecution of the Jews was deferred for an undefined period.

Attitudes did not improve even when the Second Republic had reached firm ground. Politicians for the most part turned a blind eye to the Nazis employed in the public services, and little attempt was made to bring war criminals to trial. Both the big parties, the People's Party and Social Democrats, had flirted with the neo-Nazi Union of Independents. But it was the Social Democrats who, for tactical reasons, secretly helped in 1963 to finance the right-wing party's successor, the Freedom Party; and it was Kreisky, as Chancellor, who was first to consider the idea of bringing the Freedom Party into government as a coalition partner. No matter that Kreisky was able to govern between 1970 and 1983 without a coalition partner, and that his plan to govern in tandem with the

Freedom Party did not need to be tested: what counts is that he evidently had no inherent inhibitions against co-operation with the far right. It was all part of his preference for an amnesiac approach to the Nazi era. Like his predecessors, he appeared to cling to the view that consensus was all-important, that the national identity could only be secured by drawing a line under the past, and that the Second Republic had no obligation to concern itself with Hitler's crimes. On the contrary, he always argued that 'coming to terms with the past was just irrelevant talk'.

Others thought differently: unsurprisingly, there is a school which holds that Austrians could only find their true identity when they accepted responsibility for their actions during the Nazi era. Even if Austria could not be considered a legal entity after the Anschluss, the nation itself had not been dissolved, and it had continued to exist between 1938 and the end of the war. I doubt that Bruno Kreisky would have concurred with such arguments. He would surely have asserted that his policy of inclusiveness, and his populist strategy of stressing patriotism and pride in Austria's post-war achievements, was a far better way of cementing national identity. Kreisky was always more concerned with the present and the future than the past, even though his character and politics were greatly influenced by his awareness of the forces that broke up the First Republic, and by his experiences, including imprisonment, as a socialist student before the Second World War.

— * —

I first met Kreisky in the 1970s. During election campaigns I had ample opportunity to observe the charismatic appeal he had for voters. It was also plain that his handling of Austria's neutrality status was cleverly managed to give the country maximum exposure abroad. He was astute in the handling of relations with the Soviet Union, deferring to the Kremlin over its refusal to countenance Austrian membership of the EEC, but rarely compromising over the pro-Western ethos that permeated Austrian society. In Kreisky's Austria, economic progress had become the envy of other European countries, and its leader made himself a significant figure at home and abroad.

Analysing reactions to Kreisky during his various incarnations in government – as State Secretary in the Foreign Office during the latter stages of the State Treaty negotiations, as Foreign Minister, and above all during his 13 years as Chancellor – there can be no doubt that he, more than any of his predecessors, understood the need to catapult Austria into the modern world. He gave the country a new self-confidence, and the conviction that Austria enjoyed international respect.

Kreisky was the first in Austria to break the political domination of the conservative People's Party and get the Social Democrats accepted as a party capable of taking charge of government, even though it was on the left of the political spectrum. His commitment to education strengthened the country's economic competence and produced long-lasting dividends from which Austria continues to benefit. He broke the monopoly of the People's Party on links with the Roman Catholic Church in Austria, and achieved a warm working relationship with its Archbishop, Cardinal Franz König.

However, my admiration for Kreisky dimmed while I was working on the biography of Simon Wiesenthal. Researching in the Kreisky Archive in Vienna I came up against some of the uglier manifestations of the Kreisky phenomenon: his tempestuous nature, his vindictive irrationality, his determination to dominate debate. The portrait that emerges is of a brilliant politician who allowed himself to be blown off course by revelations and strictures from a source – Wiesenthal – beyond his power to silence.

Kreisky became incandescent when Wiesenthal claimed that Friedrich Peter, the leader of the Freedom Party with whom he was secretly negotiating a political deal, had been a member of the Waffen SS. Wiesenthal hit out at Kreisky for consorting with an alleged war criminal. The Chancellor retaliated with a vitriolic campaign to destroy Wiesenthal's good name. Fortunately he did not succeed.

I could see a similar drive at character assassination in the way Kreisky took aim at his erstwhile crown prince, Hannes Androsch, after they fell out over economic policy. The relationship was obviously made worse because Kreisky convinced himself – on the flimsiest of evidence – that Androsch was manoeuvering to oust him from the chancellorship. As I see it, Kreisky's way of dealing with his largely self-inflicted dilemma was to launch himself into a campaign to destroy his lieutenant's good name and to allege that Androsch was guilty of corruption and tax evasion. As with his drive against Wiesenthal, Kreisky again allowed himself to be driven by his worst instincts, even though he was warned that the ousting of Androsch risked undermining the favourable economic rating that Austria had secured abroad.

Connoisseurs of the Austrian scene know that the Androsch controversy has never died down, and that the long legal saga surrounding charges of tax evasion has created a trail of bitterness on both sides of the divide. But to my mind it remains incontrovertible that the Kreisky era owed much of its standing with the international community to the economic policies pursued during the years when Kreisky and Androsch were working in tandem – and in partnership with the trade unions' and employers' organisations – to promote social welfare, full employment, low inflation and sound education. Those policies firmed up the foundations that have enabled Austria to remain remarkably recession-proof. It has long been an open question whether Kreisky, by divesting himself of Androsch, scored an own goal and deprived himself of one of his more valuable assets. Afterwards, there was nobody strong enough to restrain Kreisky from clinging to inefficient nationalised industries and using deficit spending to subsidise full employment. And there was no-one of sufficient standing to make Austria's official voice heard in the major international financial institutions. It took Kreisky's successors years to overcome these mistakes, to restructure the economy, and to regain influence on the internatioanl economic circuit.

One of Kreisky's big achievements was to make himself a familiar figure on the world stage. Thanks to him, Austria acquired a distinctive personality. World leaders enjoyed stop-overs in the country, and found it an agreeable setting for high-level diplomatic encounters. But Kreisky's ability to influence international debate can be over-emphasised. There were always distinct down-sides to Kreisky's extensive involvement with foreign affairs. For example, contrary to the widely-held impression, it was Eisenhower, not Kreisky, who dreamed up neutrality for Austria as a formula to break the deadlock during the closing stages of the State Treaty negotiations.

The Socialist International never became the important instrument of Middle East diplomacy that Kreisky wanted it to become. The Austrian Chancellor was more of a footnote in the history of the Middle East than the major peace-broker he skilfully projected himself as. Though he was well ahead of other Western leaders in realising that the PLO would have to be brought into Middle East peace negotiations, he badly misjudged Washington's reaction to his decision to befriend Yasser Arafat.

During the Schönau incident, and again during the OPEC hostage crisis, Kreisky lost his nerve too easily, and created for himself the image of being soft on terrorism. He deprived himself of the remnants of influence in the Middle East peace process by welcoming the Libyan leader, Colonel Gadhafi to Vienna.

In retirement, Kreisky came to rue his backing for Waldheim's successful bid to become UN Secretary-General. He also preferred to forget that he had once even toyed with the idea of sponsoring Waldheim for the Austrian presidency. In 1971, when it could still have made a difference, Kreisky did not use his government's resources to look into Waldheim's past, and never questioned where Waldheim's servility might have taken him in his wartime army career. All that mattered to Kreisky at the time was that an Austrian would head the UN, that this was bound to enhance Austria's profile in the international community, and that Waldheim as UN Secretary-General could be relied on to help promote Vienna's nomination as the UN's second capital in Europe, after Geneva. With Waldheim in the top post at the UN, it was inevitable that awareness of Austria would grow. But the favourable fall-out for the country was temporary, and was far outweighed by the negative fallout that was to come later. Within the confines of the UN, it did not take long for Waldheim's colleagues to discern that he lacked leadership qualities, and was of poor intellect, but was cunning and primarily self-serving. I was always surprised that the Israelis took him so seriously, and were worried by what they considered to be a pro-Arab stance. In fact, Waldheim had no marked influence on Middle East affairs.

The Great Powers supported Waldheim mainly because he was pliable, and appeared incapable of posing a threat to their diverse national interests. They re-elected him for a second term as UN Secretary-General because at the time that seemed easier than to struggle for consensus on a successor. At the UN few saw Waldheim as a shining example of postwar Austria. The slogan that he used in his presidential campaign in 1985 – that he was 'the man the world trusted' – had a double-edged meaning: mainly they trusted him to be bland and to avoid controversial action. There was always speculation at the UN that the Soviet Union knew something about Waldheim's wartime record that enabled them to put the occasional pressure on him as UN Secretary-General. But this was never substantiated. Until the the storm burst over Waldheim in the mid-1980s, nobody thought of looking into the UN archives for wartime information about Waldheim.

Those of us who had known him at the UN were as surprised as the rest of the world when the World Jewish Congress (WJC) came out with its charges against him as a war criminal. Its spokesmen grossly overplayed their hand. I was of that mind long before 1995, when I came into contact with senior staff at the WJC over their acrimonious relationship with Simon Wiesenthal. My exchanges with the WJC only served to reinforce my judgement that their strident campaign to prevent Waldheim's election as Austrian head of state had achieved the opposite of the desired effect.

There was a good case against Waldheim as a liar, and a strong argument that this alone made him unfit to be President. But it was going too far when the WJC portrayed him, on the basis of controversial evidence, as a monster with a proven record that fully justified a war crimes trial. Nobody will ever know whether Waldheim would have been elected in 1986 if he had not been so vilified abroad. But it would certainly have been a much more close-run race.

— * —

For a long time I subscribed to the view that the US-led campaign against the Waldheim presidency did nothing but harm to Austria, that it only reinforced the image of a nation without a conscience or concern for its past; that it would fan anti-semitism and encourage support for the far right and for Haider. I was not mistaken. But it took a while to realise that the anti-Waldheim campaign also produced a positive dividend, in that it helped to bring about a long overdue but still only partial catharsis: at last Austria was propelled into shedding the big lie.

Chancellor Vranitzky realised very quickly after Waldheim's arrival in the Hofburg that the turmoil around the new President's wartime record could and should be used to prize open the collective memory of Austria during the Nazi era. However, it took him four years, until 1991, to feel that public opinion was ready to accept his call to confront the evil that Austrians had perpetrated of their own free will, and for the nation as a whole to accelerate the process of making amends to victims. Vranitzky argues that he could not have acted more speedily. Austria was in turmoil, deeply divided over the Waldheim presidency. To be sure, the Chancellor's personal views were not in doubt, and he made a number of speeches between 1988 and 1991 pointing Austria towards the need to come to terms with history. But he hesitated until 1991 before taking the formal step of delivering a binding statement in parliament tantamount to changing the official doctrine of Austria as victim state.

I am among those who think he could have done this sooner, but in the end that is a mere quibble. What matters is that the Vranitzky government did what no previous administration had done: it gave the formal signal that Austria as a nation was ready to acknowledge the unpalatable home truths that had for so long been suppressed. To prove that this went beyond the articulation of principles, the government initiated practical measures designed to achieve reconciliation with the victims of Nazi persecution and their descendants. Since then, there has certainly been a mass of rethinking and new thinking in Austria. History books have been revised, and teaching directed towards greater understanding of the Holocaust. An annual day, 5 May, has been set aside for national remembrance of Nazi victims.

The pace has been accelerated, and there is a new eagerness to conclude unfinished business, including the return of works of art held in Austria's museums to their rightful owners, and the settlement of survivors' claims against Austria's banks and compensation for slave labour. The establishment of the International Commission of Experts, charged with producing a definitive, closely documented, account of Nazi crimes in Austria is of long-term importance in putting the Nazi era into its its rightful historical context.

Meanwhile, the Austrian media carry an endless stream of news stories and comment about Holocaust-related matters. The sharp debate about the new Holocaust memorial in Vienna due to be unveiled in the autumn of 2000 has been about its artistic merit and location. But there has been full acceptance of the need to have a prominently placed monument. Wiesenthal, once so cruelly reviled in Austria, has been turned into a national treasure, and has been heaped with honours. The Church, which stood aloof from the debate for years, has joined in, urging believers to come to terms with their recent history.

It is of course possible to argue – as many do – that all this goes only skin-deep, and that Haider's electoral advance demonstrates that beneath it all Austrians continue to cling to a distorted version of their recent history. I would like to think that such cynicism is misplaced, and that the younger generation, the men and women born after 1945, are for the greater part genuinely receptive to the lessons of the Holocaust, and understand that Austria must accept responsibility for past behaviour if it is to retain self-respect, let alone keep the respect of the outside world. I was encouraged, and found it deeply moving, to observe the mass of young people who came to Mauthausen in 1995 for the ceremonies to mark the fiftieth anniversary of the concentration camp's liberation, or those who crowded into Vienna's Odeon cinema in 1997 to watch the live production of a short opera based on Anne Frank's diary, and again in 1999 when the Vienna State Opera staged *White Rose*, the true story of two young German resistance workers, a non-Jewish brother and sister, who were executed in 1943 for distributing anti-Nazi leaflets.

It would be unfair to base moral judgements about Austria only on its handling of the past. There is widespread interest among the young in the exploration of new ideas, in human rights and in green issues, in new music and literature, in new openings to the world in contrast to the insularity of their parents. Notwithstanding growing resistance to the influx of refugees, Austria has absorbed proportionately more refugees from Eastern Europe since the disintegration of Yugoslavia began in 1991 than most of its EU partners have been willing to do. The response to the plight first of Bosnian and more recently of Albanian refugees was remarkably generous. As during the Hungarian uprising in 1956, and again after Soviet intervention in Czechoslovakia in 1968, Austria, once again, demonstrated its readiness to act as a country of asylum.

And yet in spite of so many positive indicators, Haider's presence on the political stage stands as a powerful warning against complacency. The widespread appeal of his demagoguery inevitably casts doubts on Austria's readiness to confront contemporary challenges with the realism and moral integrity they demand. Haider's startling electoral advance on the political scene throws into question the permanence of Austria's normalisation process and the effort of the past decade to portray the country as a mature democracy and reliable member of the international community.

Haider has been masterly at exploiting the deep malaise amongst Austria's grass-roots. He has made himself a plausible anti-politician, a figure able to capitalise on public cynicism about the political classes, a force able to rescue Austrians from the mistakes and misdeeds of tired, allegedly corrupt leaders. He plays hard on the widespread belief that the political establishment has allowed itself to be perverted by power, and the fear that this state of affairs has put Austrians' comfortable lifestyle at risk. Having dictated policy since 1945, the two mainstream parties no longer produce outstanding leaders capable of inspiring confidence or enthusiasm among the electorate. Haider, whose party won second place marginally ahead of the People's Party in the October 1999 election, is the beneficiary of the yearning for new faces and for new policies to confront the challenges of the new millenium. With the Freedom Party's controversial entry into government, its greatest test will be to show whether it can satisfy any aspect of the desire for change.

Haider's message also raises profound questions about the nature of Austria's democracy as it has been practised since 1945. When the nation was relaunched, it was generally assumed that a dynamic democracy can co-exist with consensus politics both at government level and at the level of policy-making between management and the trade unions. The country was deemed too fragile to sustain the rough-and-tumble of authentic parliamentary democracy. Consensus was the watchword that had to be respected at every level of the power structure. All this made sense in the earlier post-war period. Yet after more than five decades it has served to stultify Austria's democratic institutions, and to make political patronage an all-pervasive and corrosive phenomenon. It has reached the point where it can be argued that the democratic system, as it operates in Austria, has run into the buffers. While the two main parties dominated political life, Austria was turned into a democracy without an effective opposition, a mockery of democracy. There is plenty of evidence that voters whose political outlook otherwise has little in common with Haider have voted for the Freedom Party as a way of breaking the mainstream parties' hold on Austria's political life. A sizeable part of the electorate quite simply felt not only that the traditional coalition between Social Democrats and People's Party had run out of steam, but also that Haider should be given a chance to show whether he was capable of the responsible execution of power.

There is obviously something perverse in the idea that Austrians see Haider's Freedom Party as an instrument for enlivening democracy in Austria. Surely his strident populism, his brand of narrowly defined nationalism and his xenophobia are the very antithesis of the requirements of a small Central European state seeking to maintain and strengthen its position within the EU and responding to the pressures of the global economy. Outside Austria there is no sympathy for the notion that the Freedom Party deserves to be seen as an instrument of constructive change. Abroad, the decision to allow the Freedom Party to participate in Austria's federal government is perceived as a thoroughly retrograde step, and as a sign that Austria has still not fully absorbed the lessons of the Nazi era. Ludicrously, Haider has taken to comparing the latterday Freedom Party to Tony Blair's New Labour Party. He has spoken of 'amazing similarities' between the two parties, and asserted that he is a reformed character who has transformed his party's negative image into an 'Austrian patriotic movement'. Over and over, he has insisted that he has been misinterpreted or misunderstood, and that he has put behind him any sympathy for Hitler's policies or actions. This has failed to convince his critics at home or abroad, who remain deeply suspicious of his political ideas, of his xenophobic rhetoric, and of his unpredictability.

After the October 1999 election, Austria's partners in the EU warned both the outgoing Chancellor Klima and Foreign Minister Schüssel against taking either the Social Democrats or the People's Party into a coalition with the Freedom Party. They were told that such a course would have severe repercussions on the country's external relations. The Social Democrats needed little persuasion from the outside; the party would have split had Klima suggested coalition with the Freedom Party. Schüssel and his Austrian People's Party, however, had no compunction about an alliance with Haider's party. It was almost certainly the only chance Schüssel would ever have had to become Chancellor. So the deal was done.

The EU was ready to unleash its wrath, imposing diplomatic sanctions designed to isolate and ostracise Austria. No matter that Austria's head of state, President Klestil, insisted that the Freedom Party and the People's Party sign a declaration of commitment to democracy and human rights, to loyal membership of the EU, and to the speedy resolution of outstanding compensation to the victims of Nazi persecution. Haider would have put his name to any piece of paper that brought him closer to power. The EU, led by France, Belgium and Portugal, were determined to prevent the Austrian 'sickness' from spreading. Austria had to be quarantined, possibly for the duration of the Freedom Party's participation in Austria's federal government.

Haider and his supporters were not alone in claiming that this was unfair. Even among his opponents in Austria, many feared that outside pressures to dislodge the Freedom Party from the coalition government would backfire, and only serve to strengthen Haider's appeal for Austria's voters. More tangibly, there was concern that Austria's exclusion from informal consultations and negotiations among EU member countries would hamper Austria's ability to defend its vital interests, and also that the policy of isolating Austria would handicap its tourist trade, deter inward investment, and thus inflict serious damage to the economy.

Concern that sanctions might backfire is a view that I initially shared. I anticipated a repetition of the Waldheim syndrome, when so many Austrians responded to the US and WJC campaign against Waldheim's presidential candidacy by rallying behind him and voting him into office. But such comparisons may turn out to be oversimplistic. In Haider's case, outside intervention has come after an election, and not before, and it has been initiated by Austria's European partners without pressure from Jewish lobbies. Against those in Austria who fret that sanctions would be counter-productive, it is significant that there is also a wide swathe of opinion that welcomes external pressures as a way of reinforcing opposition to the Freedom Party's presence in government, and of weakening, possibly shortening the life of the People's Party-Freedom Party coalition.

There was little evidence, at least in the short term, that the Freedom Party would be able to exploit the sanctions issue to increase its popular support. Instead, the combination of the Freedom Party's presence in government and sanctions from abroad helped to precipitate a widespread national debate about the nature of Austria's democracy, about its place in the Europe and the world, about its present character and past history.

Such discourse is surely healthy. Austria, thanks to its geography and history, has a close understanding of Eastern and Central Europe. It has a cultural wealth and natural scenery that attract visitors from all corners of the world. It is a well-ordered and easy-going society, and possesses an enviable quality of life. It has attracted foreign investment and has modern industries with extensive export markets. Its future potential is considerable. But opportunities must be exploited. Otherwise Austria will be relegated to the third division, with all the old arguments about victim or perpetrator left on the agenda. What Austria needs is an injection of leadership to steer its democracy away from the buffers, and forward into a less complacent, more dynamic, future. Haider and his supporters claim he is the answer. In reality he personifies the problem.

And yet, I believe some good will come out of it. If the Waldheim crisis helped the Vranitzky government to begin the process of confronting the Austrian nation with its past, so Haider's challenge may help to complete the catharsis and enable Austria to modernise and energise its political life, and to confront the new millenium with greater assurance as an integral part of a constantly evolving, exciting European architecture.

BIBLIOGRAPHY

Albrich, Thomas, *Exodus durch Österreich: Die jüdischen Flüchtlinge 1945–1948*, Innsbruck, 1987

Andics, Hellmut, *Ironimus der 60er Jahre: Karikaturen aus den Jahren 1960–1970*, Vienna, 1970

Bailer, Brigitte, 'Ohne den Staat weiter zu belästigen... Bemerkungen zur österreichischen Rückstellungsgesetzgebung', *Zeitgeschichte* 20, Vienna, 1993

Baque, James, *Crimes and Mercies: The Fate of German Civilians under Allied Occupation 1944–50*, London, 1998

Bischof, Günter, 'Die Instrumentalisierung der Moskauer Erklärung nach dem 2. Weltkrieg', *Zeitgeschichte* 20, Vienna, 1993

Bischof, Günter and Joseph Leidenfrost, 'Die bevormundete Nation: Österreich und die Alliierten 1945–49', *Innsbrucker Forschungen* vol. 4, Innsbruck, 1988

Bischof, Günter, Anton Pelinka and Ferdinand Karlhofer (eds), 'The Vranitsky Era in Austria', *Contemporary Austrian Studies* vol. 7, New Brunswick NJ

Booker, Christopher, *A Lookingglass Tragedy: The Controversy over the Repatriations from Austria in 1945*, Duckworth, 1998

Boutros-Ghali, Boutros, *Egypt's Road to Jerusalem: A Diplomat's Story of the Struggle for Peace in the Middle East*, New York, 1997

Brook-Shepherd, Gordon, *The Austrians: A Thousand-year Odyssey*, London, 1996

Bruno Kreisky, Seine Zeit und mehr, Wissenschaftliche Begleitpublikationen zur Sonderausstellung im Historischen Museum der Stadt Wien, Vienna, 1998

Bundespressedienst (ed.), *Active Neutrality: Austrian Foreign Policy since 1945*, Vienna, 1975

Bundespressedienst (ed.), *Österreich Dokumentationen – Widerstand und Verfolgung in Österreich 1938–45*, Vienna, 1988

Burns, John, Wolfgang Hirczy and Jacqueline Vansant, *The Sound of Austria – Österreich: Politik und öffentliche Meinung in den USA*, Austrian Institute for International Politics, Vienna, 1995

Clare, George, *Berlin Days 1946–47*, London, 1990

Cordt, Herbert and Beppo Mauhart (eds), *Zurück in die Zukunft: Ein Diskussionsbeitrag über genützte, vertane und künftige Chancen*, Vienna, 1988

Das Bild Österreichs in den ausländischen Medien 1965–86, Institut für Publizistik und Kommunikationswissenschaften der Universität Wien, Vienna, 1987

Der österreichische Staatsvertrag in Karikaturen, exhibition catalogue, Vienna, 1980

Dickinger, Christian, Anton Pelinka and Herbert Schachter, 'Der Konflikt zwischen Bundeskanzler Kreisky und Finanzminister Androsch: Versuch einer Rekonstruktion', *SWS-Runschau* Heft 1/1998, Vienna

BIBLIOGRAPHY

Dor, Milo (ed.), *Die Leiche im Keller: Dokumente des Widerstands gegen Dr. Kurt Waldheim*, Vienna, 1988

Embacher, Helga and Margit Reiter, *Gratwanderungen: Die Beziehungen zwischen Österreich und Israel im Schatten der Vergangenheit*, Vienna, 1998

Ergert, Viktor, *50 Jahre Rundfunk in Österreich*, ed. ÖRF, 5 vols, Salzburg, 1974–85

Europäische Rundschau, Vienna, May 1980

Gallup, Stephen, *A History of the Salzburg Festival*, London, 1987

Gehler, Michael and Herbert Sickinger (eds), *Politische Affären und Skandale in Österreich: Von Mayerling bis Waldheim*, Vienna, 1996

Grunwald, Henry, *One Man's America: A Journalist's Search for the Heart of his Country*, New York, 1997

Haider-Pregler, Hilde and Peter Roessler (eds), *Zeit der Befreiung: Wiener Theater nach 1945*, Vienna, 1998

Hamann, Brigitte, *Hitlers Wien: Lehrjahre eines Diktators*, Munich, 1996

Hellsberg, Clemens, *Demokratie der Könige: Die Geschichte der Wiener Philharmoniker*, Vienna, 1992

Herz-Kestranek, Miguel, *Mit Ezjes bin ich versorgt*, Vienna, 1998

Hobsbawm, Eric, *Age of Extremes: The Short Twentieth Century, 1914–1991*, London, 1997

Holl, Otmar, *Österreichische Entwicklungshilfe 1970–1983: Kritische Analyse und internationaler Politik*, Laxenburg

Holzer, Gabriele, *Verfreundete Nachbarn: Österreich-Deutschland*, Vienna, 1995

Holzer, Karin, *Johann Böhm: Eine Biografie*, Vienna, 1997

Horvath, Traude and Gerda Neyer, *Auswanderungen aus Österreich von der Mitte des 19. Jahrhunderts bis zur Gegenwart*, Vienna, 1996

Jahrbücher des österreichischen Widerstands:

1986: Botz, Gerhard, *Anschluss an die Vergangenheit (Verdrängung der NS-Vergangenheit)*

1986: Neugebauer, Wolfgang, *Die Entwicklung des österreichischen Nationalbewusstseins*

1987: Neugebauer, Wolfgang et al., *Zur Entwicklung des österreichischen Nationalbewusstseins; Vranitzky-Rede anlässlich des 2. Internationalen Welttreffens ehemaliger Kriegsteilnehmer, Widerstandskämpfer und Kriegsopfer*

1989: Beer, Siegfied, *Exil und Emigration als Information*

1991: Beer, Siegfied and Edouard Staudinger, *The Morgenthau Plan*

1992: Beer, Siegfied, *Inspection of Mauthausen Concentration Camp*

1993: Bartoszewski, Wladyslaw, *Der Widerstand, ein Begriff von heute und damals*

1995: Ranshofen-Wertheimer, Ego and Leopold Kohr, *Mit der Washington Post gegen die Nazis*

1995: Rabinovici, Doron et al., *50 Jahre Kriegsende – 50 Jahre Zweite Republik – die US-Perzeption in Österreich nach 45*; Ela Hornung and Irene Bandhauer-Schoffmann, *Der Topos sowjetischer Soldaten in lebensgeschichtlichen Interviews mit Frauen*

1998: Roth, Gerhard et al., *Überlegungen zum Umgang mit der jüngsten Vergangenheit*; Wolfgang Neugebauer, *Vom europäischen Widerstand zur Europäischen Union*

Jelavich, Barbara, *Modern Austria, Empire and Republic, 1815–1986*, Cambridge, 1987

Karner, Stefan, 'Essay zur Politik der sowjetischen Besatzungs- und Gewahrsamsmacht' in Alfred Ableitinger and Siegfried Beer (eds), *Österreich unter alliierter Besatzung 1945–1955*, Studien zu Politik und Verwaltung 63, Vienna, 1998

Kausel, Anton, *Ein halbes Jahrhundert des Erfolgs: Der ökonomische Aufstieg Österreichs im OECD-Raum seit 1950*, Vienna, 1998

Keyserling, Robert, 'Anschluss oder Besetzung, 1938–45 aus der Sicht der USA', *Zeitgeschichte* 4, Vienna, 1982

Keyserling, Robert, *Austria in World War II: An Anglo-American Dilemma*, Montreal, 1988

Kicker, Renate, Andreas Kohl and Hans-Peter Neuhold (eds), *Aussenpolitik und Demokratie in Österreich: Strukturen, Strategien, Stellungnahmen*, Salzburg, 1983

Kirschbauer, Gert and Karl Müller, *Begnadet für das Schöne: Der rot-weiss-rote Kulturkampf gegen das Moderne*, Vienna, 1992

Kleindel, Walter, *Österreich: Daten zur Geschichte und Kultur*, Vienna, 1995

Knight, Robert, *Absentee Germans: The Second Austrian Republic and the Nazi Past*, Institute for German History, Tel Aviv, 1997

Knight, Robert, 'Besiegt oder befreit?' in Günter Bischof and Joseph Leidenfrost, *Die bevormundete Nation*, Innsbruck, 1998

Knight, Robert (ed.), 'Ich bin dafür, die Sache in die Länge zu ziehen', *Die Wortprotokolle der österreichischen Bundesregierung 1945–1952 über die Entschädigung der Juden*, Vienna/Cologne/Weimar, 1999

Kos, Wolfgang, *Eigenheim Österreich – zu Politik, Kultur und Alltag nach 1945*, Vienna, 1995

Kreisky, Bruno, *Zwischen den Zeiten: Erinnerungen aus fünf Jahrzehnten* (memoirs, part 1), Vienna/Berlin, 1988; *Im Strom der Politik: Erfahrungen eines Europäers* (memoirs, part 2), Vienna/Berlin, 1988; *Der Mensch im Mittelpunkt* (memoirs, part 3), ed. Johannes Kunz and Margit Schmidt, Vienna, 1996

Kriechbaumer, Robert (ed.), *Österreichische Nationalgeschichte 1: Die Spiegel der Erinnerung: Die Sicht von Innen*, Vienna, 1998

Kurth Cronin, Audrey, *Great Power Struggle over Austria, 1945–1955*, Cornell Studies in Security Affairs, Cornell, 1986

Le Carré, John, *A Perfect Spy*, London, 1986

Lendvai, Paul, *Auf schwarzen Listen: Erlebnisse eines Mitteleuropäers*, Hamburg, 1986

Letwin, Shirley (ed.), *Morality and Politics in Modern Europe*, Harvard Lectures by Michael Oakshot, Cambridge MA, 1993

Luther, Kurt Richard and Iain Ogilvy, *Austria and the European Union Presidency: Background and Perspectives*, London, 1998

Luther, Kurt Richard and Peter Pulzer (eds), *Austria 1945–95: 50 Years of the Second Republic*, London, 1998

Lynn, H. Nicholas, *The Rape of Europa*, London, 1994

Meir, Golda, *Mein Leben*, Frankfurt am Main/Vienna, 1983

Meissl, Sebastian et al. (eds), *Verdrängte Schuld, verfehlte Sühne: Entnazifizierung in Österreich*, Vienna, 1986

Menschen nach dem Krieg, Schicksale 1945–55, catalogue of exhibition at the Schallaburg: Oliver Rathkolb, 'Über Denazifizierung und Wiedergutmachung';

Siegfried Beer, 'Die Geheimdienste im besetzten Österreich', Schallaburg, 1995

Mitchell, Ian, *The Cost of a Reputation*, London, 1998

Niemals Vergessen! Ein Buch der Anklage, Mahnung und Verpflichtung, Vienna, 1946

Österreichische Zeitschrift für Aussenpolitik, 1971, 1972, 1973, 1974, Vienna

Österreichs Nachbarstaaten: Innen- und aussenpolitische Perspektiven, Schriftenreihe des Zentrums für Angewandte Politikforschung vol. 12, 1997: Georg Winckler, *Die wirtschaftlichen Beziehungen Österreichs zu seinen Nachbarstaaten*; Otmar Holl, *Die aussenpolitischen Beziehungen Österreichs zu seinen Nachbarstaaten*, Vienna, 1997

Parkinson, E. (ed.), *Conquering the Past, Austrian Naziism Yesterday and Today*, Detroit, 1989

Pelinka, Anton and Erika Weinzierl (eds), *Das grosse Tabu – Österreichs Umgang mit seiner Vergangenheit*, Vienna, 1987

Pelinka, Anton and Robert Wistrich, *Wandlungen und Brüche: Von Herzls 'Welt' zur 'Illustrierten Neuen Welt', 1897–1997*, ed. Joanna Nittenberg, Vienna, 1997

Pelinka, Anton and Sabine Meyr (eds), *Die Entdeckung der Verantwortung: Die Zweite Republik und die vertriebenen Juden*, Vienna, 1998

Peres, Shimon, *Battling for Peace: Memoirs*, London, 1994

Pick, Hella, *Simon Wiesenthal*, Reinbek bei Hamburg, 1997

Portisch, Hugo, *Österreich II*, 3 vols, Vienna, 1989–96

Prawy, Marcel, *Die Wiener Oper: Geschichte und Geschichten*, Vienna, 1969

Prutsch, Ursula and Manfred Lechner (eds), *Das ist Österreich – Innensichten und Aussensichten*, Studien zur Gesellschafts- und Kulturgeschichte 11, Vienna, 1997

Rathkolb, Oliver, *Bruno Kreisky in the Perspectives of US Top-level Decision Makers, 1959–1983*, Contemporary Austrian Studies, Vienna, Autumn 1993

Rathkolb, Oliver, *Die Wiedererrichtung des Auswärtigen Dienstes nach 1945*, Vienna/Graz, 1985

Rathkolb, Oliver (ed.), *Gesellschaft und Politik am Beginn der Zweiten Republik*, Vienna/Graz, 1985

Rathkolb, Oliver, *Washington ruft Wien: US Grossmachtpolitik und Österreich, 1932–1963*, Vienna/Graz, 1997

Rathkolb, Oliver, Georg Schmid and Gernot Heiss, *Österreich und Deutschlands Grosse: Ein schlampiges Verhältnis*, Salzburg, 1990

Rauchensteiner, Manfried and Wolfgang Etschmann (eds), *Österreich 1945: Ein Ende und viele Anfänge*, Forschungen zur Militärgeschichte 4, Graz/Vienna, 1997

Rechtsextremismus in Österreich nach '45 – Österreichischer Widerstand, Vienna, 1981

Rot-Weiss-Rot-Buch: Gerechtigkeit für Österreich! Darstellungen, Dokumente und Nachweise zur Vorgeschichte und Geschichte der Okkupation Österreichs, 3 vols, Vienna, 1946

Rotbacher, A., M. Zemanek and W. Hargassner (eds), *Österreichs europäische Zukunft*, Vienna, 1996

Schärf, Adolf, *Erinnerungen aus meinem Leben*, Vienna, 1963

Schärf, Adolf, *Österreichs Erneuerung: 1945–1955*, Vienna, 1955

Schmidl, Erwin A., 'The Airlift that never was: Allied Plans to Supply Vienna by Air, 1948–1950' in *Army History Bulletin of Arms History*, Washington DC, Winter 1998

Schweiger, Günter, Österreichs Image in der Welt: Ein weltweiter Vergleich mit Deutschland und der Schweiz, Vienna, 1992
Schweiger, Günter (ed.), Österreichs Image im Ausland, Vienna, 1988
Sternfeld, Albert, Betrifft: Österreich – von Österreich betroffen, Vienna, 1990
Stourzh, Gerald, Kleine Geschichte des Österreichischen Staatsvertrages, Graz, 1975
Stourzh, Gerald, Österreich, Deutschland und die Mächte: Internationale und österreichische Aspekte des 'Anschlusses' vom März 1938, Vienna, 1990
Stourzh, Gerald, Um Einheit und Freiheit: Staatsvertrag, Neutralität und das Ende der Oste-West-Besetzung Österreichs 1945–1955, Vienna/Graz, 1998
Stourzh, Gerald, Vom Reich zur Republik: Studien zum österreichischen Bewusstsein im 20. Jahrhundert, Vienna, 1990
Sturmthal, Adolf, Zwei Leben: Erinnerungen eines sozialistischen Internationalisten zwischen Österreich und den USA, Vienna, 1989
Sunjic, Melita H. and Patrik-Paul Volf, Echte Österreicher: Gespräche mit Menschen, die als Flüchtlinge ins Land gekommen sind, ed. UNHCR, Vienna, 1995
Szirtes, János, Austrian Foreign Policy, 1945–85, Vienna, 1986
Taylor, Alan J., Europe – Grandeur and Decline, London, 1967
Thalberg, Hans J., Von der Kunst, Österreicher zu sein, Vienna, 1984
The Salzberg Seminar – the First 50 Years, Salzburg, 1997
Trenkler, Thomas, Der Fall Rothschild, Vienna, 1999
Waldheim, Kurt, Der österreichische Weg: Aus der Isolation zur Neutralität, Vienna, 1971
Waldheim, Kurt, Worauf es mir ankommt: Gedanken, Appelle, Stellungnahmen des Bundespräsidenten, 1986–1992, ed. Hanns Sassmann, Graz, 1992
Weinzierl, Ulrich (ed.), Lächelnd über seine Bestatter: Österreichisches Lesebuch von 1900 bis heute, Munich, 1989
Weltcircus – Zeitgeschehen in Karikaturen, Vienna, 1977
Wheatcroft, Andrew, The Habsburgs: Embodying Empire, Harmonsworth, 1998
Wohnout, Helmut, Aussenpolitik – Staatsvertragsverhandlungen, Archiv Vogelsang Institut, Vienna
25 Jahre Staatsvertrag – Protokolle der Staats- und Festakte der Jubiläums-Veranstaltungen, Vienna, 1981

INDEX

Acheson, Dean 26
Adenauer, Konrad 13, 27, 50–52, 67–70, 110, 153, 175, 203–204, 228
Adler, Viktor 200
Alter, Henry 89
Amin, Idi 183
Andrews, Julie 87
Andropov, Yuri 154
Androsch, Hannes 101–102, 106, 137–9, 141–8, 154
Arafat, Yasser 6, 115, 127, 131–2, 134, 198
Attlee, Clement Richard 37, 93
Avilov, Victor I. 75

Bahr, Egon 70
Ball, George 112
Begin, Menachem 128–31, 133
Benya, Anton 139, 141, 143, 145
Berman, Karel 97
Bernard, Thomas 168
Béthouart, Emile 25
Bettelheim, Bruno 9
Bevin, Ernest 26, 93
Bidault, Georges 26
Blair, Tony 103–104, 233
Blum, Yehuda 159
Böhm, Karl 88–90, 94, 96
Bormann, Martin 88
Borodajkewycz, Taras 225
Braithwaite, Rodric 44, 46–7
Brandauer, Klaus Maria 97
Brandt, Willy 52, 67–70, 112, 127, 145

Brecht, Bertolt 209
Brendel, Alfred 9
Brezhnev, Leonid 115–16, 154
Brittan, Samuel 140
Bronfmann, Edgar 155, 163, 168
Brook-Shepherd, Gordon 72
Bush, George 134

Carlos 'the Jackal' (Ilich Ramirez Sanchez) 129–30
Carreras, José 97
Carter, Amy 115
Carter, Jimmy 6, 102, 111, 115–16, 118, 131,
Castro, Fidel 74
Cézanne, Paul 70
Chamberlain, Neville 38
Chirac, Jacques 185
Christie, Agatha 175
Churchill, Winston 16, 18, 21–2
Clare, George 44–6
Clark, Mark 12–13, 36–7
Cocteau, Jean 95
Craig, Gordon 165

Damm, Helene van 134
De Gaulle, Charles 15–16, 77
Delors, Jacques 192
Dermota, Anton 88
Dinitz, Simcha 125
Dobrynin, Anatoly 28
Domingo, Placido 97
Douglas, Eugene 132
Drucker, Peter 9

241

Dubcek, Alexander 78
Dulles, Eleanor 6
Dulles, John Foster 1, 6, 27, 29, 31, 52, 56, 60–61, 211–12
Dunn, James 21–2

Eden, Anthony 16
Eisenhower, Dwight D. 27, 29, 56–8, 66, 74, 229
Eisenmenger, Rudolph Hermann 95
Eisler, Georg 176
Eliav, Arie 126, 133
Erhardt, John 42
Eshkol, Levi 121
Eyskens, Mark 193

Fahmi, Ismail 125
Ferrier, Kathleen 94
Figl, Leopold 1–2, 12–13, 15, 31, 62, 204, 207–8, 225
Fischer, Harry 174–5
Fischer, Heinz 98–9
Fischer, Jutta 9
Fischer, Wolfgang 9, 174–5, 178–9
Fischler, Franz 196
Ford, Gerald 110, 113, 118, 130–31
Fraser, Nicholas 186
Freud, Sigmund 200
Frid, Grigori 99
Frischenschläger, Friedhelm 153, 155–8, 166
Fulbright, James William 124
Furtwängler, Wilhelm 88, 90, 94, 175–6

Gadhafi, Colonel 128–9, 132, 153, 161, 198, 229

Gallia, Hermine 177
Garbo, Greta 95
Gat, Israel 121
Gehrer, Elizabeth 217–18
George VI, King 93
Genscher, Hans Dietrich 193
Gerassimov, Genardi 192
Giacometti, Alberto 178
Giscard d'Estaing, Valéry 110
Glenny, Misha 186
Globke, Hans 69
Goebbels, Joseph 88
Goldenberg, Jakuv 42
Goldmann, Nahum 60–61, 210–12
Gorbach, Alfons 75
Gorbachev, Mikail 110, 159, 191
Göring, Hermann 87–8, 95
Gratz, Leopold 142, 156
Greene, Graham 171–2
Gromyko, Andrei 14, 69–70, 114, 158
Gruber, Karl 12, 28, 56
Gruberova, Edita 97
Grunwald, Henry 187
Güden, Hilde 88
Gufler, Bernard 69
Gütersloh, Albert Paris von 177

Haider, Jörg xi, xii, xiii, 2, 86, 90, 104, 155, 163–4, 168, 170, 182–190, 204–5, 220, 223, 230, 232–5
Hamilton, Duke of 175
Havel, Vaclav 162
Hayek, Friedrich 9
Healey, Denis 102, 139
Heller, Clemens 84–5

INDEX

Hellsberg, Clemens 92, 94, 95
Helmer, Oskar 206–7, 214
Herz, Martin 206
Herzl, Theodor 200
Herzstein, Robert 165
Hilberg, Raoul 216
Hilton, Tim 179
Hiscocks, Charles 36
Hitler, Adolf xi, 8, 16–20, 31, 38, 73, 87, 95, 119, 156, 173, 182, 183, 185, 218, 234
Hochhauser, Victor 94
Hodl, Carl 168
Hofmannsthal, Hugo von 87, 223
Hogg, Sarah 139–140
Holender, Ioan 95–9
Horowitz, Vladimir 88
Hotter, Hans 88
Howe, Geoffrey 193
Hull, Cordell 16
Hundertwasser, Friedensreich 178
Hurdes, Felix 90, 208
Hussein, King (of Jordan) 161
Hussein, Saddam 183

Innitzer, Cardinal 50

Jankowitsch, Peter 86, 166–7, 214
Jaruzelski, Wojciech 111
Jellinek, Gustav 211
John XXIII, Pope 78
John Paul II, Pope 162
Jonas, Franz 80–81, 142

Kallir, Otto 174, 177, 178
Karajan, Herbert von 89–90
Kaysen, Karl 85

Kennan, George 21
Kennedy, Jackie 70
Kennedy, John F. 56, 66, 70–72
Keyes, Geoffrey 24–6, 42, 208
Khomeini, Ruhollah Mussawi 132
Kirchschläger, Rudolf 10, 79, 114, 116, 142
Kissinger, Henry 102, 110, 125, 127, 145
Kitaj, R.B. 99
Klaus, Josef 79, 81–2
Klestil, Thomas 185, 201, 234
Klima, Viktor 195–6, 201, 220, 234
Klimt, Gustav 170, 173–6
Knight, Robert 165–7, 214–16, 226
Koch, Ed 155
Koestler, Arthur 174
Kohl, Helmut 154
Kokoschka, Oskar 95, 173–6, 178
Kolb, Ernst 206
Kollek, Teddy 123
König, Cardinal Franz 40, 77–8, 156, 201, 220, 228
Korda, Alexander 171–2
Koren, Stephan 139
Körner, Theodor 205–6
Krauland, Peter 206
Kraus, Joseph 206
Kraus, Karl 200
Krause, Axel 7
Krauss, Clemens 88–9
Kreisky, Bruno xii, 3–11, 13–14, 28–31, 56, 59–60, 62–82, 83–99, 101–117, 118–134, 134–8, 141–8, 149–156, 159, 170, 198, 204, 212–13, 223, 226–9
Krips, Josef 94

243

Krushchev, Nikita 14, 21, 27–31, 51, 52, 59, 66–7, 69–72, 76–7
Krushchev, Nina 70
Kunz, Erich 88

Lauder, Ronald 161, 168, 218
Le Corbusier 95
Le Carré, John 44, 47
Le Pen, Jean-Marie 188
Lederer, Erich 178
Lehmann, Lotte 87
Leopold, Rudolf 177, 179–180
Levai, Kurt 175
Lever, Harold 145
Lewis, Flora 98
Lippmann, Walter 72
Lloyd, Frank *see* Levai, Kurt
Löhr, Walter 160
Looram Rothschild, Bettina 217
Loos, Adolf 175
Luce, Henry 51
Lügner, Richard 92
Luns, Joseph 110

Macmillan, Harold 1–3, 5–6, 31, 50, 151
Mahler, Gustav 92–3, 99, 175
Mahler-Werfel, Alma 175, 211
Mair, John 36–7
Major, John 139
Marboe, Peter 152
Masterman, Sue 7
McGovern, George 134
Meany, George 212
Medzini, Meron 126
Meir, Golda 119–21, 124–8
Menuhin, Yehudi 89, 94

Metternich, Count 196
Mikoyan, Anastas 52, 61–2
Mindszenty, Joszef Kardinal 78
Mitterrand, François 138, 195
Mock, Alois 191–3
Molden, Fritz 10
Molotov, Vyacheslav 1, 16, 18, 22, 26, 28–31, 51
Mortier, Gerard 90
Mozart 170–71, 173
Mueller-Graaf, Carl-Hermann 50
Muskie, Ed 6
Mussolini, Benito 73, 182

Nasser, Gamal Abdel 72, 120–21
Nehru, Jawaharlal 28
Neumann, Robert 209
Nirenstein, Otto *see* Kalir, Otto
Nixon, Richard 60, 102, 110, 115, 118, 124, 128
Nowotny, Eva 86

Oistrakh, David 71
Olah, Franz 24
Öllinger, Hans 106

Palme, Olaf 112, 127
Paul VI, Pope 108
Peres, Shimon 130, 132
Pérez de Cuéllar, Javier 163
Peter, Friedrich 105–8, 153–4, 228
Pinay, Antoine 5, 31
Pius XII, Pope 78
Podgorny, Nikolai 76
Pompidou, Georges 77
Poncet, Jean François 1
Popper, Hans 174

Popper, Karl 9
Portisch, Hugo 197–9, 215

Raab, Julius 28, 30, 54–5, 60–64, 210–13
Rabin, Yitzhak 128, 131
Radice, Giles 151
Rathkolb, Oliver 97, 167, 214
Reagan, Ronald 6, 110, 118, 132–4, 154
Reder, Walter 155
Reed, Carol 171–2
Reinhardt, Max 87–8
Renner, Karl 12, 20, 35–6, 39, 204–5
Reuter, Ernst 52
Reuther, Walter 212
Riess-Passer, Susanne 189
Roifer, Mathilda 187
Roll, Eric 9, 145
Roosevelt, Franklin D. 16, 18
Rösch, Otto 130
Rosen, Jane 159
Rosenbaum, Eli 160
Rostow, Elspeth 85
Rostow, Walt 85

Sadat, Anwar 11, 15, 125, 127, 130–31
Salcher, Herbert 145
Sartawi, Issam 127, 133
Schärf, Adolf 24, 51, 208, 215, 225
Scheich, Manfred 191–2
Schiele, Egon 170, 173–80
Schirach, Baldur von 88, 177
Schmidt, Helmut 102, 143, 145
Scholl, Hans 99
Scholl, Sophie 99

Schultz, George 162
Schumann, Elizabeth 87
Schüssel, Wolfgang 189, 201, 234
Schwarzkopf, Elizabeth 89
Secher, Pierre 146
Seefried, Irmgard 47, 88
Seibel, Richard 37
Selznick, David O. 171–2
Shamir, Yitzhak 128
Sharett, Moshe 211
Sharon, Ariel 128
Shevardnadze, Edouard 158, 191–2
Sinowatz, Fred 151–9, 186
Speer, Albert 88
Spiel, Hilde 9
Stalin, Joseph 8, 14, 16–19, 21–3, 26, 27, 35, 39, 41, 51
Steger, Norbert 151, 154, 163, 182
Stemmer, Arthur 178
Steyrer, Kurt 159
Strauss, Johann 170
Strauss, Richard 87
Stravinsky, Igor 95
Sukarno, Ahmed 74

Tauber, Richard 93
Taylor, A.J.P. 37
Thalberg, Hans 70
Thatcher, Margaret 154
Thompson, Llewellyn 56, 71–2
Tito, Josip Broz 21, 27
Tolbukhin, Fedor Iwanowitsch 38
Torberg, Friedrich 209
Toscanini, Arturo 87–8, 89, 96
Trapp, family von 172
Trudeau, Pierre 151
Truman, Harry S. 21, 25, 26, 41

Vranitzky, Franz 82, 98, 153, 161, 163, 167, 181, 186, 190, 195, 196–201, 215–216, 231

Waldheim, Kurt xii, 2–3, 9, 15, 20, 65, 74, 78–9, 90, 94, 102, 113–15, 122, 134, 150, 153, 159–168, 170, 181, 187–8, 197–9, 201, 214–15, 223–4, 229–231, 235
Walker, Kara 99
Walter, Bruno 88–9, 93–4, 96, 211
Watson, Hugh Seton 49
Webhofer, William 186
Weidenfeld, George 9–11
Weizman, Ezer 130
Whitman, Walt 85
Wiesel, Elie 155

Wiesenthal, Simon 5, 37, 81–2, 98, 101, 106–8, 120, 142, 163, 201, 216, 219, 228, 230, 231
Wilder, Billy 9, 174
Wilson, Harold 110, 128
Winterton, John 24
Wittgenstein, Ludwig 200
Wobisch, Helmut 94
Wollte, Wolfgang 193
Wylie, Alexander 211
Wyszynski, Cardinal Stefan 78

Yamani, Sheikh Ahmed Zaki 129–30
York, Duchess of 92

Zimmermann, Udo 99
Zweig, Stefan 200